M

Pete Rose

Pete Rose

Baseball's All-Time Hit King

WILLIAM A. COOK

McFarland & Company, Inc., Publishers
Jefferson, North Carolina, and London

Library of Congress Cataloguing-in-Publication Data

Cook, William A., 1944–
    Pete Rose : baseball's all-time hit king / William A. Cook.
        p.   cm.
    Includes bibliographical references and index.

    ISBN 0-7864-1733-1 (softcover : 50# alkaline paper)

    1. Rose, Pete, 1941–   2. Baseball Players—United
States—Biography.   I. Title.
    GV865.R65C66   2004
    796.357'092—dc22   2003019128

British Library cataloguing data are available

Cover photographs: (top) Pete Rose with the 1962 Macon Peaches
(Middle Georgia Archives, Washington Memorial Library, Macon, Ga.);
(middle) breaking the all-time hits record (Online Sports); and (bottom) sliding into home (National Baseball Hall of Fame Library, Cooperstown, N.Y.)

Manufactured in the United States of America

McFarland & Company, Inc., Publishers
    Box 611, Jefferson, North Carolina 28640
        www.mcfarlandpub.com

Rose was perhaps the most versatile player of all time, having ve hundred or more games at five different positions in his 24-year eague career (1B 939, 2B 628, 3B 634, LF 671, RF 595). Despite the ous major league records he had set in his career (most games played, most at-bats, 14,053; most hits, 4,256; as well as holding seventeen modern and all-time records and being second in career doubles, 746; h in runs scored, 2,165; and ninth in base on balls, 1,566), Pete Rose, use he was on the ineligible list of major league baseball, was persona grata for entry into the only place he ever wanted to be in his life: the tional Baseball Hall of Fame at Cooperstown, New York.

It would appear that this grandstand icon had toppled to the ground. onetheless the fans continued their love affair with "Charlie Hustle" regardess of the back-stabbing of the press and collusive tactics of billionaire baseball team owners. The fans never abandoned Pete, then or now. This is especially true in his hometown of Cincinnati, where he continues to be idolized to this very day with an unmatched fervor and it seems he can do no wrong. To the average American baseball fan, Pete Rose personified a blue-collar work ethic and was someone with whom they could identify in their everyday lives. From a humble beginning he had raised his stature in life by virtue of hard work and brute determination to succeed. He was a hero from the heartland, the kid from next door who made it big. America was his oyster.

Regardless of his exile from baseball, forced upon him by major league baseball and enforced by three uncompromising commissioners, wherever Rose traveled fans still flocked to see and meet him. The fans were not going to let the major league baseball barons keep a good man down. They would not forget him and let him languish the way another banned icon, Shoeless Joe Jackson, had for most of the twentieth century. In 1999 Pete Rose was elected by a vote of fans nationwide to baseball's All-Century Dream Team. Commissioner Bud Selig, in an unlikely move, temporarily lifted the ban, allowing Rose to participate in the ceremonies that took place prior to the second game of the World Series. When Rose's name was announced, the Atlanta crowd gave him an overwhelming ovation.

In early 2002, thirteen years after Rose's ban from baseball, hundreds of fans and well-wishers of all ages jammed Menlo Park Mall in Edison, New Jersey, lining up outside a memorabilia shop to gladly pay $50 or $100 for Pete's autograph on a baseball, bat or photo. Since his banishment from baseball, Pete Rose has participated in scores of these dog and pony shows all across the nation, and the results are always the same: near hysteria by fans wanting to be close to him, many of them too young to have ever seen him play, but eager to pay homage and fork over $50 to meet the fallen star.

In Cincinnati on September 23, 2002, a special ball game paid tribute

Contents

Introduction

On the evening of September 11, 1985, with a sellout crowd of fans on hand at Cincinnati's Riverfront Stadium and millions of others ing on television, the Reds' Pete Rose was poised to collect hit number of his long brilliant career, passing Ty Cobb as the all-time career hits le Cobb's record had stood for 57 years.

Rose came up to bat in the first inning against the San Diego Padre Eric Show and on the fourth pitch lined a clean single to center. As he reached first base, thousands of camera flash bulbs fired off rapidly, his teammates mobbed him, fireworks exploded above the stadium and the crowd overwhelmed him with an unprecedented seven-minute standing ovation. Rose, who stood on first base with tears in his eyes, later said that he was looking up into the sky and saw two visions, one of Ty Cobb and the other of his late father, Harry Rose. At that moment Pete Rose was on top of the world. Less than four years later the world would be on top of him.

Rose was banned for life from baseball in 1989 for allegedly betting on major league games. By virtue of signing an agreement that he didn't completely understand with then baseball commissioner Bart Giamatti, Rose was no longer welcome in any minor league or big league stadium. His friends in baseball deserted him one by one: Johnny Bench, Joe Morgan, the press that had once idolized him quickly abandoned him. Soon after he would face indictment for tax evasion in federal court and serve time in prison. He had achieved everything that he had wanted in life through baseball, and suddenly he was an outcast from the game he loved so much.

to Cinergy Field (formerly Riverfront Stadium), which was about to be demolished after a new ballpark (the Great American Ball Park) was built directly behind the left field fence. Pete Rose was invited to participate in a celebrity softball game that was organized by his business agent, Warren Greene, and with the stadium's owners. Many of his former Reds teammates from the days of the "Big Red Machine" attended such as Johnny Bench, Joe Morgan, George Foster, Tony Perez, Cesar Geronimo, and Ken Griffey, Sr. The former Reds players were opposed by other legendary players, such as Steve Carlton, Steve Garvey, Mike Schmidt and Ryne Sandberg. Although one-third of the Cinergy Field seating was already demolished to allow for construction space for the new stadium, a sellout crowd of 41,092 turned out for the game, and though the focus of the event was supposed to be a farewell for the old ballpark, Pete Rose, as usual, stole the show.

Throughout the stadium there was a continuous chorus of the ever-familiar crowd chant of *Pete! Pete! Pete!* while once again flashbulbs popped like fireworks. One fan, 14-year-old John Lloyd, demonstrating his wish that Pete Rose be allowed into the Hall of Fame, held up an Ohio license plate that read "LET 14 IN," referring to Pete's major league jersey number. When Rose was announced to the crowd, former Reds slugger George Foster took Pete's arm and raised it high in the air as the fans gave him a three-minute standing ovation. Even Marge Schott, who was deposed from her majority stockholder position with the Reds in the middle 1990s by Bud Selig and his henchmen, was there and gave Rose a big hug during the introductions. It all was simply one big Pete Rose lovefest.

Pete Rose—Charlie Hustle, the Hit King, the local kid from the west side of Cincinnati who had made it big—had come home one last time to the stadium that was scene of so many of his historic achievements and was subsequently saluted royally by his fans. Even the *Cincinnati Enquirer* had heralded his homecoming with a quarter-page advertisement hawking a limited edition 18" × 24" full-color lithograph of Pete Rose, personally signed, for $195. In the exhibition contest, although he failed to reach base in his first two at-bats, Pete didn't let the fans down. In the sixth inning of the exhibition game, a pudgy Rose, now 61 years old, tagged up at second base and, to the delight of the huge crowd, made a determined try to reach third, coming in with a signature head-first slide under a widely grinning Mike Schmidt.

Just one day before, when the Cincinnati Reds had played the Philadelphia Phillies in the last game ever to be played in Cinergy Field, Rose was not permitted to participate in any of the official ceremonies because of his lifetime ban from baseball. While many of his former teammates, including Tommy Helms, Clay Carroll, Davey Concepcion, and Johnny Bench, and players he managed during his tenure as field general of the Reds, like

Tom Browning, Eric Davis, Rob Dibble, and Barry Larkin were introduced, Rose watched the final tribute to the stadium on television. Nonetheless he was in the stadium in spirit. Ray Knight, now a coach for the Reds, was the player who had replaced Rose at third base when he left Cincinnati after 16 seasons, signing as a free agent to play for the Philadelphia Phillies in 1979. In a tribute to Pete, Knight had placed a red rose behind home plate inside the wishbone "C" that was crafted into the stadium grass.

While the fans' admiration for Rose is straight from the heart, it can be argued that in reality these planned events are about economics, not tribute. Was the celebrity softball game in the rusted and doomed cavern of the former Riverfront Stadium about nostalgia, or was it scheme on the part of Warren Greene to use the event as a clever marketing opportunity for his client Pete Rose?

Regardless of the possible motivations of the bean counters, Pete Rose remains an acknowledged part of baseball history, at least for the fans. But one question remains: When will Pete Rose be formally reinstated by baseball and thus be made eligible for election to the Hall of Fame? It seems that as long as Rose remains outside looking in at Cooperstown, the controversy will continue.

Does Rose himself foster some of this of controversy? Rose claims that he is treated like a leper by the commissioner's office and that for years the office would not even return his agent's telephone calls. Indeed, at times since his banishment from major league baseball, circumstances surrounding Rose have bordered on the absurd. A case in point is an incident that occurred in early 2000 when his son, Pete Rose Jr., was being given a tryout in spring training by the Philadelphia Phillies for a possible assignment to their AA Reading team. Pete Jr. was scheduled to play in a split-squad spring training game, and he left two tickets for the game at the stadium gate window for his father. However, Phillies executives were so concerned about what major league baseball might think or do if Pete Sr. attended the game that they actually placed a call to the office of the commissioner of Major League Baseball to ensure that Pete's banishment from baseball did not preclude him from using the tickets for a spring training game.

The story of Pete Rose, the legend, is part triumph and part tragedy. It is also the story of an evolution in the person of Pete Rose. In fact it is the story of two Pete Roses. For as Pete Rose got more hits, became more famous and accumulated more wealth, his personality changed, and not necessarily for the better. Slowly he became as obsessed with placing bets as he did with getting base hits. He went from Charlie Hustle to Charlie hustled.

Scandal in baseball did not begin with the allegations that Pete Rose bet on his own in team to win in 1988. Scandals are as old as the Grand Old

Game itself. Even at the dawn of professional baseball in the amateur National Association in September 1865, a game between the New York Mutuals and Brooklyn Eckfords was alleged to have been fixed. The Mutuals lost the game to the Eckfords, 28–11. Later it was revealed that two of the Mutuals' players, Ed Duffy and William Wansley, had enticed their own teammate, shortstop Thomas Devyr, with a bribe to throw the game. When news of the scandal broke, the National Association launched an investigation. Consequently, both Duffy and Wansley were banned from playing in the association. However, as the Mutuals were in dire need of a shortstop, Devyr was allowed to continue playing. By 1870, both Duffy and Wansley were also reinstated.

Many of the stoic faces on the bronze plaques hanging on the hallowed walls of the National Baseball Hall of Fame in Cooperstown have had to deal with scandals in their past. Babe Ruth, Ty Cobb, Tris Speaker, Leo Durocher, Eddie Collins, Ray Schalk, Rube Waddell, Joe DiMaggio, and Mickey Mantle, just to name a few, have all have been implicated in unsavory events during their careers in baseball. But for some reason they were all purified by the baseball lords, while Pete Rose is treated differently. The virtues of justice and fairness in baseball seem to have seldom heard the name of Pete Rose. Later in this work, a synopsis of the controversy surrounding some of these players named above will be presented for the purpose of comparison with the case involving Rose and his eligibility for the Hall of Fame.

While it may be somewhat difficult for outsiders to understand the blatant blind loyalty that the average Cincinnati fan has for its favorite son Pete Rose, a diligent attempt to explain that allegiance in terms of relevance to the reinstatement of Rose will be made in this work. But to arrive at a point where an argument can be made for or against the reinstatement of Rose by major league baseball, it is necessary to first look at the major league career of Pete Rose. The common argument heard so often in the Rose matter today is that his personal life should not be permitted to nullify what he accomplished on the field as a player.

There is a conspicuous irony in the circumstances of Shoeless Joe Jackson and Pete Rose in that they both seem to have become fallen stars due to tainted friendships. Jackson was banned from baseball for life and from eligibility for the Hall of Fame for allegedly accepting money from gamblers in a conspiracy to throw the 1919 World Series to the Cincinnati Reds. In my book *The 1919 World Series: What Really Happened?* (2000), I looked at each one of the eight alleged conspirators on the Chicago White Sox to assess the degree of their individual involvement in the alleged fix of the series. I came to the conclusion that Joe Jackson was duped into association with the scandal. Jackson himself said years later that the only thing he was guilty of was choosing the wrong friends, referring to his roommate Claude "Lefty" Williams, who was alleged to be one of the primary conspirators.

It has been nearly fourteen years since Pete Rose was banned from major league baseball. Fourteen years in which he has had to endure constant humiliation, degradation and defamation. All because of the allegations of a few small-time degenerates that he befriended in the middle 1980s, such as Paul Janszen, Tommy Gioiosa and Ron Peters. These allegations are used by men like Bud Selig, who may have an agenda against Rose that goes far beyond gambling, to keep him out of Cooperstown. It can be argued that fourteen years in exile is a long and cruel sentence, and the fans, for the most part, want Pete Rose in the Hall of Fame.

Perhaps Pete Rose has suffered enough and it is time that long overdue justice came calling on his behalf. On the other hand, perhaps the Rose banishment symbolizes the need to protect the integrity of the national pastime from unsavory sources. Either way, my motivation in this work is simply to put forth the facts, as we have them, of Rose's life and career. The reader doubtless will arrive at his own conclusions about Rose's place in the game's history and in Cooperstown.

I

Pete's Journey to the Big Leagues

Peter Edward Rose was born in Cincinnati, Ohio, on April 14, 1941, at the Deaconess Hospital on Straight Street in Clifton Heights. He was the first son born to Harry and LaVerne Rose in a family that would eventually include four children: two daughters, Jackie and Caryl, and another son, David. He grew up at 4404 Braddock Avenue in the hillside neighborhood of Sedamsville, which ran along the edge of the Ohio River on the west side of Cincinnati, and attended Saylor Park Elementary School. Sedamsville is described in *The WPA Guide to Cincinnati*, published in 1943 as a "grimy little community wedged between the bluffs of Mount Echo Park and the Ohio River."

Because of the topography of the neighborhood of Rose's youth, more often than not writers and journalists unfamiliar with the city's neighborhood culture think that it is clever to refer to Rose in their works as a "river rat." But the term "rat" was commonly used in Cincinnati in the 1940s and 1950s to refer to free-spirited teenagers and identify the neighborhood where they were domiciled. There were the Corryville rats, the Mohawk rats, etc. However, as almost any native Cincinnatian can assure you, there was not then and there still is not today any cultural difference between the Sedamsville of Rose's youth and other Cincinnati neighborhoods, with the exception of the basin district, which for decades was split between migrating Appalachian whites and southern blacks. If Pete Rose is to be identified differently from a Cincinnati cultural perspective, then it would be more accurate to identify him as a west sider. Nonetheless, Pete used to correct people, explaining that he was not from Western Hills, but rather Riverside. Whatever, it's a fact that east is still east and west is still west, even in Cincinnati.

Rose honed his early skills at playing baseball in nearby Bold Face Park, and even today Rose still acknowledges the fact that the dimensions of the park were challenging for him as a youthful player when at bat. Today that facility is named in his honor as Pete Rose Park. Later he played high school baseball at Western Hills High School under coach Paul Nohr, who sent twelve players to the major leagues during his three decades at the school.

There are a couple of versions of the story of how Rose became a switch hitter. One has it that at the insistence of his uncle Buddy Bloebaum, he began switch hitting. The other story is that his father, Harry Rose, had told young Pete's Knothole baseball coach that if he let his son become a switch hitter he would promise never to take him on a vacation during the season. Whatever the case, each evening during his youth, before retiring, Rose religiously swung a bat one hundred times from the right side and one hundred times from the left side. Other than playing baseball and accompanying Harry Rose to the various athletic events that he participated in— baseball, football, basketball—Pete spent a lot of time near the banks of the Ohio River, employed as a toll taker from cars using the Anderson Ferry to cross the river from Cincinnati to Northern Kentucky. Shortly after breaking Ty Cobb's all-time hits record in 1985, Rose stated in an interview, "All I am is my father, one generation later with a bigger and better opportunity."[1]

Going all the way back to the 1869, when the Cincinnati Red Stockings— the first professional baseball team in America—finished the season undefeated with a record of 69–0, Cincinnati has always been a baseball town, and everyone seemed to play some sort of organized ball. When Pete Rose was a young boy, there were knothole teams, American Legion teams, and municipal leagues, as well as junior and senior high school teams. Many major-league players have had their beginnings in Cincinnati, including Ken Griffey, Jr., Barry Larkin, Buddy Bell, Jim Wynn, Rich Dotson, Roger McDowell, Dave Parker, Claude Osteen, Ron Oester, Garry Maddox, David Justice, and others. However, the neighborhood on the west side of Cincinnati commonly known as Western Hills is an area very well known for having produced a significant number of major league ball players over the years including Clyde Vollmer, Don Zimmer, Russ Nixon, Art Mahaffey, Dick Drott, Herm Wehmeier, Jim Bolger, and others. At the time that Rose was graduating from Western Hills High School at the age of 19 in 1960, the west-side baseball fans and scouts in Cincinnati were actually more interested in another Western Hills High graduate by the name of Ed Brinkman, who had played shortstop alongside Rose at second base. Brinkman was signed by the Washington Senators for $75,000 and played in the major leagues for 15 years for the Senators and Detroit Tigers. While Brinkman became known for his slick fielding and laser-like throws to first, his batting average was consistently in the low .200s and he finished his career with a .224 lifetime batting average. Thus, he never achieved the long-term notoriety of his high school teammate, Pete Rose.

The Cincinnati that Rose grew up in during the 1940s and 1950s was an aging, dowdy and worn-out industrial city that was well known for a lot of close inner-city living. Yet it was still considered a good place to live and raise a family. It had a certain old-world charm about it and was a city of tightly connected neighborhoods. For the most part, people didn't work far from their neighborhoods, and a large number of people owned their homes, purchasing them through neighborhood building and loan associations where their bankers were also their neighbors. There was, overall, a certain subtle civic pride expressed by the people of Cincinnati.

For the most part, though, the city's business and political agendas were dominated by old-line money from families that controlled some of the community's key industries, such as Procter & Gamble, Emery Industries, the First National Bank, and Cincinnati Milling Machine. Following World War I, a so-called political reform movement was advanced in Cincinnati, led by some of the city's wealthiest families, including the Emerys, Tafts, and Seasongoods. Under the guise of replacing corrupt politicians like the notorious Republican party boss George B. Cox, these elitists created a third party known as the Charterites and led a movement that eventually replaced the voting ward system and direct election of the mayor with a repressive form of municipal government that elected officials with at-large elections using proportional representation. The result of the so-called reform movement was that the average voter in Cincinnati was disenfranchised, having no true representation by his officials, as most elections produced results that found half of the nine-member city council residing in the same or nearby neighborhoods. Almost always, these council members resided in the more affluent neighborhoods rather than working-class or poor neighborhoods.

Notwithstanding the bogus political reform movement of the 1920s, overall the city had not changed much since the early part of the century, and although it was a northern city, it had a lot of southern influence in it—especially when it came to race relations of the time. The Cincinnati of Pete Rose's youth was a heavily segregated city. Dr. Martin Luther King had once called Chicago the most segregated city in the north. If that was a fact, then Cincinnati had to be considered a close second. Nearly all of the neighborhoods in Cincinnati in the 1940s and 1950s were segregated by race. This circumstance led to a system of de facto segregation in most of the public schools. Since a neighborhood was either populated by an all-white or all-black population, the neighborhood schools' enrollment also followed that racial trend. Since most blacks living in Cincinnati in 1940s and 1950s did not have the financial resources to own single-family homes, it followed that they would rent apartments or houses. Consequently, the housing market was segregated as well, and all the Cincinnati daily newspapers, the *Enquirer*, *Post* and *Times Star*, carried classified advertisements for housing listed by racial preference until 1964. The first Cincinnati Reds of color to break the segregated housing system in the city were Tony Perez and Chico Riuz and their families. In 1967, both ballplayers and their families moved into a new apartment building on Fairview Avenue, located in the all-white neighborhood of Clifton Heights, without incident.

Likewise, in the 1950s, recreational facilities in Cincinnati were segregated. Popular swimming clubs like the Phillips pool, the Coney Island amusement park, and even some bingo games run by veterans' fraternal organizations were either "Whites Only" facilities or they systematically segregated black patrons with separate seating arrangements within the bingo hall. When Hank Aaron first came to Cincinnati with the Milwaukee Braves in the early 1950s, he was refused service in downtown Cincinnati restaurants. Jackie Robinson had received death threats when he first came to the city with the Brooklyn Dodgers in 1947, and the Reds did not bring up their first African-American ball player, Chuck Harmon, to the majors until 1954.

Since the high schools in Cincinnati were caught in the trap of de facto segregation, it is highly unlikely that Pete Rose played much baseball against people of color until he started his professional career in the minors. Western Hills High School was a nearly all-white school when Rose attended there. In fact, in most Cincinnati high schools in the late 1950s, there were no black players on the varsity baseball teams. Perhaps the only high schools in Cincinnati during the 1950s that had more than a few black athletes participating in any sport were Taft High School, a nearly all-black high school in the notorious ghetto of the West End, and perhaps a few black athletes at Withrow High School and Woodward High School, on the city's east side.

Despite this rather gaping hole of social isolation in Rose's youthful background, he has never shown the slightest trace of intolerance for people of color, then or now. As a matter of fact, Rose has, over the years, befriended many black athletes and is well respected by people of all races who have had contact with him socially and on the ball field.

Another interesting aspect of the Cincinnati of Rose's youth is that it was void of organized crime. There was very little vice in Cincinnati, then or now. However, a footnote should be included for the infamous Cincinnati bootlegger George Remus, who sold $75 million worth of booze in a two-year period in the 1920s before being convicted and carted away to the federal penitentiary in Atlanta. However, there were some bookmakers, primarily on the west side of town, and of course fifteen miles east of Cincinnati was and is the beautiful River Downs race track. But just across the Ohio River from Cincinnati in Northern Kentucky, it was a whole different world. In the 1940s and 1950s, in towns directly across the river such as Newport, Bellevue and Covington, casino gambling was legal. In addition, there was also a large thoroughbred race track at Latonia. Bawdy nightlife, gambling and prostitution were in abundance just a bridge away from clean-living Cincinnati. This gambling and vice activity continued until the late 1950s, when local ordinances were passed and the gaming industry of Northern Kentucky packed up and moved west to Las Vegas. In the 1940s, some of the Brooklyn Dodgers who were well-known gamblers such as Leo Durocher, Hugh Casey and Kirby Higbee, were frequent patrons of the casinos in Northern Kentucky when the team was in town to play the Reds.

Howie Schultz, who was Higbee's roommate with the Dodgers in 1943, recalled one unfortunate trip of Kriby's to the Northern Kentucky gambling joints. "The last series we played was in Cincinnati, and we got our paychecks. He [Higbee] went down to the hotel and cashed his, and he had thirteen $100 bills, and he went across the river into Covington, Kentucky, and the next morning he had to borrow tip money from me."[2]

Pete Rose was introduced to horse racing at about the same time he was introduced to baseball. His father, Harry Rose, a gifted amateur athlete in his own right who played semipro football in the rough-and-tumble Feldhaus League and softball with Don Zimmer, was a hard-working, devoted family man who was employed as a bank clerk for the Fifth Third Bank in downtown Cincinnati. However, Harry Rose had another passion besides sports. He liked to gamble, and he frequently packed up the whole Rose family and took them to River Downs race track on Saturday afternoons. Subsequently, young Pete Rose became familiar with the world of laying down a $2 bet at an early age.

Tommy Helms has known Pete Rose for forty years. Helms played with Rose in the minors at Macon and in the big leagues at Cincinnati, then later became a coach under Rose when he managed the Reds. His theory about Pete's introduction to gambling at an early age is the following: "If your daddy's a fisherman, then you'll be a fisherman too. Pete's daddy liked to gamble, so when Pete grew up, that's what he liked to do."[3]

Dave Bristol had been in the Cincinnati Reds organization since 1951, starting out as a minor-league infielder. He never made the big club, but in one way or another he was destined to be associated with Pete Rose for about 40 years. Bristol was Rose's manager at Macon in 1962, then was a coach on the Reds in 1966 and took over the team as manager in midseason after Don Heffner was fired. He continued to manage the team, which included Rose, until the end of the 1969 season. In 1982 and 1983, Bristol was a coach with the Philadelphia Phillies when Rose played there and later was a coach for Rose in 1989 when he managed the Reds.

Rather than speak about the possible influence that Harry Rose might have had on Pete's penchant for gambling, Bristol chose to describe him in another way. "Yeah, I knew his father,"[4] said Bristol. "He was a nice man. He played football until he was 42 years old. He was really gung ho! I'm sure that Pete inherited some of that from him too."[5] Perhaps Harry Rose, despite his small size, could have played professional football if he had gone to college. He was certainly tough enough and skilled enough. But throughout the history of the NFL, nearly all of the players have been former college players. One notable exception was Harry Ferguson, who played for the Green Bay Packers in the 1950s.

The Roses weren't the only family who wagered on the horses in Cincinnati. Thoroughbred horse racing was popular in Cincinnati then and remains so today. On any given day in the summer, you can find upwards of 10,000 people at the daily program out at River Downs, the picturesque race course nestled between the green hills of Ohio and Kentucky right on the Ohio River, fifteen miles east of Cincinnati. Among the crowd at the track you can count on finding ballplayers and celebrities too. As a matter of fact, River Downs was a favorite spot for Hall of Fame member Frank Robinson to relax in the afternoon and place a few bets during his playing days with the Reds.

Pete Rose did not play baseball for Western Hills High School in his senior year, due to the fact that he had repeated the 10th grade and was ineligible. Therefore, to fill the gap, he played on a semipro team out of Dayton, Ohio. Following his graduation in June 1960, his uncle Buddy Bloebaum, who was a scout for the Reds, went to see farm director Phil Seghi. Up until high school, Rose had been a catcher. Now he was a second baseman, and there was concern about his ability to field his position. There was also concern about Pete's size, as he was about 5'9" and perhaps 145–150 pounds at most. Nonetheless, Bloebaum convinced Seghi to give young Rose a try, and the Reds offered him a contract for $12,000—$7,000 was a bonus, and $5,000 was to be paid if he remained on a big-league roster for at least 30 days. Immediately he would be paid $400 a month and assigned to the Reds' farm club in Geneva, New York. There is some disagreement in the previously published chronicles of Rose's career regarding whom he first encountered upon arriving at McDonough Park, where the Geneva Redlegs played. But whether it was Asa Brooks, who was general manager of the Geneva Redlegs, or Reno DeBenedetti, the manager, Rose is credited with stating to whomever, "I'm your new second baseman."[6]

The Macon Peaches 1962: Pete Rose at third from left bottom row, Tommy Helms at fourth from left bottom row, Art Shamsky at fifth from left bottom row, Dave Bristol at eighth from left top row. (Courtesy of the Middle Georgia Archives, Washington Memorial Library, Macon Ga.)

Two other Reds hopefuls playing at Geneva in 1960 with Rose were Art Shamsky and Tony Perez. Reflecting on his memories of Rose at Geneva, Perez stated in a thick Cuban accent, "He was not that good hitter. He hit .277. He was terrible playing second base. I don't know how they not kill him on double plays. Every time he pivots, they hit him. All he do is hustle and work hard. He go out before every game and take ground balls at second base. He told me he was catcher in school, but he work and become a good second baseman."[7]

Rose and Shamsky roomed together during the season in a private boarding house. The Geneva Redlegs finished in the cellar that year in the New York–Penn League. However, Rose, in his first year in professional ball, showed promise. He played in 85 games and hit .277 in 321 at-bats with 89 hits, including eight doubles, five triples and one home run. In addition, he drove in 43 runs and stole 18 bases. At the end of the season, he was eligible to be drafted by other teams, but there were no takers. Rose had also made 36 errors and was clearly not ready for the big leagues. Former big-league pitcher Tom Ferrick was then a scout in the Reds organization. After seeing Rose play a game in left field at Geneva, Ferrick put in his report:

that this guy had marginal skills and was going to have a tough time of it if he made it to the majors.

But Rose was determined, and over the winter of 1960–61 he took a job loading boxcars for the post office. By the time spring training came around, he had added about twenty pounds of bulk to his frame. In 1961, the Reds assigned him to play at Tampa of the Class A Florida State League, where in 130 games he hit .331 and led the league in hits with 160 and triples with 30. Johnny Vander Meer, the Reds' pitcher, who had hurled back-to-back no-hitters in 1938, was the manager at Tampa, and although he was impressed with Pete's hustle, he wanted to move Rose off second base and play him either at third base or in the outfield. Phil Seghi, the Reds' farm director, was against the move.

However, Rose's performance at Tampa was good enough for the Reds to move him up to the Class A Macon Peaches for the 1962 season. Macon was in the South Atlantic League, i.e. the Sally League. Bob Bonifay, general manager of the Peaches in 1962, remarked that "the Sally League in 1962 was considered a strong A."[8] Macon was where the Reds were grooming some of their top prospects.

Harley Bowers was a longtime sports writer for the *Macon Telegraph* and an advocate for baseball in Macon. He stated that "in addition to Rose playing on the Peaches in 1962, the Reds had other top prospects, like Tommy Helms, Art Shamsky, Ted Davidson and Mel Queen playing there."[9] Bonifay also stated that Gus Gil was on the team as well. Gil remained in the Cincinnati organization through 1966 and then was sold to Cleveland. He went on to play four years in the American League between 1967 and 1971 for the Indians and the expansion Seattle Pilots, who became the Milwaukee Brewers in 1970.

"Tony Perez was also supposed to play for the Peaches in '62, but he wound up at Rocky Mount,"[10] added Bowers. Perez did join the Peaches for the 1963 season.

However, the Reds weren't the only team in the Sally League in 1962 that had some players with big-league potential. The New York Mets' Ed Kranepool was playing for Knoxville, while Dave DeBusschere, who went on to have a brilliant career in the NBA, playing for the New York Knicks, was having a very good year on the mound with the Savannah White Sox, or the SavSox, as the team was commonly called. Also on the Savannah squad were three other Chicago White Sox hopefuls: J. C. Martin, who was being converted from an infielder to a catcher, and outfielders Don Buford and Jim Hicks.

The Minnesota Twins had Tony Oliva assigned to the Charlotte Hornets. Dave Bristol said of Oliva, "He was a very good player; you could see 'big league' written all over him."[11] Tony Oliva would play 15 years in the major leagues for the Minnesota Twins and win three American League batting titles, finishing his career in 1976 with 1,917 hits, 220 home runs and a career batting average of .304.

There were also a few players in the Sally league on the downside of their careers, like former Chicago, Cleveland and Baltimore shortstop Chico Carrasquel. Now 36 years old, Carrasquel had played 10 years in the American League and was hanging on for the love of the game, playing Class A ball with Greenville.

From the start in Macon it was apparent that Pete Rose had big-league potential; everyone was optimistic about the kid. He roomed with Tommy Helms and was all business. "He was a hustler,"[12] said former Peaches general manager Bob Bonifay. "He paid attention to baseball, and there were no race tracks or dog tracks in Macon." Peaches manager Dave Bristol said that there was a certain excitement in the dugout created by the way Rose played the game. "When I turned in my reports—I did that twice a year—I mentioned that he was a big-league prospect and going to be a good player. Phil Seghi felt the same way."[14] "He was just like he was in the majors at Macon, a real tough guy on the field, boom, boom, boom all the time," added Harley Bowers.[15] In fact, the fans around the Sally League had taken notice of Rose's head-first slides and gallops down the first base line on walks and dubbed him "Hollywood."

Rose modeled his all-out-hustle style of play after former St. Louis Cardinals and New York Yankees great Enos "Country" Slaughter. Slaughter ran out every ball he hit, ran down to first on walks, and ran at top speed off the field from the outfield in between innings. According to former *Cincinnati Post* sports writer Earl Lawson, Joe Morgan, who played with Rose on the Cincinnati Big Red Machine teams of the 1970s, used to hassle Rose by telling him, "The old ladies in their 60s and 70s loved him, because you play like the ballplayers they used to watch when they were young."[16] Actually, Rose couldn't have picked a finer role model than Slaughter, who in 19 years in the major leagues wound up his career with a .300 batting average and 2,383 hits. In 1985, Slaughter was elected to the National Baseball Hall of Fame.

The bulk that Rose had added to his body was starting to pay dividends. In a game the Peaches won 4–2 against the Savannah White Sox on July 13, 1962, Rose hit a towering home run on 3–2 pitch over the scoreboard in right center. The ball cleared the wall at the 375-foot mark, dropping over the 30-foot-high scoreboard behind the barrier. It would be his ninth and final home run of the season. However, at that time, he led the Peaches in that category. On August 11, Rose had five hits (a double and four singles) in a 5–4 Peaches victory over the Asheville Tourists.

On August 16, the Peaches were defeated by the Knoxville Smokies, 7–4.

Pete Rose with the Macon Peaches, 1962. (Courtesy of the Middle Georgia Archives, Washington Memorial Library, Macon, Ga.)

A packed house of 8,991 fans, the largest crowd ever in Knoxville's Bill Myer Stadium, was on hand for the game as the Smokies won their 11th game in a row. However, in the account of the game the next morning in *The Macon Telegraph*, Rose was praised even in defeat. "Pete Rose, an All-Star infielder if there is one in the league, led Macon's hopes with a triple and two singles and scored three runs. His triple was the only extra-base hit for the Peaches."[17] In the Peaches' final home game of the 1962 season on August 25, they defeated Portsmouth 16–10. Rose, winding up a great year in Macon, had four hits in six at-bats.

Nineteen sixty-two was a banner year for the Macon Peaches and general manager Bob Bonifay. The ball club drew 100,035 fans to Luther Williams Field, while finishing third in the Sally League but winning the league playoffs. On August 28, Harley Bowers, writing in *The Macon Telegraph*, said, "With only the playoffs remaining, one can look back on the 1962 baseball campaign as the most successful in recent Macon history. The attendance total is something to crow about, too, but assures Macon of continued support from Cincinnati. In looking ahead, one can reasonably expect to see quite a few of this year's stars back for another season in Class A.

Which should assure the Peaches of a much stronger club in 1963, one that will be a genuine threat."[18]

However, Pete Rose had a different vision for the 1963 season. He finished the 1962 season in Macon with a .330 batting average, got 178 hits with nine home runs, and led the league in runs scored (136) and triples (17). Rose's 136 runs scored were the highest total in the South Atlantic League since 1940, when Hooper Triplet of Columbia scored 133 runs. At that time, in 1962, only eight league leaders in runs scored in the history of the Sally League, since it began in 1904, had scored more runs in a season than Rose. Ironically, Pete's roommate Tommy Helms, whom the Reds considered their top prospect, had actually out hit him in 1962, finishing with a .340 average. But Pete Rose had proven that he could meet the challenge, and the Cincinnati front office took notice.

II

The Cincinnati Kid

When Pete Rose reported to the Cincinnati Reds' training camp in Tampa, Florida, in March 1963, he was slated to be on the roster of Reds' AAA farm club in San Diego. Tommy Helms had also been invited to camp but held out for more money. Helms's contract tug-of-war with the Reds' front office might have cost him a chance to make the Reds' roster that year. Eventually he was assigned to San Diego.

As for Rose, no one really expected big things out of him at the training camp. In one of his first exhibition starts on March 12 against Philadelphia, Rose looked weak at bat against Ray Culp as he took a third strike with two runners on base in a 12–6 Phillies victory. But Pete was already Pete Rose, and he played determined to make the big club. One person who took notice of his hustle was Reds manager Fred Hutchinson. Another was New York Yankees pitcher Whitey Ford. During an exhibition game between the Yankees and the Reds, Ford was standing next to Mickey Mantle when Rose drew a walk and proceeded to run down to first base at full throttle. "That," observed Ford, "is 'Charlie Hustle.'"[1] The name stuck, and for the next twenty-four seasons, Pete Rose would build the legend of Charlie Hustle into an American sports icon.

Rose made the team that spring and was headed to Cincinnati to fulfill his boyhood dream of playing with his hometown Reds. He had also fulfilled the dreams of his parents, Harry and LaVerne Rose. However, not everyone was happy about Rose taking a spot on the Reds' roster. The 1963 Cincinnati Reds for the most part were a veteran ball club. Most of the players were

18

holdovers from the 1961 National League championship team: Gordy Coleman, Eddie Kasko, Leo Cardenas, Frank Robinson, Vada Pinson, Johnny Edwards, Joey Jay, Bob Purkey, Jim O'Toole, Gene Freese and Don Blasingame. In fact, Don Blasingame had been the Reds' regular second baseman since 1961 and in 1962 had an outstanding year for the Reds, hitting .281 with 139 hits, while in the field he made just 17 errors in 352 attempts, winding up the season with a .976 fielding average. Blasingame was married to a former beauty queen and was very popular among his Reds teammates. Now his job was threatened by a young, cocky, hometown guy who had been signed to a contract by his uncle and was attempting to make the big jump from Class A ball to the major leagues.

On the day that Pete Rose played his first game in the major leagues, an event was taking place in Georgia that, oddly, was a harbinger of things to come for Rose. The attorney general for the State of Georgia, Eugene Cook had concluded that former University of Georgia athletic director Wallace Butts was not connected with a gambling ring. The attorney general concluded that while Butts had disclosed information that could have affected the outcome of Bulldogs football games, the only evidence that he had of Butts being involved in the gambling ring was a series of telephone calls that Butts had made to persons who had done some gambling. Twenty-five years following Rose's major league debut, his telephone calls would become the primary evidence in the allegations by the major league commissioner's office that he had bet on baseball and had bet on his own team, leading to his lifetime banishment. But Pete began gambling almost as soon as he arrived in the big leagues. According to author Michael Y. Sokolove in his book *Hustle—The Myth, Life and Lies of Pete Rose*, in his rookie season Rose spent nearly every off day at River Downs in Cincinnati. He was even there before night games, catching half the race card before heading for Crosley Field.

Despite Don Blasingame's status with the ball club, Fred Hutchinson inserted Rose at second base in the opening day lineup. Rose was actually surprised at being in the lineup and didn't even know that he was going to start until he noticed his number on the outfield scoreboard prior to the game. A lot of writers like to play down the major league debut of Pete Rose on April 8, 1963, because he didn't get a hit in the game. While there was nothing that Rose did in his major league debut that would have suggested that he was going to be a future candidate for the Hall of Fame, the fact of the matter is that Rose played a key role in the Reds' 5–2 victory over the Pittsburgh Pirates. The jam-packed crowd of 28,896 at Crosley Field received Rose warmly as he started two double plays and was on the pivot end of another. When Rose made his first major league appearance at bat, the hometown crowd gave him an ovation that would be repeated hundreds of

Pete Rose. (National Baseball Hall of Fame Library, Cooperstown, N.Y.)

times to come in major league stadiums all across America during the next 24 years. In the first inning, after being walked and dashing down to first base, he scored the first of 2,165 runs in his career when he crossed home plate on a home run by Frank Robinson.

However, Rose was under the gun. One anonymous veteran on the team told *Cincinnati Enquirer* sports editor Al Heim, "He'll [Rose] have to play good ball because he's got a fine ballplayer sitting on the bench ready to come in if he slows down."[2] The next morning in the *Cincinnati Enquirer*, sports writer Lou Smith predicted that Pete Rose would become the 1963 National League Rookie of the Year: "The Reds' Pete Rose. He promises to become another Enos Slaughter. He not only reeks with color but has loads of ability."[3]

Following the opening game in Cincinnati, the Reds hit the road for Philadelphia, where they dropped two games. Rose didn't get a hit, and Phillies manager Gene Mauch rode him unmercifully from the bench. In the first game at Philadelphia, Rose went 0 for four against fellow Cincinnatian Art Mahaffey, grounding out, flying out and striking out twice while leaving four runners on base. The following night, the Reds lost 10–7, and Rose failed to hit the ball out of the infield in five at-bats. However, in the fourth inning, Rose drew a walk from Phillies pitcher Jack Hamilton and immediately sprinted down to first base. Seeing Rose jet out of the batter's box and head full steam to first raised the ire of Phillies manager Gene Mauch, who called him a "hot dog." From that point on, Mauch was relentless in his riding of Rose every time he came to bat. "I couldn't understand why he was always yelling at me,"[4] Rose said later. "I'd never done anything to him."[5] Finally, on Saturday, April 13, 1963, in a 12–4 loss to the Pirates at Forbes Field in Pittsburgh, Rose got his first major league hit—a triple off of veteran pitcher Bob Friend, breaking his 0-for-12 for debut.

His rough start against Phillies pitching notwithstanding, Rose would go on to thrive against Philadelphia pitching, finishing his career with a .340 batting average against them, his highest lifetime average against any National League team. As for Gene Mauch and his bench tactics against Rose, by July Rose was hitting .347 against Phillies pitching, and Mauch just dropped it. Later Mauch was to say that "riding Rose only made it tougher for us get him out."

Meanwhile a lot of players on the team were giving Rose the cold shoulder, particularly Gene Freese and Don Blasingame. To them he wasn't "Charlie Hustle" but "Charlie pain-in-the-ass." Gordy Coleman remarked that following a road game, the Reds' team bus would pull up to the hotel and a lot of the veteran players would go one way and Rose the other. Some of the resentment of Rose by his teammates was fueled by his over-zealous hometown rooters. Harry and LaVeren Rose, as well as a mighty contingent of fans from Western Hills, flocked down to Crosley Field for every home game and boisterously rooted for the local kid. Over the years, Rose has convinced a number of sports writers like Earl Lawson and authors such as Roger Kahn into believing that his experience of rejection by the veteran players was unique. However, Dave Bristol has a refreshingly different twist on the hazing of Rose. "Just Pete's personality sometimes could cause that. Freese and Blasingame were toward the end of their careers. That kind of hazing in baseball at that time was common, they always gave a rookie a hard time. Hey, Rose took Blasingame's position. I'd be mad too, wouldn't you?"[6]

Since all the white veteran ball players on the Reds, notwithstanding Jim O'Toole, would not socialize with him, Rose was befriended by the black players on the team, mainly Frank Robinson and Vada Pinson, who took him out to dinner on the road and kidded around with him in the clubhouse. "Here was this kid," Pinson says, "who wanted to be a major leaguer more than anything in the world. But he was so raw, he just didn't know how. Frank Robinson and I took a little time to show him. Dressing. Tipping. Basics like that. No big deal. Just a little kindness to a youngster."[7] According to Frank Robinson, "Nobody had to show Pete how to hit, but they wouldn't show him how to be a major leaguer. So we did."[8]

Robinson was all too familiar with the negative attitudes of his teammates. While he was the acknowledged team leader of the Reds on the field, he was still resented by some of the white veteran players on the team. According to Bernie Stowe, the Reds' equipment manager for decades, "Robinson and Pinson were both self-centered when they came up. It was 'I this and me that.' They both went to the same high school, and it became them against the rest."[9] Perhaps Robinson and Pinson fueled some of the dislike for themselves among the Reds' veterans; they made the most money and really didn't care what others thought about them. Left-handed pitcher Jim O'Toole was aware of this personality split on the team and attempted to counsel Rose, telling him that to be accepted by the white players on the team all he had to do was distance himself from Robinson and Pinson. However, Pete didn't do that, and the resentment it created reached all the way up to the level of the Reds' front office.

As for his rookie-year hazing, Rose states, "They didn't want a rookie on second base, because they had veterans in all other positions. And the only guys that treated me with any dignity and decency was Frank Robinson and Vada Pinson, the black guys. It was a cliquish team in those days. That's why they didn't win. The black players were just like me when I was a kid. No car, no money, no suit of clothes. All they had to do was play sports."[10]

Now there are some authors and sports writers who believe that it was manager Fred Hutchinson who forced the issue of Rose's fraternization habits into the Reds' front office claiming that he personally had a problem with the fact that Rose, Robinson and Pinson had become too chummy for the limits of his racial tolerance. But Rose himself has never implicated Hutchinson in the matter. However, it remains a fact that Reds president and general manager Bill DeWitt also had a problem with the relationship, did call Rose into his office and subsequently question the value of his continuing association with the black ballplayers on the team. It was at that meeting that Rose informed DeWitt of the social isolation he was faced with on the team, with veterans Gene Freese and Don Blasingame being the ringleaders of the plot against him. Early on, both Hutchinson and DeWitt saw marquee quality in Rose, and swift action was taken to protect the young rising star. Gene Freese was eventually sent down to the minor leagues with the Reds' AAA affiliate club at San Diego, and on November 26, 1963, he was sold to Pittsburgh. On July 1, 1963, Don Blasingame was sold to the Washington Senators. For the rest of the team, like it or not, Pete Rose was their second baseman, and he went on to become the 1963 National League Rookie of Year. In Pete's first year in the major leagues, he played in 157 games, hit for a .273 average with 170 hits and scored 101 runs. In 1963, the Reds led by fire-balling pitcher Jim Maloney (23–7), finished in fifth place one game behind the Philadelphia Phillies and a distant fourteen games behind the pennant-winning Los Angeles Dodgers.

Although Pete Rose was a big league ball player, for the most part, as he cruised around the streets of Western Hills in his mint green Corvette, he was like most other 22-year-old men in Cincinnati. He was focused on building his career, perhaps starting a family, and also not adverse to seeking some adventure in life. One afternoon during the 1963 season, while on an outing to Cincinnati's River Downs race track, Pete met Karolyn Ann Englehardt. They began to date and quickly fell in love. During the off season, on January 25, 1964, Pete and Karolyn were married. As she had been raised a Catholic, the wedding took place at St. William's Church in the Western Hills neighborhood of Price Hill, and a picture of the happy couple being showered with rice ran on the front pages of Cincinnati newspapers the next day. Following the wedding, Pete reported to Fort Knox, Kentucky to participate in military training with the Ohio National Guard.

Rose reported to spring training in Tampa, Florida in March 1964, in an awakened America that was suddenly taking stock of its soul. During his rookie year in June 1963, the civil rights movement had come into full bloom with Governor George Wallace of Alabama defiantly standing in the schoolhouse door at the University of Alabama, attempting to block the enrollment of black students, while millions watched on television. Civil rights leader Medgar Evers had been gunned down in Mississippi, and in August, Dr. Martin Luther King delivered his "I Have a Dream" speech at the Lincoln

Frank Robinson. (Photo File, Inc.)

Memorial in Washington, D.C., that made the nation refocus on the plight of black Americans. Then on November 22, the unthinkable happened: President John F. Kennedy was assassinated in Dallas and the nation mourned.

Rose had a relatively normal and productive spring training in 1964, but the season ahead was to be a humbling experience for him. Fred Hutchinson, the Reds' manager, was diagnosed with cancer before the 1964 season began. It was Hutch who had seen the raw potential in Rose and played him ahead of a capable veteran second basemen like Don Blasingame in 1963. Now Hutch wanted to take his mentorship of Rose to the next level. Hutchinson had not yet found resolution in the issue of Rose's fraternization with the black players on the team. To that end, he was convinced that it was in the best interest of Rose that he take action to separate him from the fellowship and advice of the black ballplayers, namely Pinson and Robinson, who seemed to be so much of a thorn in the sides of Hutchinson and Bill DeWitt, Sr. Therefore, Hutchinson approached DeWitt and convinced him to hire an extra coach, a white coach to act as an adviser to Rose and help him with developing certain aspects of social etiquette. Former Reds All-Star second baseman Johnny Temple was chosen for the task and signed as a player-coach. Hutchinson was convinced that Temple was the right person for the job. Hutchinson later told sports writer Earl Lawson, "I'd want him to go out to dinner with Pete on the road...polish him up a little."[11] Johnny Temple was a classy dresser and knew how to order a meal in a fine restaurant. Temple fit in well with the crowd at Toots Shor's in New York City, which was an environment light years away from Rose's usual family dining experience at the Trolley Tavern, a gritty family seafood restaurant and bar down along the Ohio River at Anderson Ferry in Cincinnati. Through the Johnny Temple intervention must have been a humiliating experience for Rose, he played along. He was still a dewy-eyed kid from Sedamsville, just happy to be a big league ball player making $15,000 a year, and his days of making waves in the Reds' front office were years away yet.

The Reds lost the opening game of the 1964 campaign at home to the Houston Colts, 6–3, and Rose went 0–4. The opening game was also a disappointment for Rose's father-in-law, who had given anyone interested 2–1 odds that he would get a hit in the opening game. On April 23 when the Reds visited Houston, Rose went 0–4 again but played a key role in a very odd historical event. Going into the top of the ninth inning, the score was tied 0–0. Houston pitcher Ken Johnson had a no-hitter going. Rose led off the ninth and tapped a bunt just to the right of home plate. Johnson quickly fielded the ball, but then threw wildly to Pete Runnels at first base, and Rose scampered down to second on a two-base error. Chico Ruiz then grounded out, and Rose reached third base. Vada Pinson followed by hitting a routine grounder toward second base. Future Hall of Fame member Nellie Fox attempted to field the ball but wound up booting it, thus allowing Rose to score, giving the Reds a 1–0 lead. In the bottom of the ninth, Joe Nuxhall shut down the Colts, and Ken Johnson had become the first pitcher in major league history to pitch a no-hitter and lose the game.

Rose struggled at the plate early in the season as the sophomore jinx set in. He wound up the month of May by going 0 for eight in a doubleheader with the Cardinals, and by June he was not hitting much more than his weight. Consequently, Hutchinson benched him and inserted Bobby Klaus into the lineup at second base. Distraught, Rose called his uncle Buddy Bloebaum for advice. According to author Roger Kahn, writing in *Pete Rose: My Story*, Bloebaum told Pete he was swinging the bat defensively. He said to lower his hands and attack the ball.

Nonetheless, while Rose continued to ride the wood, he made contributions, getting in the game as a late-inning replacement for Klaus. On June 20, he came up to bat for Klaus in the bottom of the eighth in a game against the Dodgers and laid down a squeeze bunt off of Don Drysdale that drove in the deciding run as Leo Cardenas scampered across the plate to give the Reds a 5–4 lead. By June 30, Rose was back in the lineup and spared the Reds the humiliation of having a second no-hitter tossed against them in the 1964 season, this time by the Cubs' Larry Jackson, when he led off the seventh with a single for the only Reds hit in the game. By July 4, Rose was hitting .253, which was actually a higher average than a few other players in the Reds' lineup, including Gordy Coleman and Tommy Harper.

On July 19, Bobby Klaus was sold to the New York Mets, and Rose had

Pete Rose, 1964. (The Topps Company, Inc.)

second base all to himself. On August 28, the Reds released Johnny Temple. Pete Rose was now going to have to order his own meals too. The nurturing of Rose was finished, and he completed the 1964 season playing in 136 games and hitting .269 with 139 hits. From that point on, he did not have fewer than 176 hits in a season until the strike-shorted year of 1981, when he got 140 hits in 107 games.

As a result of a monumental September swoon by Philadelphia, the Reds wound up in a battle for the pennant that year. The Philadelphia Phillies after leading the league for most of the season, collapsed in September, blowing six and a half-game lead by losing ten games in a row with twelve games remaining on the schedule. However, the Reds eventually lost out in the pennant race to the St. Louis Cardinals on the last day of season, finishing in a second-place tie with the Phillies, just one game behind.

There was a sad epilogue to the 1964 season for Rose, as he lost a true friend in manager Fred Hutchinson. Hutchinson's health had deteriorated so badly that in August he had to step down as Reds manager and turn the reigns over to Dick Sisler. Following a courageous battle Hutchinson succumbed to his cancer on November 12, 1964.

In 1965, Dick Sisler officially took over as manager of the Reds, and Pete Rose came into his own. On September 16 at Shea Stadium in New York, Rose got the 500th hit of his career off of Al Jackson. That season he hit .312, which was the fifth highest batting average in the National League, and he led the league in hits with 209. Pete also became a father in 1965 with the birth of his daughter, Fawn.

However, the Reds finished in fifth place, eight games behind the Los Angeles Dodgers. As a result of the Reds' lackluster performance, Dick Sisler was fired as manager and replaced by Don Heffner for the 1966 season. Then on December 9, 1965, Bill DeWitt, Sr. would make one the most boneheaded trades in baseball history when he shipped perennial team leader Frank Robinson to Baltimore for pitchers Milt Pappas, Jack Baldschum and outfielder Dick Simpson. DeWitt had stated publicly that he considered Robinson to be an old thirty. Old, indeed. In the 1966 season, all that old man Robinson did was win the triple crown (.316 batting average, 49 home runs and 122 RBIs) and lead the Orioles to the American League pennant and world championship over the Los Angeles Dodgers in a four-game sweep.

In 1966, Rose was moved to third base by manager Don Heffner. Brooding and disgruntled, Rose went into a slump and after 16 games was hitting below .200. However, after his old Macon roommate Tommy Helms took over at third he was moved back to second base and once again flourished. He had another fine year, hitting .313 with 205 hits. Also in 1966, the Reds began to assemble the players who would make up the Big Red Machine teams of the 1970s. Tony Perez had taken over first base, and of course Helms joined the team, playing third base while hitting .284 and was named National League Rookie of the Year. However, as the team began to falter once again, after 83 games with the Reds' record at 37–46, Don Heffner was fired and replaced as manager by another familiar face from Rose's Macon experience, manager Dave Bristol. The Reds went on to finish fourth in 1966, 18 games behind Los Angeles.

Assessing the impact of the trade of Frank Robinson in 1966, Dave Bristol said, "you could feel the loss of Robinson on the team. He was one of the best players that ever played. As a matter of fact I played with him in the minors at Ogden. There really wasn't a team leader on the Reds that year."[12] When Bristol was asked if Pete Rose was considered the new team leader on the Reds, his reply was "No."[13] Despite the fallout that resulted from the controversial trade of Frank Robinson, Bristol still does not speak ill of Reds president and general manager Bill DeWitt, Sr. "He was just a frugal person. He was in a small market and trying to make a living. I doubt that he would believe it today if he saw the salaries."[14] Bristol went on to say that he really enjoyed being reunited in Cincinnati with so many of his players from the Macon Peaches. In addition to Pete Rose there were Tommy Helms, Art Shamsky, Tony Perez and Mel Queen, and Ted Davidson was there too. "We all came up through the system together. It was God send."[15]

At least on paper, the Reds were a good ball club going into the 1967 season. In 1967, more pieces of the Big Red Machine were added to the roster. Lee May joined the club to take over first base, so that called for some changes in the lineup. At the request of Bristol, Pete Rose made the switch from second

Pete Rose. (National Baseball Hall of Fame Library, Cooperstown, N.Y.)

base to left field. This permitted Bristol to move Tony Perez to third base and insert Tommy Helms at second base, alongside All-Star shortstop Leo Cardenas. Pitcher Gary Nolan joined the team as well, and at the end of the 1967 season, a nineteen-year-old catcher by the name of Johnny Bench was called up from the minors and played in 26 games. Nonetheless, the Reds came up short in the pennant race again, finishing in fourth place with a record of 87–75, 14½ games behind the pennant winning St. Louis Cardinals.

Pete Rose had another good year in 1967, averaging .301 with 176 hits. He now had 899 hits for his first five years in the major leagues. No one was paying any attention to the matter at the time, but Rose's 899 hits in his first five years had eclipsed the total of another ballplayer by the name of Tyrus Raymond Cobb, who had 764 hits in his first five years in the big leagues.

In 1968 and 1969, Rose won back-to-back National League batting titles. He won the crown in 1968 with a .335 average, led the league with 210 hits and finished second in doubles with 42 and runs scored with 94. Coming down the stretch in the 1968 season Rose found himself in a head-to-head battle for the batting title with the Pirates' Matty Alou, when in the last week of the season he suddenly went into a slump. Then his roommate Tommy Helms, who was home in North Carolina nursing a fractured wrist, showed up at Crosley Field, it raised Rose's spirits, and he went five for five in the second to last game of the season. Rose clinched the batting title on the last day of the 1968 season when he went one for three against San Francisco pitcher Ray Sadecki while Alou went hitless in four trips to the plate against the Chicago Cubs. According to Rose, "I had a guy posted in the bleachers at old Crosley Field. He must have had a hot line to Chicago, because he told me what Alou did every time he was bat."[16]

But once again, the Reds, sprinkled with talent all over, failed to win the pennant, finishing fourth in 1968 despite the fact that Rose had won the batting title and Johnny Bench had been named National League Rookie of the Year. Pete had been voted to a starting spot on the All-Star team outfield that year, but had to sit the game out with a severely sore shoulder. Willie Mays substituted for him and scored the only run of the game in a 1–0 National League victory at the Houston Astrodome.

In 1969, division play was introduced into the Major Leagues, and the Reds finished third in the National League West Division. Rose won his second batting title with an average of .348 in another close race with Pittsburgh's Roberto Clemente. He was also first in runs scored with 120, second in hits with 218, second in triples with 11 and fourth in total bases with 321. On November 16, 1969, Pete and Karolyn Rose were graced with the birth of their son Pete Jr. (aka Petey).

Despite the fact that Pete Rose was now a big league star of considerable stature, he had yet to play on a pennant-winning team. That was about to change, as the Big Red Machine was now built and ready to roll off the assembly line. In addition to Rose, now playing in right field and winning his second batting title in the 1969 season, first baseman Lee May, "the Big Bopper" as his teammates referred to him, had hit 38 home runs and had 110 RBIs. Tony Perez, known as "the Big Dog" playing at third base, had 37 home runs and 122 RBIs. Johnny Bench, the catcher known as "the Little General," had hit 26 home runs with 90 RBIs. Bobby Tolan, playing center field, batted .315 and hit 21 home runs with 93 RBIs. Even Alex Johnson playing in left field had hit .315 with 17 home runs. Rounding out the starting eight were Tommy Helms at second base and Woody Woodward at shortstop. The Big Red Machine was loaded! Even their pitching staff looked promising in 1969, with veterans such as left-hander Jim Merritt, Clay Carroll, and Jim Maloney, at the end of his career but with three no-hitters during the decade of the 1960s, along with promising young hurlers such as Gary Nolan and Wayne Granger.

Unfortunately, manager Dave Bristol didn't get the chance to see his ball club become the powerhouse that it was destined to be. He was fired following the 1969 season and replaced with a virtually unknown fellow by the name of George Lee "Sparky" Anderson. Nonetheless, it was Dave Bristol who had built the Big Red Machine, position by position, from 1962 through 1969 at Macon and in Cincinnati. Bristol, the quintessential professional, has no regrets and holds no ill will toward Bob Howsam. Howsam had taken over as general manager of the Cincinnati Reds in 1967 after the team was sold by Bill DeWitt, Sr. to a group of local investors for $7 million. Referring to Howsam, Bristol remarked, "He was a good baseball man."[17] As for his successor as manager, "I told Sparky Anderson at the World Series that year [1969], you're

Dave Bristol. (National Baseball Hall of Fame
Library, Cooperstown, N.Y.)

getting one hell'va ball club and they know how to win. That was the best team a man could have dreamed to have. The next year at the World Series [1970] Sparky told me, 'Dave, you were 110% correct.'"[18]

By 1969, Pete Rose had become more than just a household name to the Cincinnati fans and general population of the city. He had developed into a genuine local hero. He was the "Cincinnati Kid;" he was one of theirs, and the people in Cincinnati embraced him and were immensely proud of his accomplishments. By 1969, WCET, a public education station in the city, had already made a documentary film about the life of Rose that was an hour long and hosted by former New York Yankees pitcher, Reds radio broadcaster and Hall of Fame member Waite Hoyt. The devotion to Rose in the city was growing stronger. In September 1968, the expansion Cincinnati Bengals were making their debut in the city, but they had to share the spotlight with Pete Rose going neck and neck with Matty Alou for the National League batting championship. In September 1968, Pete Rose took center stage over any other sporting event in Cincinnati, come hell or high water, until the baseball season was over.

Seven months later, in early April 1969, on a Sunday evening, the rather raucous rhythm and blues band Wayne Cochran & the CC Riders arrived in Cincinnati and were appearing at a local nightclub called the Inner Circle, located in the Cincinnati neighborhood of Corryville, just west of the University of Cincinnati campus. This was the place to be, and upon entering the Inner Circle that evening, one quickly discovered that it was jam-packed, extremely loud and in a state of high energy. When Wayne Cochran finally appeared on the stage that Sunday evening, almost immediately he and the band drove the audience into a frenzy. Then, about forty-five minutes into the show and in between songs, as a profusely sweating Cochran began to

Pete Rose. (National Baseball Hall of Fame Library, Cooperstown, N.Y.)

ease back towards the microphone to sing a slow ballad, all at once, from the back of the club, a chorus of loud cheers began to flow forward over the smoky tables. It was Pete Rose! He and his wife Karolyn had just arrived at the Inner Circle from the airport, with Pete fresh from playing a doubleheader that afternoon in Atlanta. The Inner Circle was to Cincinnati what the Copa Cabana was to New York City. The second wildest rhythm & blues band in the world next to James Brown had come to Cincinnati, so it was only fitting that Cincinnati's favorite son had come to pay homage. Everyone in the club that night thought that they were experiencing something very special—and perhaps they were. For a few hours in the spring of 1969, the rowdy but tightly controlled club seemed like it was the center of the universe. To the patrons of the Inner Circle that night, the ravages of the Vietnam war and the assassination of Martin Luther King seemed momentarily forgotten. Maybe it was only coincidental that Wayne Cochran and Pete Rose were both there together that night for a few hours. Maybe it was only coincidental that anyone was there, but to many it all seemed natural for the glorious celebration that was at hand. The presence of Pete Rose had not upstaged Wayne Cochran, but had actually enhanced his appearance, and it was suddenly difficult to distinguish which was the real star of the show.

Such was the stature that Pete Rose gained around Cincinnati in 1969. At the time he was just seven years and 1,327 hits into his career and was a regular guy who wanted to be part of his hometown and the town in turn wanted him to be part of it. It was a mutual civic love affair that would only grow larger with time. There was no arrogance in Rose's demeanor then. He was a very public person; he knew who he was, was not snobbish and relished the limelight. A fan could rub shoulders with him at the race track, or on any given Saturday morning in the off season you might even find Pete having breakfast at a table with various blue-collar workers at the Wheel Cafe, a now defunct diner in downtown Cincinnati. If you were driving around Western Hills, you might look to see if one of his fancy cars were parked outside the Gay 90s Restaurant in the satellite community of Cheviot. Maybe the Inner Circle, the Wheel Cafe and the Gay 90s were not exactly at the level of grandeur of the Toots Shor's experience that Rose was forced into with Johnny Temple, but it was home and Pete Rose and Cincinnati, and back then it all seemed perfect together.

III

Rose and the Big Red Machine

In January 1970, Rose signed a contract with the Reds for $105,000 per year. He thus became the highest-paid player ever to wear a Cincinnati uniform. Furthermore, Rose and the Cincinnati Reds were about to enter the decade of the 1970s with an elite ball club and a shinning new stadium. The Reds also had a new manager, Sparky Anderson, who was about to inherit the powerful Reds ball club built by Dave Bristol during the 1960s. For Anderson, the 1970 Cincinnati Reds would be the very first major league team that he would manage in an odyssey that would take him all the way to a spot in the National Baseball Hall of Fame in Cooperstown, New York.

Sparky Anderson decided to get things rolling when he named Pete Rose captain of the Reds. With the appointment, Rose became the first player ever to be officially named captain on a Reds team in their 101-year history, dating back to 1869. Anderson said that when he first met Rose after being named manager, the two of them had just gotten on a bus to go out on one of the Reds' winter marketing caravans. "He [Rose] came up to me and said, 'Skip, remember this. I make the most money on this team and the guys follow me. So just tell me what you want done.'"[1] Rose had the most player seniority (seven years) of all the Reds and was now a veteran. By evolution, he had become one of the class of ballplayers that use to harass him as a rookie. But Rose was secure in his status on the team and used his position to motivate rather than agitate.

Whether or not Pete Rose was the true leader of the "Big Red Machine" is open to debate. In actuality the extraordinarily talented Reds teams of the

Sparky Anderson. (National Baseball Hall of Fame Library, Cooperstown, N.Y.)

1970s had many of leaders besides Rose. Johnny Bench was a leader; Joe Morgan, who joined the team in 1972, would become a leader by steady production, and of course the man they called the "Big Dog," Tony Perez, is more often than not acknowledged as the supreme leader and motivator of the "Big Red Machine." Sparky Anderson once said that Tony Perez was the leader who kept all the other leaders on the Big Red Machine in harmony.

The power-laden 1970 Reds got off to fast start, beating the Expos 5–1 on opening day. The last game was played at historic but cozy little Crosley Field, where the deepest part of the park was 390 feet in right center field on June 24, 1970, with Lee May and Johnny Bench belting back-to-back home runs in the eighth inning off of Juan Marichal to beat the San Francisco Giants 5–4. The final out in the old park came when Wayne Granger got Bobby Bonds on a ground ball back to the mound. Pete Rose had a triple, which of course was the final three-base hit in the 58-year history of the ballpark. Ironically, when the Reds played their first game at the new Riverfront Stadium on June 30, 1970, before 51,051 fans, defeating the Atlanta Braves 8–2, Pete Rose again tripled, thereby getting the first three-bagger in the history of the new ballpark. For the record, Henry Aaron hit the first home run at Riverfront Stadium.

Two weeks later, on a very sticky, hot evening of July 14, 1970, the Major League All-Star Game would be played at the Reds' new stadium in Cincinnati, and the city's native son, Pete Rose, would take center stage. By contrast to the way the Bud Selig All-Star Games are played in the new millennium, in 1970 the game was still played for real. Players took pride in their leagues and in being named to the All-Star teams. There was no way that an All-Star game would wind up in a fiasco such as that which took place in 2002 at Milwaukee with the game ending in a tie. The players played with zeal, and going into the 1970 All-Star Game, the National League had won seven games in a row dating back to 1963. The 1970 All-Star Game was first one for which the fans had voted for the starting players since 1957. President Richard M. Nixon had come to Cincinnati, was in the stands at Riverfront Stadium when the game began, and was still present when the game entered the bottom of the 12th inning with the score tied 4–4.

With two outs in the bottom of 12th, Pete Rose hit a single and then went to second on a single by the Dodgers' Bill Grabarkewitz. Then the Cubs' Jim Hickman singled into center field, and Rose took off full-speed for third as Leo Durocher, coaching at third, waved him home. Rounding third, Rose looked over his shoulder and saw the Royals' Amos Otis fielding the ball and getting ready to unleash a throw to the plate. As Rose approached the plate with a head full of steam, he momentarily thought about making a head first slide. But the Indians' catcher, Ray Fosse, was positioned up the third base line and had home plate blocked, so Rose decided to run through Fosse and hopefully knock the ball loose. Rose approached Fosse at the same time that the throw from Otis was arriving at the plate, so he bent forward and drove his left shoulder hard into Fosse, knocking the ball loose. Fosse fell backward from the force of the collision, and the ball rolled all the way to the backstop as Rose fell over him onto the plate, scoring the winning run.

As a result of the collision, Fosse suffered a separated and fractured right shoulder. Rose, too, was shaken and missed the next three games with a bruised knee. A fallacy in the Rose-Fosse collision that has continued to exist since the 1970 All-Star Game is that following the collision with Rose, Fosse was never as good a catcher as before. But prior to the 1970 season, Ray Fosse had only played in 44 major league games between 1967 and the start of the 1970 season, hardly enough experience to make a definitive judgment on Fosse's capabilities. As for why Fosse would have put himself in harms way with a 200 pound Pete Rose charging at him full speed down the third base line, he has stated, "I was playing with guys like Brooks and Frank Robinson and Harmon Killebrew. I wanted the respect of my peers. I wasn't going to look like a fool and get out of the way."[2] One of the postscript ironies of the Rose-Fosse incident is that the night before the All-Star Game, Fosse had been a guest in Rose's home, talking baseball late into the night.

Another is that Ray Fosse's hometown is Marion, Illinois, a community that would become home to Rose for five months when he was sentenced to spend time in Marion Federal Prison in 1990 for tax evasion.

Later in the season, on August 29, 1970, Rose got the 1,500th hit of his career off of the Expos' Carl Morton at Montreal's Jarry Park. The Big Red Machine cruised to the 1970 National League West Division title, winning

102 games and finishing 14½ games ahead of the second-place Los Angeles Dodgers, then crushed the Eastern Division champion Pittsburgh Pirates in three straight games for the pennant. While Rose finished the season with 205 hits and a .316 batting average, his contributions were but part of the huge supporting cast on the team. Johnny Bench's hallmark year was 1970, and his statistics for the season were never eclipsed during his playing days. In 1970 Bench became the youngest player, at 22 years old, ever to win the National League MVP award when he led the league with 45 home runs and 145 RBIs. In addition, Tony Perez had hit .317 with 40 home runs, Lee May had 34 home runs and 94 RBIs and Bobby Tolan hit .316.

Despite all this power at the plate, three of Reds' pitchers had suffered arm injuries during the season, and Cincinnati lost the World Series to the Baltimore in five games as the Orioles outscored the Reds 33–20. For Pete Rose and all the Reds, the World Series was a huge disappointment. Playing in his first World Series, Rose hit only .250, going five for 20. Brooks Robinson, the series MVP, had one of the finest World Series that any player has ever experienced. Robinson hit .429 in the Series, tying the record with nine hits in five games, including two home runs, but what is remembered most about Robinson's Series is his spectacular fielding at third base. Time and time again, he robbed Reds batters of hits with spectacular falling-down backhand stabs, amazing leaping grabs and acrobatic throws to nail Reds runners at first base and squelch rallies.

Following the Series, the Reds' Johnny Bench said, "I never saw Pie Traynor play, but if he was better at playing third than Brooks, he had to be inhuman."

For Pete Rose, the winter of 1970–71 was to be a dark one. On December 9, 1970, as Rose sat in a barber's chair getting a haircut, he received the news that his father Harry had died of a heart attack. Harry Rose was 57 years old. Although he had the opportunity to see his son become a big league star and play in a World Series, Harry Rose passed away much too soon to see Pete rise to the enormous heights he would eventually attain in his career. The death of his beloved father would continue to haunt Pete Rose for years to come. He had been the water boy on his father's semi-professional football team, and Harry Rose had been his constant inspiration. Now suddenly he was gone.

With the 1971 season fast approaching, Rose began the first of his many battles with the Cincinnati Reds' front office over his salary. For the 1971 season, Reds general manager Bob Howsam offered Rose the same $105,000 that he signed for in 1970. Consequently Rose threatened to sit out the 1971 season, even though some of the fans expressed feelings that he was being disingenuous by turning-down a six-figure salary. But the fans took on less importance with Rose than economic matters. Suddenly he began to take them for granted. He was no longer elated about wearing a big league uniform; he was aware of his potential, he was an established star, and he knew it. In 1970, he had finished in a tie with the Cubs' Billy Williams for the most hits (205) in the National League and third in doubles (37). Rose was now well on his way to becoming Pete Rose, Inc. He had opened a bowling alley with Johnny Bench and started a family restaurant in Western Hills. While baseball was still paramount in his thinking, he was now looking beyond the day-to-day rigors of the major league schedule. Pete wanted to make money. Nonetheless, Rose settled for a token raise of $2,500 and began spring training.

The glitter of the 1970 season was now behind the "Big Red Machine," and the team looked forward to the 1971 season feeling confident that they could win it all. However, something happened on the way to the pennant: The machine ran out of gas. In the 1971 season, the Reds finished in a fourth-place tie with Houston, posting a disappointing 79–83 record, 11 games behind the division-winning San Francisco Giants. In 1970, the Reds had scored 775 runs, but in the 1971 season all they could muster were 586 runs, a drop in run production of nearly 25 percent. In addition, the Reds' pitching in 1971 had become pitiful. Lefty Jim Merritt, who had won twenty games in 1970 (20–12), won just one in 1971 (1–11). Gary Nolan had fallen from 18–7 in 1970 to 12–15 in 1971. Then there was Wayne Simpson, who had burst on the scene in 1970 with a blazing fastball, posting a record of 14–3, including a one-hitter against the Los Angeles Dodgers at cozy little Crosley Field. But in 1971, his record fell to 4–7. The only members of the 1971 Big Red Machine to continue their production of the previous year were Pete Rose, the only player to hit over .300, finishing with a .304 average and 192 hits, Lee May, who hit 39 home runs, and pitchers Don Gullet (16–4) and Clay Carroll (10–4) with 14 saves. Bobby Tolan had missed the entire season with a torn Achilles tendon suffered while playing basketball in the off season. The subpar year of the Reds regulars in 1971 was so endemic that even "The Big Dog," Tony Perez, had lost his stroke, hitting only 25 home runs with a .269 average. Following his MVP year of 1970, Johnny Bench had simply imploded in 1971. He fell into the doghouse with the Riverfront Stadium boobirds, hitting just 27 home runs and batting a paltry .238. In some Cincinnati taverns, Johnny Bench, MVP, was suddenly being referred to as "Johnny Bummer." Consequently, during spring training in 1972, Bench announced that he would no longer tip his cap to the fans after hitting a home run.

By 1971, Johnny Bench had become the matinee idol of the Reds, to the displeasure of Rose, who relished the limelight. Perhaps Bench's celebrity had contributed to his decline in production, as the handsome 23-year-old bachelor spent too many nights out on the town in Cincinnati night spots in Mt. Adams, or the Inner Circle and the Den of the Little Foxes at the Holiday Inn.

Johnny Bench had become a man about town and a scaled-down Cincinnati version of New York's "Broadway Joe" Namath. He dated pretty girls and owned an auto dealership in addition to the partnership with Rose in a bowling alley. Following his successful 1970 season, he debuted as a singer in Las Vegas, had a two-minute role in an episode of *Mission Impossible*, presented a trophy to the University of Cincinnati Homecoming Queen, appeared on the Johnny Carson show, and even toured Vietnam with Bob Hope. Somewhere along the line, in pursuit of this busy agenda, his production on the field simply took a nosedive.

However, the problem with the Reds went far beyond Bench. Something was drastically wrong with the team. Prior to the 1971 season, no other Reds team had finished below .500 since 1966. The "Big Red Machine" needed repairs, and the front office took notice. General manager Bob Howsam had to do something to rejuvenate this talented bunch of under-achievers, and he did it on November 29, 1971. He negotiated what is regarded as one of the best trades in baseball history when he sent slugging first baseman Lee May, utility player Jimmy Stewart and second baseman Tommy Helms to the Houston Astros in exchange for second baseman Joe Morgan, infielder Denis Menke, pitcher Jack Billingham and outfielders Ed Armbrister and Cesar Geronimo. To complete the re-tooling of the Big Red Machine, Bob Howsam struck another deal, acquiring left-hander Tommy Hall from Minnesota to bolster the Reds' bullpen in exchange for Wayne Granger.

The trading of All-Star Tommy Helms wasn't very popular with Reds fans at the time. Most loyal Reds fans were somewhat confused by the intended value of the trade. The believed that the Reds could win a pennant without Lee May at first base, but that Tommy Helms was another matter. A look at statistics for Helms and Morgan in 1971 didn't seem to justify the trade. Joe Morgan had hit .256 in 1971; Tommy Helms had hit .258. Morgan had batted in 56 runs, and Helms had batted in 52. Morgan had a fielding average of .986, Helms, .990. Joe Morgan was a virtually unknown player in Cincinnati. His reputation coming out of Houston was that of a moody ballplayer and a troublemaker of sorts who couldn't get along with his manager Harry "the Hat" Walker. Therefore the average Cincinnati Reds fan was a little bit skeptical of the trade.

Pete Rose was a little skeptical, too. Tommy Helms had grown up in the Reds organization and played shortstop alongside of Pete Rose at second base with the Macon Peaches in the minors. When Helms came up to majors as a full-time player in 1966, he played primarily at third base. However, in the 1967 season Pete Rose moved to right field to make room for Helms to play at second. Helms was Rose's roommate on the road, and when he first came up to majors, he lived in a spare bedroom in the Roses' home. Helms was big on the city's night life scene, too. He operated a disco in downtown Cincinnati on Walnut Street called "Tommy Helms' Dugout" that was located directly across from smut king publisher Larry Flynt's "Hustler Lounge." Tony Perez, another good friend of Rose's, said when he joined the Reds, "He [Rose] ran with Tommy Helms then, we never see him. They crazy."[4] In 1970, a reporter asked Pete Rose what he would like to do when he was finished as a player. Rose replied, "I'm going to manage the Reds and Tommy Helms is going to be one of my coaches."[5] To this very day, Helms still feels a deep sense of loyalty to his friendship with Rose and takes extreme caution to not involve himself in anything that may have the potential to cause any controversy for Rose.

The 1972 major league season was delayed by a players' strike that lasted for thirteen days. When play began, the retooled "Big Red Machine" picked up where they left off in the 1971 campaign and finished April with 5–8 record. By May 10, the Reds were 8–13 following a 4–2 loss at Riverfront Stadium to the Chicago Cubs. Sparky Anderson said, "That night following the game as usual I went straight to the clubhouse and into my room. Then I turned around and came back into the clubhouse and I told the players, I want everyone out of here as quickly as you can get out. I want you to shower and get out. I want no one to worry about one single thing. I give you my solemn promise that we will win this thing. Then I walked back in my room and from that day forward we never looked back."[6]

On May 12, the Reds beat the St. Louis Cardinals 5–4 and began a nine-game winning streak. Then on May 28, as the Reds began a twelve-day road trip, they had a record of 18–17 and were in third place, four and a half games behind the Houston Astros. On May 29, the Reds arrived in Houston, and Tommy Helms sought out his friend Pete Rose. "You just ain't as big as you used to be," said Helms.[7] "What do you mean?" asked Rose.[8] "Well, the other night they had it on the scoreboard, 'Come See The Big Red Machine. Tony Perez, Johnny Bench, Bobby Tolan and Little Joe [Morgan].' They didn't even mention you. What are you hitting anyway?"[9] "More than you," answered Rose. I'm hitting .250."[10] "Well, then we're even, because I'm hitting .250 too," said Helms.[11] Rose went on to tell Helms that despite his slump, when he started to hit again, he was going to confuse his son Petey, because he thought that all he was supposed to do was hit the ball, run to first, and turn right and head for the dugout. "When I start making that left turn and sliding he's going to have ask what I'm doing."[11]

The Reds swept the Astros in that four-game series and left Houston in second place, trailing the Los Angeles Dodgers by two games. On June 25, the Reds beat the Astros at Riverfront Stadium in Cincinnati, took over first place, and never relinquished it for the rest of the season, cruising to the National League West Division title by 10½ games over second-place Houston.

Pete Rose did start to hit again and finished the 1972 season with a .307 batting average and 198 hits, most in the National League. However, the thirteen-day players strike cost Pete another 200-hit season. He lost eight games and possibly 34–38 at-bats. It was without a doubt another season of solid Rose contribution to the Reds' success. But however hard Rose may have tried in 1972, the season belonged to Johnny Bench.

The long slump that Bench had found himself in during the 1971 season carried over into the 1972 season, and he had only one single in his first 22 at-bats. Consequently, the Riverfront Stadium boobirds were unrelenting in their torment of Bench. Despite the possibility that Bench was suffering some anxiety about the poor health of his mother, many fans simply chalked up his poor performance to nothing else but arrogance. But Bench started to come out of his season-long slump when the Reds made the road trip to Houston in May. Between May 30 and June 3, Bench hit seven home runs in five games, tying a National League record set in 1929 by Jim Bottomley of the St. Louis Cardinals. At one point he had an eleven-game hitting streak, in which he hit .447 with 21 hits in 47 at-bats, driving in 18 runs.

On July 10, 1972, *Time* magazine proclaimed Bench as baseball's best catcher and featured his likeness on their cover. From there it was nowhere but up for Bench. In September, Ralph Edwards surprised him by making him the subject of his show *This Is Your Life* and even taped the episode at home plate in Riverfront Stadium. Bench finished the 1972 season with a league-leading 40 home runs and 125 RBIs, winning his second MVP award in three years. The Reds clinched the 1972 National League West Division title in Houston on September 22 in a showdown with the Astros, defeating them 4–3 as both Pete Rose and Johnny Bench hit home runs.

Johnny Bench capped his memorable season by hitting what is considered the most dramatic home run in Cincinnati Reds history off of Pittsburgh relief ace Dave Giusti in the ninth inning of game five of the National League Championship Series to tie the score 3–3. *Cincinnati Enquirer* writer John Erardi states that Bench's home run took place in the days before Bench and Rose began feuding. "When Bench connected on his home run, Rose, who had been called upon in the eighth inning to lay down a sacrifice bunt and delivered, shot out of the dugout and actually beat Bench to first base. Rose was there waiting to slap palms with Bench when the ball sailed over Clemente's head in right field and over the wall."[12]

Following Bench's home run, both Tony Perez and Denis Menke singled, and Reds manager Sparky Anderson sent George Foster in to run for Perez. Now the huge crowd at Riverfront Stadium was standing and cheering wildly as the next batter, Cesar Geronimo, worked the count to two balls and no strikes. At that point, Pirates manager Bill Virdon summoned Bob

Moose from the bullpen to replace Giusti. Geronimo then flied out to Clemente; however, Foster tagged up at second and sprinted into third base. Menke held at first. Darrel Chaney was coming up to hit as Bill Virdon made a trip to the mound to confer with Moose. The move worked, and Chaney popped up to Gene Alley in short left field for the second out. Sparky Anderson then sent Hal McRae up to hit for Clay Carroll. McRae swung at the first pitch from Moose—strike one! The next pitch from Moose was a hard slider slightly wide of the plate and low. Manny Sanguillen, the Pirates' catcher, attempted to backhand the ball, but it hit the dirt and skidded all the way to the backstop as George Foster came galloping down the third base line with the winning run and the pennant for the Reds. Regardless of Johnny Bench's dramatic home run in game five, Pete Rose led all the regular position players in hitting in the 1972 NLCS with a batting average of .450, going nine for 20. Bench hit .333.

The Big Red Machine then met the Big Green Machine, the Oakland A's in the 1972 World Series. The Series went seven games, but for the second time in three years, the Reds pulled up short of becoming world champions, losing the series to the A's four games to three. For both Rose and Bench, it was a miserable World Series. Pete hit .214, going six for 28, and Johnny had .261, six for 23.

The fact that Pete Rose had led the National League in hits in 1972 and hit over .300 for the eighth straight year didn't seem to matter much when it came to the Cincinnati Reds' publicity department. It was as if they took Rose's contributions to the team for granted. When the 1973 Cincinnati Reds yearbook was published, he was noticeably missing from the cover. Featured instead was a collage of caricatures that included Clay Carroll (Fireman of the Year), Sparky Anderson (Manager of the Year), Bobby Tolan (Comeback Player of the Year), Joe Morgan (All-Star Game MVP) and Johnny Bench (NL MVP). In fact, you had to go to page 22 of the publication to find Pete Rose, who was featured right after the page on Denis Menke.

Nonetheless, if 1972 was Johnny Bench's year, then 1973 belonged to Pete Rose. He had what is considered the finest year in his long, illustrious career. On June 19 at San Francisco's Candlestick Park, Rose got the 2,000th hit of his career with a base hit to center off of Ron Bryant as the Reds beat the Giants 4–0 behind the pitching of Fred Norman. It was Rose's third hit of the game, and the Candlestick crowd gave Rose a standing ovation. Reds radio broadcaster Joe Nuxhall regularly did a "star of the game" show following all Reds games. You would have thought that with Rose getting his 2,000th hit it would have been a no-brainer selection to have him on the program, but once again Nuxhall, like everyone in the Reds franchise just seemed to take lightly all the contributions and milestones that Rose was making. Nuxhall had Fred Norman on his postgame show as the star of the game.

Johnny Bench. (National Baseball Hall of Fame Library, Cooperstown, N.Y.)

Then on September 22 at Dodger Stadium in Los Angeles, Pete set a new record for the most hits by a switch hitter in a single season when he hit his fifth home run of the season off of Dodger pitcher Gregg Shanahan for his 224th hit of the season and number 2,145 of his career. The previous season record for switch hitters was 223, set by Frankie Frisch with the New York Giants in 1923. For Shanahan, at least, it was a way of getting into the record books, as he pitched in a total of eleven big league games over the course of two years with no won-lost record. As for Rose, he was finally given a shot at appearing on Nuxhall's postgame show.

At one point in the 1973 season, Cincinnati had been 11 games behind Los Angeles, but the Reds kept on coming and eventually won the National League West Division title by three and a half games over the Dodgers. Pete Rose had a fantastic year, winning his third batting title with an average of .338, and he led the league in hits with 230 while also setting a new club record for hits in a season, eclipsing the old Reds record of 219 by Cy Seymour set in 1905. With such a sterling season, Rose was named National League MVP for 1973.

The Reds lost the 1973 NLCS to the New York Mets three games to two. The Reds split the first two games, played in Cincinnati. In the first games, they beat Tom Seaver 2–1, but they lost the second game to Jon Matlack, 5–0. In the third game, played at New York, Rose was involved in one of the most memorable postseason incidents in baseball history. In the fifth inning, the Mets were leading the Reds 9–2 when Rose led off of the inning with a single off New York pitcher Jerry Koosman. Joe Morgan then hit a bouncing ball down toward first that John Milner fielded. Rose then charged into second with a hard stand-up slide, crashing into shortstop Bud Harrelson in an attempt to break up a double play. Harrelson, upset by what he considered unnecessary roughness, immediately sprayed Rose with a stream of profanity, calling him a cocksucker. All at once the two began wrestling on the ground, with the larger Rose winding up on top as both benches emptied and a full-scale brawl erupted on the field. Among the many infamous stories resulting from the donnybrook is the one of enraged Reds reliever Pedro Borbon chewing up a Mets cap as he was being led off the field by Andy Kosco and Phil Gagliano. Order was eventually restored, and both Rose and Harrelson remained in the game. But in the bottom of the fifth, with Rose playing in left field, a fan seated in the upper tier of the Shea Stadium grandstand hurled a whiskey bottle at Rose, just missing his head. At that point, Sparky Anderson pulled his players off the field, fearing for their safety as other fans began littering the field with trash.

The scene at Shea Stadium was reminiscent of the infamous "mauling of Medwick" in the 1934 World Series, when fans pelted St. Louis Cardinals outfielder Joe "Ducky" Medwick with eggs, fruit, bottles and garbage after he had spiked Detroit Tigers third baseman Marvin Owen. Baseball commissioner Judge Kenesaw Mountain Landis was so concerned for the safety of Medwick that he removed him from the game.

Now, with the crowd nearly out of control at Shea Stadium, the game was in danger of being forfeited when Mets players Tom Seaver, Willie Mays and others went to left field and personally appealed to unruly fans. As a calm returned to the stadium, Rose once again took up his position after NYPD officers were positioned in the left field grandstand to control the heavily alcohol-laced Mets fans. Following the game, Rose was isolated in his hotel room in the Biltmore Hotel. He had even received death threats as a result of the Harrelson incident. In regard to the melee with Harrelson, Rose stated, "Me sliding into Harrelson trying to break up a double play was baseball, the way it's supposed to be played. I'm no damn little girl out there. I'm supposed to give the fans their money's worth, and play hard, and try to bust up double plays—and shortstops."[13]

When Rose went to bat the next day in game four, every one of the 50,000 fans in Shea Stadium booed him. However, Rose got his revenge against the angry New York fans. He hit a home run off of Harry Parker in the 12th inning to give the Reds a 2–1 victory. As Rose circled the bases, he defiantly raised his arm in a clinched fist. The next day, the Reds lost game five and the pennant to the Mets, 7–2. New York banged out thirteen hits off of Cincinnati pitching to give Tom Seaver the win.

While Cincinnati fans have always held the belief that Pete Rose was a victim in the Bud Harrelson fracas, with the Shea Stadium fans getting totally out of control, New York fans have viewed the incident from a different perspective. They see Rose as a bully and the villain in the incident to this very day. After all, Rose outweighed the popular Harrelson by forty pounds, and it made no sense to the New York fans that Rose would attempt to slide so hard into Harrelson in a game that was already out of reach for the Reds, with the Mets leading 9–2. I suppose there are arguments coming out of both dugouts in this matter, but then again, this was typical play for Charlie Hustle throughout his career.

Pete Rose was now 32 years old. He had been in the major leagues for eleven years, played on two pennant-winning teams and three division-wining teams, was a Rookie of the Year, won three batting titles, had 2,151 hits, had six two-hundred-hit seasons, was an MVP and had hit over .300 for nine straight years. It's safe to say that if Rose had walked away at this point in his career, he would have been a strong candidate for the Hall of Fame. For the record, noted Hall of Fame switch hitter Mickey Mantle never had a 200-hit season in his entire 18-year career, and switch hitter Frankie Frisch, also in the Hall of Fame, had only three 200-hit seasons in his entire 19-year big league career.

Rose was rewarded for his stellar performance in the 1973 season by the Reds' front office with a new contract for 1974 that called for $160,000. According to author Roger Kahn, writing in *Pete Rose: My Story*, during the 1973 season, Cincinnati general manager Bob Howsam and Rose had breakfast together on the road at least once a week, where they talked about leadership and generally about the other players on the team—who was doing what and who needed a boost somewhere. According to Rose, "He [Howsam] looked at me as the team leader now, so I guess it was all those breakfast talks. Or it could have been the whiskey bottle that did it."[14]

The Los Angeles Dodgers had finished in second place in the National League West Division race in 1970, 1971 and 1973 while finishing third in 1972. The Dodgers needed to find a way to push their club over the top and challenge the "Big Red Machine" for the division title. They made a couple of key trades over the winter and then some strategic moves in their lineup for the 1974 season that would set the stage for one of baseball's most intense rivalries during the remainder of the 1970s. First the Dodgers sent outfielder Willie Davis to Montreal for relief pitcher Mike Marshall; then they traded pitcher Claude Osteen to Houston for outfielder Jimmy Wynn. Steve Garvey had come up to the majors as a third baseman, but seemed to play erratically at the position. Garvey had batted .304 playing in 114 games in 1973, some at first and some in the outfield, but he needed to play every day. For the 1974 season, Garvey was inserted into the lineup at first base, and Bill Buckner moved to the outfield. Suddenly the Dodgers had one of the best infields in the National League, with Garvey at first, Ron Cey at the hot corner, Bill Russell at shortstop and Davey Lopes at second. All this, combined with the solid pitching of Andy Messersmith (20–6) and Don Sutton (19–9), while Mike Marshall picked up 21 saves in the bullpen, allowed the Dodgers to get off to fast start in 1974, winning 17 of their first 23 games as Steve Garvey won the National League MVP award, hitting .312 with 21 home runs and 111 RBIs.

Consequently, Pete Rose and the Big Red Machine were chasing Los Angeles most of the season until September, when they overcame a 10½-game lead to close the gap to one and a half games. However, in a head-to-head series for the West Division crown played at L.A. in early September, the Big Red Machine sputtered and finished the season in second place, four games behind the Dodgers, who won 102 games. Nonetheless, the Reds had won 98 games and were gearing up for their most dominant years in the 1970s. In 1974, Johnny Bench had another outstanding season with 33 home runs while leading the league in RBIs with 129 and total bases with 315, while Joe Morgan hit .292, the highest average on the club, had 22 home runs and stole 58 bases. On the mound for the Reds, Jack Billingham won nineteen games (19–11) and Don Gullet seventeen (17–11).

For Pete Rose, it might have seemed as if 1974 was an off year, as he failed to hit .300 for the first time since 1964, finishing the 1974 season with .284 batting average. However, despite his 54-point drop in batting average from the previous season, he still led the league in doubles with 45 and runs scored with 110. In addition, Pete played 163 games in the outfield and had but one error, finishing the season with a brilliant .997 fielding average.

In 1975, the Big Red Machine finally began to show its awesome muscle. The Reds won 28 games in their last turn at bat. Overall, the 1975 Cincinnati Reds won 108 games in their drive to the National League West Division title, breaking the club record of 102 set in 1970. At that time, the 108 wins were the most in the National League since the Pittsburgh Pirates had won 110 in 1909. In addition, the Reds set a National League record by winning 64 games at home, breaking the old mark of 61 set by the 1962 San Francisco Giants, and also set the major league record for the highest stolen base percentage, .8235, breaking the mark set by the Los Angeles Dodgers of .8215 in 1962. At one point, the Reds played 15 games without an error, a feat that even got the attention of President Gerald Ford, who remarked about it when he came to Cincinnati to dedicate a new DEP facility built in the city. Even the Reds pitchers got in on the action, setting a major league record for allowing the fewest number of unearned runs in season—40.

Although the Reds swept the first three-game series of the 1975 season with the 1974 National League champion Los Angeles Dodgers, they otherwise started off slowly and barely played .500 ball in April, finishing 12–11 for the month. On May 3, manager Sparky Anderson went to Pete Rose and asked him to move from left field to third base to make room for George Foster in the lineup. Although Rose had not played the infield since playing 35 games at second base in 1967 and also remembered his misery when Don Heffner attempted to move him to third base in 1966, he agreed. By May 21, the Reds had a won-lost record of 21–21 and were five games behind the Dodgers. However from that point on, the Big Red Machine began to roll and won 41 out of the next 50 games. By the All-Star Game on July 15 the Reds were 12½ games ahead of the Dodgers. The Big Red Machine clinched the West Division title on September 7, a National League record for wining a title earlier than any other team in the circuit's history. Eventually the Reds won the West by 20 games over the second-place Los Angeles Dodgers.

Pete Rose had another excellent season in 1975, hitting .317 with 210 hits while leading the league in doubles with 47 and runs scored with 112. Rose's 47 doubles tied a major league record for doubles by a switch hitter. In a huge three-game series with the Los Angeles Dodgers at Riverfront Stadium in July that saw 150,000 fans pack the stadium, Pete beat the Dodgers 5–3 in one game with a home run off of Mike Marshall. Then on August 17, batting against Bruce Kison of the Pittsburgh Pirates, he got hit number 2,500 of his career as the crowd at Riverfront Stadium acknowledged the milestone with yet another standing ovation.

Rose played rather well at third base in 1975, making only 14 errors for the season. Looking back on the move following the season, he remarked that the advantage it gave the Reds, other than getting the powerful bat of George Foster into the lineup, was that it gave the Reds a set lineup to play every day. Sparky Anderson agreed with that assessment, stating that after he moved Rose to third and inserted. Foster in left he concerned himself mainly with the Reds' pitching and hardly paid any attention to the starting eight for the rest of the season.

The 1975 National League West Division victory was decidedly a team effort. Joe Morgan was voted the National League MVP and set a new Cincinnati club record for most walks in a season, 132, and also led the league in the same category. Morgan hit .327 for the season, and his 94 RBIs were a new Reds team record for second baseman as well, edging out the 93 RBIs that Tony Cuccinello had driven in during the 1931 season. Tony Perez, who had 109 RBIs, became the Reds' all-time leader in that category with 1,024, breaking the

CINCINNATI · OUTFIELD

PETE ROSE · REDS

Pete Rose, 1974. (The Topps Company, Inc.)

previous record of 1,009 set by Frank Robinson. In fact, 1975 was the 9th straight year in which Perez had knocked in 90 or more runs in a season. Johnny Bench tied the Reds club record for grand slams six, hitting two during the season while hitting 39 doubles and 28 home runs and knocking in 110 runs. It was the sixth time in the last seven seasons that Bench had exceeded 90 RBIs. Ken Griffey, Sr. also hit .305, while George Foster, after taking over in left field, wound up the season with 23 home runs and 78 RBIs while hitting an even .300. Pitching-wise, the Reds had three fifteen-game winners in Gary Nolan (15–9), Jack Billingham (15–10) and Don Gullett (15–4), while the bullpen, consisting of Will McEnaney, Rawley Eastwick, Pedro Borbon and Clay Carroll, was the best in the league.

By the time the 1975 NCLS began, the Big Red Machine was in high gear and swept the Pittsburgh Pirates three games to none. Pete Rose hit

.357 in the series, going five for 14. But in the third game with the Reds up two games to zip, the Pirates mounted a last stand, sending fire-balling rookie left-hander John Candelaria to the mound. The Pirates were ahead 2–1 going into the top of the eighth, and Candelaria already had 14 strike-outs, having given up the only Reds run on a home run to Davey Concepcion in the second inning. Then with two outs and Merv Rettenmund on base, Pete Rose hit a dramatic two-run homer off of Candelaria to give the Reds the lead 3–2. It was Pete's first hit of the year off of Candelaria.

When Rose hit that home run on the evening of October 7, 1975, a typical scene throughout Cincinnati was that of people watching the game on TV in the Bearcat Cafe on McMillan St. From inside the establishment one could hear people who lived in the apartments above the stores along McMillan Street screaming out of the windows with utter glee at the top of their lungs. It was near bedlam. Those fans knew that the death blow had been dealt to the Pirates in the NLCS. Though the Pirates came back to tie the score 3–3 in the bottom of the ninth in the top of the 10th inning the Reds took the lead back 5–3. Pete Rose scored a run with a bloop hit to right, then came home on a hit by Joe Morgan to right center. Will McEnaney then shut the Pirates down in the bottom of the 10th, and the Reds had won their third National League pennant in five years. It was on to meet the Boston Red Sox in the 1975 World Series.

The Reds split the first two games of the Series, played in Boston, then came home to Riverfront Stadium to defeat the Red Sox in a slugfest, 6–5, that saw a record six home runs hit in the game by Johnny Bench, Davey Concepcion, Cesar Geronimo, Carlton Fisk, Bernie Carbo and Dwight Evans. The Red Sox evened the series up in game four, two games each. In the fifth game, the Reds and Sox were tied 1–1 going into the sixth inning when Pete Rose singled to drive in Don Gullett with the go-ahead run. However, the night belonged to the Big Dog, Tony Perez, who broke out of an 0–15 slump in the Series, hitting two home runs and driving in four to give the Reds a 6–2 victory.

The series returned to Boston for game six, with the Reds leading three games to two, for what would be one of the most talked-about World Series games in history. The night games in Cincinnati had been played under frigid conditions so severe that commissioner Bowie Kuhn wore long underwear under his pinstriped suit to keep warm. Now in Boston, the rains came, and the Series was delayed for three days. Play was finally resumed on the evening of October 21, and Gary Nolan was named to start for Cincinnati against Luis Tiant, who had pitched a 6–0 shutout against the Reds in game one and then beat them a second time in game four by a score of 5–4. With the Series on the line, grandstand managers among the fans and in the press corp alike were asking why Sparky Anderson wasn't starting Don Gullett, who had beaten the Red Sox in game five and now had had three days rest due to the rain delay.

The Red Sox got off to a quick start in game six, scoring three runs in the first inning when American League Rookie of the year Fred Lynn hit a three-run homer off of Nolan. The Reds came back to score three runs off Tiant in the fifth and tie the score 3–3. After a walk and then a single by Pete Rose, the Reds had runners on first and third. Ken Griffey, Sr. then hit a ball to deep center field. Fred Lynn attempted to chase the ball down and smashed into the wall. Griffey wound up at third. It then took the Red Sox trainer took five minutes to revive Lynn, who stayed in the game. Joe Morgan then popped up for the second out, but Johnny Bench followed by lining the first pitch from Tiant into the "Green Monster" (left field wall at Fenway Park), scoring Griffey. In the seventh, the Reds took the lead when George Foster doubled home two runs to make the score 5–3 Reds. In the eighth, Cesar Geronimo hit a home run to give the Reds 6–3 lead. However, in the bottom of the eighth, the Red Sox erased the lead when Bernie Carbo, a former Reds player, hit a three-run pinch home run off of Rawley Eastwick, tying the game at 6–6. In the bottom of the ninth, the Red Sox loaded the bases with none out, but a double play ball kept them from winning the game. Will McEnaney had taken over on the mound for the Reds from Rawley Eastwick and gave Carlton Fisk an intentional pass to load the bases and set up a double play at any base. This brought the left-handed-hitting Fred Lynn to the plate. Lynn hit a foul ball just outside the left field foul line. Don Zimmer, the Red Sox's third base coach, sent Denny Doyle racing for home, but George Foster quickly fielded the ball with one hand and threw a perfect strike to Johnny Bench at the plate to nail Doyle for the double play.

The game now entered extra innings, and in the top of the 11th inning, Pete Rose was nicked by a pitch from Boston reliever Dick Drago. Ken Griffey, Sr. then forced Rose at second, attempting to sacrifice. This brought up Joe Morgan, who drove the ball deep to right field. Dwight Evans chased the long fly ball down, making an unbelievable one-handed catch as the momentum from his chase sent him crashing into the wall. Ken Griffey, Sr. was sure that the ball was in play, had taken off for third base, and now became an easy double play for Evans, even though his throw from the outfield was way off the mark.

The game entered the bottom of the 12th inning with the score still tied at 6–6. The Reds put two men on base in the 12th but failed to score. Then in the bottom of the 12th, Carlton Fisk was the first batter as Pat Darcy took over on the mound for the Reds. With 34,000 fans in Fenway Park clapping and yelling, Fisk drove the ball high down the left field foul line as he stood at the plate, using body English to attempt to keep the ball fair. The ball then smashed into the screen that runs along the foul pole in fair territory that was put up to keep balls from breaking windows on Lansdowne Street. Fisk had done it! Home run! All New England seemed to explode at that point, with the Boston fans jumping out of the stands onto the field as the security guards looked the other way. The home run by Fisk that beat the Reds in game six 7–6 became infamously known as "The Midnight Ride of Carlton Fisk" and is remembered as one of the greatest moments ever in World Series history. Although the Reds would win the World Series, the heroics of Carlton Fisk in game six sometimes make people think for a moment, before they remember the actual outcome of the Series, that perhaps Boston was victorious. As Carlton Fisk has often stated, Boston won that World Series three games to four.

When Pete Rose had come up to bat in the 11th inning, he had stated to Fisk, the Boston catcher, "This is some kind of game, right?"[15] Pete was still mesmerized by the game as the Reds boarded the team bus that night, and he told manager Sparky Anderson that game six of the 1975 World Series was the greatest game he had ever played in. Anderson was feeling no such immediate nostalgia and furthermore was on the hot seat for starting Gary Nolan in the game with the world championship on the line, instead of his best pitcher, Don Gullett. "Peter Edward, you're crazy,"[16] replied Anderson. "I'm not going to sleep tonight, and you call that the greatest game you've ever been in."[17] Rose then replied to Anderson, "Don't worry, we'll win tomorrow."[18]

Rose was right, of course. In game seven, the Reds overcame an early 3–0 deficit as a result of wildness by starting pitcher Don Gullet to beat the Red Sox 4–3 and thus win their first world championship since 1940. But the Big Red Machine had been winning games all year in 1975 by coming from behind. In the seventh inning, Pete Rose, with his second single of the night, had driven in Ken Griffey, Sr. with the tying run. In the ninth, Griffey, the leadoff hitter, drew a walk. Cesar Geronimo then sacrificed, moving Griffey along to second; then he advanced to third on pinch hitter Dan Driessen's ground ball. Pete Rose was then walked, bringing up the National League's MVP, Joe Morgan who singled off Boston reliever Jim Burton to score Griffey and win the game 4–3. The Reds were world champions at last.

The team was heralded in a parade down Fifth Street in Cincinnati, with confetti flowing from the windows of the office towers while 25,000-plus people jammed Fountain Square to join in a tribute to the team. The president of the University of Cincinnati, Warren Bennis, won a case of Boston Baked Beans from Harvard University president Derek Bok, and Cincinnati retail stores were soon hawking cheesy commemorative World Series mugs for anywhere from $1.75 to $3.99, depending on the size. Fans framed the front pages of the *Cincinnati Enquirer* and *Post* which proclaimed the Reds' championship. The whole city rejoiced in a massive informal celebration. The good people of Cincinnati knew they had something special in Pete Rose and the Big Red Machine, and they reveled in it.

Pete Rose was named the MVP of the 1975 World Series. Hit .370, going 10 for 27. In playing on a world championship team, Pete had accomplished one of the three original goals that he had made for himself in baseball; getting a World Series ring, matching or besting Ty Cobb's record of 200 or more hits in nine seasons and getting 3,000 career hits. "I'm a young 34, and I intend to play at least a few more years,"[19] said Rose. "So I don't see any reason why I can't attain my other goals."[20] With seven 200-hit seasons already chalked up in his career and 2,500 career hits, barring a serious injury, the other two goals looked like duck soup for Rose. However, as Rose savored the 1975 Cincinnati Reds' victory in the World Series, he could hardly fathom at that point in time that those goals would be attainted rather quickly and he would set his sights on much more lofty goals in just a few short years.

However, at the same time Pete Rose was taking aim at achieving his goals in baseball, he was changing and becoming more complex. Physically, he began to grow his hair a little longer. Gone were the military-style crew cuts he sported in the sixties and early seventies, now replaced with a sort of medieval Prince Valiant-type haircut that extended over his ears. There was also a developing dichotomy about Pete and his new personal wealth. While he owned a Porsche and now bought expensive, fancy, quasi-mod clothes—tight pants, wide collar shirts and jackets at Dino's, a trendy male boutique, in downtown Cincinnati—he still shopped with Karolyn and the kids at K-mart and pigged out on White Castles. Yes, he gambled, but he had always gambled, and going to the race track was legal.

But Pete was also starting to become deeply immersed in baseball economics as well. Suddenly, the guy who had aspired to becoming baseball's first $100,000-a-year singles hitter had been there and done that. Rose's contract for 1976 called for $188,000 and he was closely watching the withering away of the reserve clause. Jim "Catfish" Hunter of the Oakland A's had just become a free agent at the end of the 1974 season as the result of an arbitrator's declaration that his contract with A's owner Charles O. Finely had been violated. Subsequently, Hunter signed with the New York Yankees for 3.75 million dollars, and Rose took notice. As he reexamined his personal goals in baseball, he began to ask himself: Shouldn't Charley Hustle be the highest-paid player in baseball?

As the world champion Reds headed for spring training in 1976, Pete Rose was confident that the team could win it all again. "If everybody just does what they're capable of doing, nothing spectacular, Johnny Bench, Joe Morgan, Tony Perez, Cesar Geronimo, Davy [Concepcion] and me, we will

Pete Rose. (National Baseball Hall of Fame Library, Cooperstown, N.Y.)

win a lot of ball games. But pitching is the name of the game, and we have some good pitching; our relief pitching is spectacular."[21]

The Big Red Machine started off the 1976 campaign with an 11–5 win over Houston on opening day. They took over the division lead on May 30 and never relinquished it, winning the National League West Division championship for the fifth time in seven years by ten games over the second-place Los Angeles Dodgers. The Dodgers, playing their last year with legendary manager Walter Alston at the helm, finished with a record of 92–70, but otherwise there was not another club in the division that even finished over .500. The fact is that no team was going to beat the Reds in 1976. The Big Red Machine was absolutely dominating again, averaging 5.3 runs scored per game. The Reds led the National League in wins with 102, runs, 857, doubles, 271, triples, 63, home runs, 141, batting average, .280, slugging average, .424, stolen bases, 210, fewest errors, 102, and fielding average, .984. In addition, the Reds' relief pitchers led the league with 45 saves. The 210 stolen bases were the most by a Reds team since 1914.

Pete Rose had another remarkable year. Now 35 years old, he finished with a .323 batting average and led the league with 215 hits, thereby giving him eight 200-hit seasons in his career. He also led the league in doubles with 42 and runs scored with 130. He became the first player in history to lead the league in runs scored and doubles for three straight years. Following the 1976 season, he had now collected 2,762 hits, which placed him 28th on the all-time list. His place in Cooperstown was more than assured.

Johnny Bench and Tony Perez didn't play to their capacity in 1976. Bench had the worst year of his career, hitting .234 with 16 home runs, and Perez had a marginal season, hitting .260 with 19 home runs. Nonetheless, once again Perez did get 91 RBIs, thus giving him 90 or more RBIs for ten straight seasons. The subpar seasons of Bench and Perez mattered little, however; the Big Red Machine had oodles of other talent to carry the load. Besides Rose, there was Joe Morgan, who won his second straight National League MVP award, batting .320 with 27 home runs, 111 RBIs and 60 stolen bases. George Foster also hit .306 with 29 home runs and led the league with 121 RBIs. Ken Griffey, Sr. hit .336 and lost the batting crown when he sat out the final game of the season while Bill Madlock of the Chicago Cubs played and got four hits to wind up with a batting average of .339. In the pitching department, the starters included rookie Pat Zachry (co-Rookie of the Year), who went 14–7 while beating the archrival Los Angeles Dodgers five times. Gary Nolan was 15–9 and Don Gullett 11–3, while Rawley East-wick was 11–5 in relief with 26 saves.

The Reds met the blossoming Philadelphia Phillies of Steve Carlton, Mike Schmidt, Gregg Luzinski and company in the 1976 NLCS and promptly swept the series three games to none as Pete Rose batted .429 to lead all hitters.

The Reds moved on to defend their world championship in the 1976 World Series against the talented New York Yankees, who were making their first postseason appearance since 1964. The Yankees were managed by perennial baseball kook Billy Martin and lead by their talented captain, catcher Thurman Munson, who despised playing in the shadow of Johnny Bench, as well as third baseman and American League home run leader Gregg Nettles. The Yankees' pitching staff was anchored by Catfish Hunter, Ed Figueroa and National League castoff Doc Ellis. The Yankees had won the American League East Division championship by 10½ games over the Baltimore Orioles and defeated the Kansas City Royals three games to two in the ALCS.

The 1976 World Series didn't last long, though, as the Big Red Machine swept the Yankees in four straight games. Johnny Bench, rebounding, from a year-long slump, hit two home runs in the final game to seal the Bronx Bombers' fate. Overall, Bench, the Series MVP, hit .533, slightly overshadowing Thurman Munson, who hit .529 in the Series. The Yankees were so humiliated that manager Billy Martin was thrown out of the final game for throwing a ball out of the dugout in the direction of home plate umpire Bill

Deegan. For Pete Rose, the second consecutive World Series victory was bittersweet; he had his second championship ring, but he hit only a paltry .188 to earn it.

During the World Series, *Cincinnati Post* reporter Richard Hoffer decided to drop in on the neighborhood of Pete Rose's youth in Riverside, or Sedamsville if you prefer, and watch a game at Hauck's Cafe, owned by Rose's sister Jackie and brother-in-law Al Schwier. Hoffer was interested in seeing how people in the old neighborhood were handling the stardom of the most famous former resident. There were only a handful of people in the bar that night, and game three of the World Series was coming over a black and white television that was functioning, though somewhat blurred.

What Hoffer discovered in Hauck's Cafe was that there was, if anything, a sense of ambivalence towards Rose in the patrons gathered in the tavern. While there was some loyalty expressed towards Pete, most of the assembled patrons just felt that he had strayed too far away from the neighborhood to be connected any longer. Brother-in-law Al Schwier said, "He comes around when he can, but of course he's busy. He's got speaking engagements and so forth. But he'll still come around. What he'll do is bring some bats and a dozen balls, go down to the park, and start shagging flies with the kids. That's the kind of guy he is."[22] Yet on the other hand, Schwier felt that Rose had elevated himself socially from the norms of Riverside, and he now felt a barrier between himself and his famous brother-in-law. "He's out of my class socially; I don't think he's changed any, and I've seen him grow up, but we're not in the same class any more. It was different when his dad was alive. He's not as close as when his dad was around."[23]

According to Hoffer, for every Pete Rose fan in the establishment that night, there seemed to be an enemy, too. Perhaps it was the money that seemed to create a distance between Rose and the people who were once the closest to him. Pete was now making $188,000 per year, which would have taken the average resident of Riverside anywhere from 12 to 15 years at their jobs to make at that point in time. Maybe with his father gone the neighborhood had lost its sense of place in his life. Otherwise, the general population of Cincinnati still idolized Rose, and his influence seemed to be boundless in the fall of 1976.

Free agency had now come into baseball with a vengeance. Following the success of the Catfish Hunter arbitration case in 1974, baseball labor leader Marvin Miller wanted to test the limits of the reserve clause. According to Miller, paragraph 10(a) in the Uniform Player's Contract stated that an owner had a right to renew the contract of an unsigned player for one year and one year only. While the owners, contented that the contract could be renewed forever if the player didn't sign, Miller wanted to challenge the clause. To do that he found two major league players willing to play the 1975 season without signing their contracts: Andy Messersmith of the Los Angeles Dodgers and Dave McNally of the Baltimore Orioles. Both players played the 1975 season without signing a contract and subsequently were declared free agents on December 23, 1975 by a three-member arbitration panel that ruled there was nothing in the players' contract that stated it could be renewed for more than one year. Baseball's infamous reserve clause, which had been in effect since 1879, was dead. The owners decided not to appeal the ruling to the U.S. Supreme Court, and consequently Messersmith signed a three-year $1 million contract with Ted Turner's Atlanta Braves. In line with a new players' agreement signed in 1976, players with six years of major league service could now opt to declare free agency by not signing their contracts, and the club losing the player would be entitled to a draft selection from the club that signed the free agent. At the conclusion of the 1976 season, twenty-four players who had played out their options participated in baseball's first free agent reentry draft. Among those players participating in the inaugural re-entry draft were Joe Rudi, Rollie Fingers, Bobby Grich, and Bill Campbell. The New York Yankees signed the Reds' Don Gullett, who had beaten them in game one of the 1976 World Series. They also signed slugger Reggie Jackson to a five-year $2.9 million contract.

The Reds had anticipated that Pete Rose, coming off of another fine season in 1976 in which he once again had gotten more than 200 hits and batted .323, would probably ask for at least $225,000 to play in 1977. Reds management was prepared to offer Rose a $425,000 two-year deal. The organization had an option for his contract, and if they invoked it Rose would play again in 1977 for $188,000, but then, according to the recent ruling, he would become a free agent at the end of the season. But when Rose walked into the Reds' front office, he shocked assistant general manager Dick Wagner by asking for $400,000 to play in 1977 alone. Rose had also hired an agent to represent him, Cincinnati lawyer Reuven Katz. When negotiations with the Reds' front office broke down, Rose headed for Florida and spring training 238 hits shy of the coveted 3,000 career hits mark, unsigned and determined to play out his option year if necessary.

It was at spring training that year in March 1977 that Pete Rose met a person who would have a profound impact on his future in baseball: nineteen-year-old Tommy Gioiosa. Rose and his family (wife Karolyn, daughter Fawn, son Petey and Rose's Doberman pinscher Dobby) traditionally stayed at the King Arthur's Inn during spring training camp in Tampa, Florida, and that was where fate brought Rose and Gioiosa together. Tommy Gioiosa was from New Bedford, Massachusetts, where he was an all-state high school baseball player. In March 1977, Gioiosa just happened to be in Tampa with the Massasiot junior college baseball team, for whom he played second base, when he met Rose's son Petey at the pool and befriended him. It was young

Petey who introduced Gioiosa to Rose. Both Rose and wife Karolyn found Tommy Gioiosa to be a great kid and liked the way he had formed a relationship with their young son. Looking back on the incident a few decades later, Karolyn Rose remarked, "I liked Tommy because he reminded me of a young kid that wanted to make something of himself."[24] Rose and Gioiosa soon formed what seemed to be symbiotic relationship that would eventually become a disaster and lead to severe problems in both their lives.

As of April 5, with the start of the season just six days away, Pete Rose had not yet been signed by the Reds. He stood firm and was determined to prove to the Reds' front office that he was worth every cent of the price he was asking. The Reds' front office continued to mull over the potential public relations nightmare of allowing Rose to play the season without a contract and losing him to the free agent re-entry draft. The eyeball-to-eyeball standoff between Rose and the Reds' front office continued and was played out in the press and on the radio. On April 11, just a few days before the season opener with Houston, the Reds' brass blinked. Rose signed a two-year contract for $725,000. While the contract momentarily satisfied Rose, he still was concerned that he was no longer the top-paid player with the Reds, as that distinction now belonged to Joe Morgan.

At the beginning of the 1977, the Reds' pitching collapsed, and the Los Angeles Dodgers, under their new personable manager Tom Lasorda, came charging out of the gate, winning 17 of their first 20 games and then pushing their record to 22–4. Consequently, the Reds were forced to play catch-up ball all year long and never quite mounted a serious threat, finishing 10 games behind the Dodgers despite manager Sparky Anderson's pipe dream that Los Angeles would fold. "The Dodgers don't have a finishing kick ... they're playing over their heads ... they'll fade just like before,"[25] said Anderson. But the Dodgers were a different team in 1977. For the past twenty years, the Dodgers had relied on a combination of pitching and speed to win games. Suddenly, in 1977, they added power to that equation, with four players hitting more than thirty home runs: Steve Garvey, 33, Reggie Smith, 32, Ron Cey, 30, and Dusty Baker, 30. Tommy John led the L.A. pitchers, returning from elbow surgery to post a 20–7 record. On his first trip to Cincinnati, Tom Lasorda let the local press know that he was a kinder and gentler sort of Dodgers manager than they had previously known with the stoic Walter Alston and also more approachable than local manager Sparky Anderson. To prove the point, Lasorda set up a wine and cheese party for the press in the Dodgers' Riverfront Stadium clubhouse.

Meanwhile, the Reds had made a critical off-season blunder when they traded Tony Perez along with relief pitcher Will McEnaney to the Montreal Expos for pitchers Woody Fryman and Dale Murphy. The trade was a disaster in more ways than one. First, Perez was more than just a steady RBI and clutch hitter for the Big Red Machine. In fact, he was the team leader. While many would have thought that role belonged to Pete Rose, slowly during the 1970s Rose conceded that responsibility to the Big Dog. It was Tony Perez who kept everyone loose in the clubhouse and on the field. He was often described as the heart and soul of the Big Red Machine. Nonetheless, the Reds' front office felt that it was an opportune time to give Dan Driessen, nine years younger than Perez with a .260 average in 1976, his chance to play every day at first base. Prior to the trade, Anderson had made ridiculous public comments to the extent that by keeping Perez with the Reds he was robbing the kid (Driessen). Likewise, another "trade Perez" campaign was launched by a naive *Cincinnati Enquirer* sports writer by the name of Bob Hertzel, whose columns advocating a trade displeased many of his readers.

When the trade occurred on December 16, 1976, the general community in Cincinnati was saddened. The local newspapers ran the story of the trade on the front pages and wished Perez well in Montreal. Pete Rose was saddened, too, having played with Tony his first year in professional baseball at Geneva in 1960 and then throughout nearly all of his big league career. Furthermore, the Rose and Perez families had become good friends, with their sons, Petey Rose and Eduardo Perez, becoming good buddies too. Dan Driessen, at first, handled the awesome responsibilities of replacing the popular Perez very well in 1977, hitting .300 with 17 home runs and 91 RBIs, but the psychological damage done by the Perez trade to the spirit of the Big Red Machine was irreparable.

Woody Fryman, the 37-year-old left-hander who was supposed to fill the void in the Reds' pitching rotation left by the departure of free agent Don Gullett, wound up being a total bust. In fact, Fryman couldn't handle the pressure of being on a contending team, and after appearing in 17 games with a 5–5 record, he walked out of the Reds' clubhouse and headed for his farm in Kentucky.

For a moment in June, things started to look up again for the Reds when they acquired Tom Seaver. Seaver came to the Reds on June 15 from the New York Mets in a trade for Pat Zachry, Doug Flynn, Steve Henderson and Dan Norman. Seaver had gotten into the doghouse with Mets general manager M. Donald Grant in arguments over his contract and demanded a trade. He finished the season 14–3 for the Reds and 21–6 overall, but his presence was not enough to overcome the rampaging Dodgers.

Several Reds players had great years in 1977, beginning with a monster season for George Foster, who batted .320 and hit 52 home runs with 149 RBIs. In addition to leading the league in home runs and RBIs, Foster was also the leader in total bases, 388, runs scored, 124, home run percentage, 8.5, and slugging percentage, .631. For his gargantuan efforts, Foster was named the National League's MVP, the sixth time a Cincinnati Reds player had won the award in the previous eight years. Ken Griffey, Sr. hit .318, and Johnny Bench rebounded from the doldrums of 1976 to hit .275 with 31 home runs and 109 RBIs.

Pete Rose hit .311 and got 204 hits in 1977. On September 28, Rose got a single off of San Diego's Dave Tomlin for his 200th hit of the season, thus tying Ty Cobb's mark of nine 200-hit seasons. He seemed to be worth of every cent of that big contract dispute he had had with the Reds' front office prior to the season. Now he was just 34 hits shy of the 3,000 mark. With a two-year contract, there was no battle to wage with the Reds' front office over the winter of 1977-78, so Pete concentrated on getting ready for the forthcoming season. Once again at spring training in Tampa, Florida, Rose met up with Tommy Gioiosa at the King Arthur's Inn, where Gioiosa had again been lodging with his junior college baseball team. This time Rose invited Gioiosa to visit him in Cincinnati at some future date. It was also during spring training in 1978 that Rose became involved with a 25-year-old woman in Tampa by the name of Terri Rubio, who later in the year gave birth to a child whom she claimed was fathered by Rose.

The Big Red Machine wound up losing the National League West Division again in 1978 to the Los Angeles Dodgers, this time coming in second, two and a half games behind. Actually, the 1978 season in the West had been a three-team race as the Reds and San Francisco Giants went head to head in the first half until July, when the Dodgers pulled ahead of the Reds. The Reds challenged in September, but eventually came up short. Injuries were the key element in the Reds' inability to catch the Dodgers, with Joe Morgan playing in only 132 games. Morgan had the worst year in his career, hitting only .232, while Johnny Bench played in only 120 games, hitting .260 with 23 home runs.

There were some members of the team who had outstanding years and kept the Reds in the race. George Foster again led the National League with 40 home runs and had 120 RBIs, while Davey Concepcion hit .301, thus becoming the first Reds shortstop to hit .300 since Joe Tinker in 1913. Also, on June 16, Tom Seaver pitched the only no-hitter of his career when he beat the St. Louis Cardinals 4–0.

But 1978 in Cincinnati belonged to none other than Peter Edward Rose. He batted .302 with 198 hits, led the league in doubles with 51, and was second in runs scored with 103. That was only for openers. On April 29 at Shea Stadium against the New York Mets, with Rose closing in on 3,000 hits and not known for his power hitting, he had a huge day. He got five hits, including two singles and three home runs, giving him a total of 2,996 hits for his career. The game was nationally televised from New York, and one person watching it was Rose's friend and former teammate Tony Perez, who now playing for the Montreal Expos. "That sonofagun is amazing," said Perez.[26]

"Three home runs in one game. Pete Rose. I mean I watch in my hotel room in Houston and he hit two. I go to eat. I know he ain't going to hit no more. I'm in there eating and this lady, she comes running in yelling 'He hit another one.' I say, 'Who? and she say 'Pete Rose' and I say she is crazy. But she not crazy. He hit three in one game. No way. Amazing."[27]

On Friday evening, May 5, Rose got the 3,000th hit of his career. At 37 years old, he was the youngest player to have achieved that milestone and he became only the 13th player in history at that time to have 3,000 career hits. He joined the likes of Ty Cobb, Hank Aaron, Stan Musial, Tris Speaker, Honus Wagner, Eddie Collins, Willie Mays, Nap Lajoie, Paul Waner, Cap Anson, Al Kaline and Roberto Clemente. Rose's historic hit came in the fifth inning when he singled to left field off Montreal's Steve Rodgers. As Pete slapped hit number 3,000 into left field, the 37,832 fans at Riverfront Stadium all stood up and cheered wildly for their hometown hero. So did the Rose family, little Petey, all decked out in a Reds uniform, daughter Fawn and wife Karolyn. Everyone stood and gave Rose a rousing and well deserved four-minute ovation. While the mainstream press focused on the fact that Rose's former Reds teammate and friend Tony Perez was there at first base embracing and congratulating him, Expos pitcher Steve Rodgers appeared to be utterly disgusted with himself for giving up the historic hit. Rodgers was kicking the rubber and slamming the rosin bag down on the mound. Though the crowd was justly happy for Pete, the avid competitor in Steve Rodgers was visibly angry over the event.

It was ironic that one of the local newspapers seemed to link Pete's 3,000th hit with his penchant for thoroughbred horse racing. Former *Cincinnati Enquirer* sports reporter Bob Hertzel reported the next day that "He [Rose] lives for action. The horses. He loves them. Other sports. He follows them all."[28] In another column, the writer stated, "They can go ahead with the 104th Kentucky Derby today in Louisville. Pete's at 3,000 and counting."[29] Even Rose himself seemed to have horse racing on his mind as moved in on hit 3,000, offering his prediction for the historic hit: "Friday night, he [Rose] says. I don't want to upstage the Kentucky Derby."[30] With all the nag banter going on, it almost makes you wonder if Pete Rose had placed any bets on when he would get his 3,000th hit.

Regardless, the accolades were numerous for Pete. But the absolute finest testimony to Rose that evening came from Montreal Expos radio broadcaster Duke Snider. "The greatest competitor I ever saw was Jackie Robinson. But I don't think he was any greater competitor than Pete Rose."[31]

After Pete got his 3,000th hit, one would think that it would be difficult to top that. But for Charlie Hustle, there was still another historic event about to commence just a few weeks ahead that would also captivate the nation. Pete Rose was about to launch an assault on one of baseball's most

Pete Rose. (National Baseball Hall of Fame Library, Cooperstown, N.Y.)

sacred records, held by consummate baseball idol "Joltin' Joe" DiMaggio: his 56-game consecutive hitting streak. It all started quietly on June 14 with a pair of singles, hits number 3,035 and 3,036 off of Chicago Cubs pitcher Dave Roberts, but a streak had begun. On June 16, Tom Seaver pitched his no-hitter against the St. Louis Cardinals, and Rose had two hits off of John Denny for a two-game hitting streak. The streak continued throughout the rest of the month of June and into July. By July 18, Rose passed the Cincinnati club record of hitting in 31 straight games, which had stood for 80 years. On July 25 he set a new modern record, hitting in 39 consecutive games in the National League with three hits against Craig Swan of the New York Mets. The old modern record of 38 consecutive games, set in 1945, had been held by Tommy Holmes of the Boston Braves. The quest continued.

On July 31, Pete got a single off the Atlanta Braves' Phil Niekro and thereby tied the all-time National League record of 44 consecutive games set by Wee Willie Keeler of the Baltimore Orioles in 1897. The nation was now watching Pete Rose, and he brought a World Series–like atmosphere to Atlanta Stadium, as 45,000 fans had showed up to see the consecutive-game hit streak continue. Phil Niekro was pumped up for it and freely admitted that the game had special meaning. The atmosphere is "something we haven't had here since '69 when we won the West, and we owe it to Rose."[32] On Rose's first trip to the plate against Niekro, the pitcher threw knuckleballs and fell behind in the count 3–1. Then he followed with a fastball that was out of the strike zone for a walk, as the Atlanta fans rowdily booed their own pitcher—they wanted to see Pete hit. In the third inning, Rose lined out hard to shortstop Jerry Royster. The hit that tied Keeler's record came on Rose's third trip to the plate, when he hit a two-strike, no-balls pitch on the ground to the right of Niekro. As Rose reached first base, fireworks exploded in the stadium, and he was presented with a floral arrangement of roses shaped in the number 44 while Braves shortstop Jerry Royster came over and shook his hand.

The following evening, August 1, Rose was poised to set a new all time National League record for consecutive-game hits and continue his quest for Joe DiMaggio's major league record 56-game hitting streak. To do it, he would have to best a pitcher he had not faced all year; rookie left-hander Larry McWilliams. It was a hot steamy night in Georgia as 31,159 fans turned out at Atlanta Stadium for the event, and millions of others watched on television. On his first trip to the plate, Rose lined out hard to McWilliams on the mound. Next Rose hit a vicious line drive down toward third base, directly into the glove of the Braves' Bob Horner, that was turned into a double play. Finally Rose came up to the plate in the top of ninth, having gone 0 for three and was now faced Atlanta relief pitcher Gene Garber, who was cruising with a 16–4 Braves lead in the game. The Atlanta fans rose from their seats and began to chant "Pete, Pete, Pete" hoping to help Pete keep the streak alive. On the first pitch from Garber, Rose tried to bunt and fouled off the pitch. He fouled off the next as well. Then Garber shook off the sign from catcher Joe Nolan and threw Rose a sidearm breaking ball. He swung and missed—strike three. Immediately, Garber leaped into the air, and the streak had ended. Nonetheless, the Atlanta fans called out for Rose to make a final curtain call, and he obliged them by coming out of the dugout and taking a bow.

In the clubhouse, wearing a T-shirt that read "Hustle Made It Happen," Pete's frustration was apparent as he addressed the press following the game. Pete, the ultimate competitor, surely knew that Garber was not going to groove a pitch him to hit, so it was a little uncharacteristic for Rose to complain as he did. "I was a little surprised that in a game that was 16–4, he pitched me like it was the seventh game of the World Series. I guess he thought it was Joe DiMaggio up there. It's easy to make pitches like that when you're winning 16–4. I just hope to get to see him tomorrow in a one-run game and hit a rope up the middle."[33]

Gene Garber was unapologetic in his remarks following the game. "I would like to congratulate him [Rose] on a fantastic contribution to baseball, as well as on his record. I don't need to comment on anything he might have said. This is Pete's moment. And what a great streak it was. I pitched him just like I would have pitched anyone else. That's the way I have to pitch if I expect to feed my children. I have a job to do, and I have to do it."[34]

So with 56 games left in the 1978 season, Pete's quest for "Joltin' Joe's" 56-game hitting streak had ended. The following night, Rose got four hits: two singles, a double and home run. Since his 44-game streak, had begun on June 14, Rose had got 70 hits and batted .376 and became a hero to millions of new fans across America as he passed little-known Tommy Holmes and ancient Willie Keeler, then challenged the sacred Joe DiMaggio. Whether Rose knew it or not, on the hot evening of August 1, 1978, Charlie Hustle had passed through that invisible membrane in a major league career where a star suddenly becomes an icon. Yes, suddenly Pete Rose, from down along the Ohio River in Sedamsville, had become a baseball icon, no less than Babe Ruth, Mickey Mantel, Willie Mays or Stan Musial.

However, in the Cincinnati Reds' front office, Rose was a problem. He was coming to the end of his two-year $752,000 contract and was already publicly talking millions. Now Rose was in the midst of completing a historic season, and the Cincinnati fans were more behind him than ever, creating yet another huge public relations problem for vice president Bob Howsam and general manager Dick Wagner. Also, there was a certain arrogance that had surfaced in Rose, who acted as if he had suddenly become the franchise. Now he was challenging the status quo on many official policies of the front office, such as having the players' sons on the field during batting practice. Rose wanted his son Petey to be able to shag balls in the outfield during batting practice, much to chagrin of the Reds' front office, which had an official policy that children remain off the field, citing a liability problem. This and other little petty battles with the front office were all having a snowball effect on Rose's chance of signing another contract with the Reds. Rose wasn't helping matters, either, as following his 44-game hitting streak, he began to appear on various television talk shows from the local Bob Braun Show on WLW-T in Cincinnati to the nationally televised and syndicated *Phil Donahue Show*, rubbing salt in the wounds of the Reds' front office by boasting about needing a truck to haul all the money away he was going to make with next year's contract, whether it be the Reds or some other club.

In essence, in early August Pete Rose had already unofficially declared himself a free agent. To that end, on October 1, 1978, the Reds' front office made a final contract offer to Rose for $800,000 for two years, stating that the he would become the highest-paid Reds player in the history of the franchise. Privately, the front office was less concerned that Rose had become the ninth leading player in hits (3,164) in the history of the game and had achieved that distinction in a Cincinnati Reds uniform, but rather were questioning just how many more productive years he had left, considering that he would be 38 years old when the next season rolled around.

On October 25, Rose joined the Big Red Machine as the Reds made a 17-game exhibition tour of Japan. At that point, the negotiations between Rose's agent Reuven Katz and the Reds' front office were almost nonexistent, so Charlie Hustle was making his farewell tour with the Cincinnati Reds in a foreign country. The end came on November 3, 1978, with Rose still touring in Japan, when he was drafted in the first round of baseball's annual re-entry draft by five teams: the New York Mets, Atlanta Braves, San Diego Padres, Texas Rangers and Philadelphia Phillies. Rose had already publicly stated that the only teams that he would seriously entertain negotiations with other than the Reds were the Boston Red Sox, California Angels, Kansas City Royals, Los Angeles Dodgers and New York Yankees. According to the rules of the re-entry draft, up to twelve teams besides the Reds were eligible to select Rose. Subsequently Rose could then negotiate with those teams as a free agent and was eligible to sign with the one making the most lucrative offer. After sixteen glorious summers that had fulfilled his boyhood dream of playing before admiring fans with his hometown, Pete Rose, aka the Cincinnati Kid, aka Charlie Hustle, was about to pack his bags and leave home, turned away by the team that he had helped take to national and world-wide recognition, considered too old, too expensive, expendable and a potential administrative problem by the front office.

IV

Philadelphia Freedom

The high-stakes baseball stampede to sign free agent Pete Rose was on. He was demanding a $450,000-per-year career non-guaranteed contract from the Cincinnati Reds. Simply stated, that meant that the Reds would pay Rose $450,000 per year for every year he continued to play in a Cincinnati uniform. In 1978, the Cincinnati Reds had drawn 2.5 million in home attendance and 2.3 million fans on the road. So it was not a question of the Reds not having the money to meet Rose's contract demands; it was simply a matter of their not wanting to. The Reds' front office had their own agenda in the re-entry draft. The Reds desperately needed pitching, and they were attempting to sign left-hander Tommy John, who would eventually be lured into a New York Yankees uniform by free-spending owner George Steinbrenner.

While Rose continued to tour Japan with the Reds, he was already getting telephone calls from Ted Turner, the flamboyant owner of the Atlanta Braves, and also a contingent of representatives from the Philadelphia Phillies, including Bill Giles, executive vice president, Paul Owens, vice president for player personnel and club president Ruly Carpenter, son of Phillies owner Bob Carpenter. Meanwhile the Reds' front office was silent. They were standing pat on their final contract offer to Rose of $800,000 for two years, although there were rumors circulating that the Reds had upped the offer to $1.2 million for two years and that Rose had turned it down, stating that it did not meet other offers he had already had. In fact, Reds president Dick Wagner was also traveling with the Reds in Japan, and he all but totally ignored Rose. According to Rose, all that Wagner had said to him was, "Let's get together when we get back to Cincinnati. You give me a call."[1]

Rose's agent, Reuven Katz, had told the *Cincinnati Post* that he knew nothing of any new offer by the Reds, had no plans to meet with Dick Wagner, and hadn't even seen him since the World Series. The reality was that there had been no new offer by the Reds; they had already written Pete Rose off and were moving on without him. The Reds' management and Rose had been at each other's throats for years now. At times, circumstances between the parties would even elevate to the point of nitpicking. According to Rose at one point the Reds' management told him not to drive his Rolls Royce to the ballpark any more, because it made the fans mad. "I told them to go to hell,"[2] said Rose. "I worked hard for that car. They didn't tell Joe Morgan and those guys not to drive their $20,000 Corvettes and Cadillac to the ballpark."[3]

The Reds concluded their 29-day trip in Japan and returned to Cincinnati on Wednesday, November 22, 1978. While on the tour, the Reds had won 14 games and lost only two. Johnny Bench had belted nine home runs in the sixteen games, a pace that would have given him 85 home runs over the course of a 162-game National League schedule. Pete Rose batted .329 on the tour, and while away he was drafted by 13 teams in the re-entry draft.

As the Reds and their traveling party deplaned at Greater Cincinnati-Northern Kentucky International Airport from Japan, the Rose children, Pete Jr. and Fawn, were there to meet their parents. Karolyn Rose came out of the jetway sporting a blouse that had the word "Yokohama" emblazoned across the breast. "Over there, they call me the Yokohama mama,"[4] said Karolyn. Pete spoke briefly with the press, making no statement about his pending contract talks, but simply stating, "It's first time I've ever visited someplace for 28 days and never saw anybody act mad. There wasn't one single person who even looked unpleasant at any time."[5] The first order of business for Rose that day was to hold a meeting at the Holiday Inn in Covington, where he presented various Reds coaches, such as Ted Kluszewski, George Scherger, trainer Larry Starr and equipment manager Bernie Stowe, four-wheel-drive Jeeps. He referred to these people as his MVPs. In essence, they were going-away presents from Pete to people he considered good friends and important to his success while in a Cincinnati Reds uniform.

By the following Monday, the bad feelings were mutual between the Reds and Rose, and he had officially written off Cincinnati as a place to play baseball in 1979. Consequently Rose, together with his agent Reuven Katz, hit the road, hustling, if you will, the best deal he could get. Rose rented a Learjet for the trip, and Katz prepared a twenty-minute promotional video tape. They planned to visit ten cities in their quest for cash. The Rose-Katz contract hustle began in Atlanta on Monday and moved to St. Louis and

Kansas City on Tuesday, then Pittsburgh on Wednesday before heading for Philadelphia later in the week. Their goal was to reach a decision by December 5. The following spring the contract odyssey would be memorialized by *60 Minutes* CBS correspondent Morely Safer referring to Rose and Katz as the best big city bandits since Bonnie and Clyde. While Rose was ready to play in another city, he maintained that his permanent residence would remain in Cincinnati. "I don't think the shock of not playing baseball in Cincinnati has set in yet,"[6] said Rose. "And it probably won't until I sit down and put on another uniform. I'm leaving with no hard feelings. We have great fans here, great people to work with. I'm going to miss them all."[7]

The Rose family had mixed emotions about Pete's departure from the Queen City. "I can't believe the time has come when Pete won't be playing with Cincinnati,"[8] said Karolyn. "The shock of leaving won't set in until later. The main thing is for him to be happy."[9] As for the kids, "Little Petey still wants to go to Montreal to be with Tony Perez's kids," added Karolyn.[10] Pete Jr. was also hopeful that perhaps his dad would wind up in Boston, where Don Zimmer was manager, and he even went to school before the Roses departed for Japan wearing a Red Sox cap. However, it was a pipe dream for Little Petey, as the Red Sox had passed on Rose in the re-entry draft.

While Rose began his road trip for millions, the Reds were busy making changes. Now that they had washed their hands of Rose, their next move was to fire manager Sparky Anderson and four of his coaches and replace him with John McNamara. The Reds' office felt that Anderson had lost control of the Reds' clubhouse and wanted a more hands-on leader to run the club. When told of the firing of Anderson, Rose had arrived in Kansas City, and he responded, "I can understand why they can't get together with me, because it is a matter of economics. But it wasn't Sparky's fault that we finished second. Without him we would have probably finished third. It's no easy task managing the Reds. I used to think I wanted to be a manager; not now. It's too tough. You try to discipline guys and they go over your head. Sparky was a fair guy. He treated a man like a man and boy like a boy. Maybe it's because I played every day that I never had any trouble with him. Some guys should be standing in front of a mirror and ashamed of themselves for what happened to Sparky because of them."[11]

Evidence of Rose's contention that some of his teammates had not given 100 percent: During spring training in 1977, Anderson had allowed some of the complaining star players on the team, to cop out on long road trips from Tampa to Fort Myers, Cocoa Beach and Vero Beach. Later, Anderson allowed those same stars to also beg off of shorter road trips to Orlando and Lakeland. The front office took notice of this, and when the Reds got off to slow start in the beginning of the 1977 season and had to play catch-up to the Los Angeles Dodgers all summer long, it cast a bad light on Anderson's leadership capabilities.

The firing of Anderson wasn't the only thing that surprised to Rose. He was almost tickled pink with the enormous contract offers that he and Katz were receiving during their trip. Everyone seemed to have their checkbooks open waiting to fill in any amount if Pete would just say yes. He had received a huge offers from Ted Tuner in Atlanta, John Galbreath in Pittsburgh, Gus Busch, Jr. in St. Louis and Ewing Kauffman in Kansas City, who truly believed that Rose had a chance to beat Ty Cobb's all-time hit record and offered him a four-year contract with options for a fifth and sixth year. Gus Busch sweetened his offer to Rose by offering to throw in a Budweiser Beer distributorship when he retired. Gus Busch was in the hospital at the time that Rose and Katz arrived in St. Louis; nonetheless his lawyer accompanied the contract hustlers back to the airport and told Rose that Gus Busch wanted him to play for the Cardinals. "He told me that Mr. Busch wants me to play for the Cardinals; that he's 79 years old and wants one more World Series in his lifetime. All he wanted me to do was that when I get my top offer to let them know and they will fly to Cincinnati and promised me I won't be dissapointed."[12]

The day before the meeting with Kauffman in Kansas City, Rose and Katz had spent six and a half hours visiting with Pirates owner John Galbreath, being treated like crown heads of Europe while touring his sprawling Darby Dan Farm near Columbus, Ohio, which included a 1.75-mile thoroughbred race horse training track and an enormous barn that housed 24 of Galbreath's prized thoroughbreds. Two horses owned by Galbreath, Chateaugay and Proud Clarion, had won the Kentucky Derby; another, named Roberto after Roberto Clemente, had won the English Derby at Epsom downs in England. "Mr. Galbreath told me that walking into the winner's circle at Churchill Downs after his two [Kentucky] Derby winners gave him the biggest thrill of his life,"[13] said Rose. "He told me it's a feeling he couldn't describe and I can believe him."[14] While Galbreath was wise enough to know Rose's vulnerabilities, he did not make an immediate contract offer. The Pirates' owner knew that he was not going to be able to compete with Gus Bush and Ted Turner. Ultimately, Galbreath offered Rose about the same salary he would make in Cincinnati, but with a bonus: he would throw in a couple of mares with good bloodlines and the use of stud service by some of his top stallions at Darby Dan Farm. Thus Rose would have a chance to become a horse breeder.

The next direction for the contract ramblers in the Pete Rose sweepstakes was east. The New York Mets had announced through general manager Joe McDonald that they were willing to cough up a three-year contract worth $1.5 million to get Rose. However, the Philadelphia Phillies had already offered Rose a three-year guaranteed contract calling for $1.8 million in total compensation, and Rose had stated that he preferred the Phillies. Meanwhile, the New York Yankees and San Diego Padres dropped out of the bidding process for Rose. The caravan for cash pulled into Philadelphia on November 30.

Meanwhile, back in Cincinnati, Rose's fans wouldn't let go of their idol without mounting a fight. The topic of Rose's departure was debated in every corner saloon in the city, while Fred W. Fehr, Jr. of the Richter & Phillips Company took out advertisements daily in the *Cincinnati Post* urging the Reds' front office to listen to the fans. Local resident Mary Helwig hung Reds president Dick Wagner in effigy on her front porch. At the Holiday Inn downtown, manager Jeff Ruby ordered that all of the Reds posters be taken down in the lobby, the schedules thrown out, and said he would only allow Reds paraphernalia back in the hotel when Dick Wagner was no longer with the Reds.

Indeed, Dick Wagner was a cat on a hot tin roof. He had casually dismissed Rose, the most popular player in the 109-year history of the Cincinnati Reds, and fired Anderson, the club's winningest manager in its history. Then to top it off, he failed to save some face by not signing free agent Tommy John. While Wagner stated that he had conferred with Bob Howsam, former Reds president, on the negotiations with Rose, the decision to fire Anderson was his alone. In an interview with *Cincinnati Post* staff reporter Earl Lawson, Wagner attempted to justify his actions. "I feel I have a job to do. I'm trying to put the best club possible on the field with the best possible leadership we can have. I can't control the Rose negotiations. We made him what I believe was an outstanding offer early in October. Rose's decision to leave the Reds was his. He wasn't forced to leave. I'll never understand why he didn't accept our offer. We made an outstanding offer to [Tommy] John. Even he admitted we were one of several clubs who offered him more money than the Yankees, with whom he signed. But when you're bidding against 12 other clubs for a player, all you can do is go with your best. And if you don't get the player you're seeking, you don't become despaired if you lose him. You take other routes in attempting to improve your club. I want to assure you that the change in managers was related in no way with our losing Rose and failing to sign John."[15]

In Philadelphia, despite the Phillies' genuine interest in Rose, things did not go well at first. Rose and Katz met with Phillies owner Ruly Carpenter and general manager Paul Owens and presented them with a contract figure that was in line with the top offers they had received so far. However, Carpenter simply responded that the Phillies could not go that high. Nonetheless, Rose admitted that the Phillies' offer was not too shabby and would make him the highest-paid player in the game. In fact, it was believed that the Phillies' offer would make Rose the highest-paid athlete at that time in professional sports, surpassing the $800,000 a year that was being hauled down by NBA star David Thompson of the Denver Nuggets.

With the numbers for Rose's services now well known around major league baseball, teams began dropping out of the running. First it was the New York Mets, then the Los Angeles Dodgers. However, Ted Turner in Atlanta called Reuven Katz and told him not to count the Braves out of the running. Kansas City and Pittsburgh were still hanging in there too. As a matter of fact Rose and Katz were planning a trip on Saturday, December 2, to visit John Galbreath in Lexington, Kentucky, where he had 44 of his prize thoroughbred horses quartered. Galbreath was convinced that the more he appealed to Rose's sense of association with the sport of kings, the more likely it was that he could sign him. Then on Sunday, Katz planned to sit down with his accountant and analyze all the offers made to Rose. Meanwhile Rose would take off for Florida, where he was being honored as major league player of the year by the National Association of Professional Baseball, then would leave for California to film an episode of *Sports Legends* a documentary television show hosted by Tom Seaver.

Back in Cincinnati, reality had set in with Dick Wagner and the Reds' front office about the future of the team, and they began to sign remaining components of the Big Red Machine to multiyear contracts. Danny Driessen, despite that fact that he hit only .250 in the 1978 season, was signed to six-year contract. Davey Concepcion, Tom Seaver and Johnny Bench were signed to five-year contracts. The five-year contract with Bench almost assured that he would finish his career in a Reds uniform and not create the public opinion firestorm that had sprung up over the Reds' failure to sign Pete Rose.

On Monday, December 4, Reuven Katz informed Ewing Kauffman, owner of the Kansas City Royals, that Pete Rose was declining his multiyear offer of $700,000 a year, as he had decided to remain in the National League. With 3,164 hits, Pete felt that he definitely had a legitimate shot at surpassing Stan Musial's all-time National League record of 3,630 hits. So that left three teams still bidding in the Pete Rose sweepstakes: Pittsburgh, Atlanta and St. Louis. However, there was speculation that Pittsburgh had also been dropped from the list by Rose, even though John Galbreath was willing to throw in a brood mare. Furthermore, Rose wouldn't deny that the Pirates had been dropped from the running. "I can't deny I did that,"[16] said Rose. "But that doesn't mean they didn't counter [make a counter offer]."[17]

Actually the best offer still on the table was from Ted Turner in Atlanta, who was offering Rose a million dollars a year for as long as he could continue to play in addition to stock in Turner's cable television station CNN, but in Philadelphia, wheels were starting to turn. Just a few days ago, Rose

had turned down a $1.8 million contract offer from the Phillies, but during his trip to the airport with Bill Giles, he was expressing disappointment. Now the Phillies had called off a news conference in Orlando, Florida, where the major league winter meetings were taking place, and there was speculation that general manager Paul Owens and owner Ruly Carpenter did not want to expose themselves to the Philadelphia press regarding the Rose question. Nonetheless, Phillies shortstop and Rose friend Larry Bowa told the Associated Press, "Unless something unbelievable happens, and I don't foresee that happening, Pete Rose should be a Phillie tomorrow."[18] Rose stated that he would have an announcement to the press on his decision the following day in Orlando.

Pete Rose. (National Baseball Hall of Fame Library, Cooperstown, N.Y.)

On Tuesday, December 5, all the bidding for Pete Rose came to a close as the Philadelphia Phillies came back with a new offer of a four-year, $3.2 million contract, paying him $800,000 a year and thereby making Rose the highest-paid player in baseball. Several dynamics contributed to the final deal. First, the Phillies, after winning the National League East Division title for the last three years, had failed to make it to the World Series, losing to the Cincinnati Reds in 1976 and then to the Los Angeles Dodgers in 1977 and 1978. There was a lot of speculation in the Phillies' front office that having a leader such as Pete Rose on the team could be the missing link to get them over the hump. Furthermore, Rose had stated that he wanted to play for the Phillies, having three very good friends on the team in Greg Luzinski, Mike Schmidt and Larry Bowa, and also he was convinced that the club could make it to the World Series. So it was virtually a love affair between the Phillies and Rose, and all that was needed to make it a done deal was to find the necessary funds to meet his contract demands. To that end, Bill Giles worked out an arrangement with WPHL-TV in Philadelphia for them to ante up some of the missing cash, in the amount of $600,000, that the Phillies needed to sign Rose. Giles went to Ruly Carpenter and told him that if they could get another $600,000 a year, they could sign Rose. Carpenter, of course, was convinced he couldn't afford Rose. But Giles, the Phillies' vice president for business operations, called WPHL-TV and told them that if the Phillies signed Rose, then the ratings for the station would go up and they would make more money, so it made sense for them to kick in some extra money to sign Rose. The deal was done. According to Giles, "That was one of my prouder moments. People were lined up in the middle of the winter waiting to buy season tickets. We paid for his contract right away."[19] In fact, the Phillies were convinced that with the addition of Rose they would draw three million fans into Veterans Stadium in 1979, an attendance figure at that time that was the exclusive domain of one team in the history of the game: the Los Angeles Dodgers.

Rose was now the highest paid member of the Philadelphia Phillies, topping slugging third baseman Mike Schmidt. Rose had achieved his objective. He had his truck load of money and was also the highest-paid player in the major leagues. His contract, calling for $800,000 a year, eclipsed that of Reggie Jackson of the New York Yankees, who was hauling in $600,000, his new teammate Mike Schmidt at $575,000, Larry Hisle of the Milwaukee Brewers at $525,000, Oscar Gamble of the San Diego Padres at $475,000 a year, and Tommy John of the Yankees, who had a new contract calling for $466,667 a year.

All that the Cincinnati Reds received for the loss of Rose was the Phillies' first choice in the amateur draft the following June. The Reds fans were still upset, but beginning to accept the fact that their native son had jumped ship. There was, however, some fallout from the Rose contract sweepstakes around Major League Baseball. Pirates owner John Galbreath's offer to of include brood mares in a contract did not sit well with a lot executives and managers. If Rose had accepted the offer from Galbreath, it is conceivable that the thoroughbreds offered him in the deal could have been worth megabucks in the near future. Phil Seghi, general manager of the Cleveland Indians, stated, "I can remember the day when we in baseball were referred to as a bunch of horse traders."[20] Herman Franks, manager of the Chicago Cubs, remarked, "It's a sad day when owners start bringing in horses as an inducement to sign players. All I can say is more power to Pete if he got what they say he got."[21]

But what really struck fear into the hearts of the executives was seeing how Rose could control the market of major league baseball. They became greatly concerned about the long-term ramification of free agent bargaining and what it would do to baseball as a whole if left unchecked. The legendary Frank Lane was now working for the California Angels and weighed in with his opinions on the Rose contract sweepstakes. "At Pete's age I'd rather be selling him than buying him. He's a great offensive player. He'll attract at the gate to justify the first year the money he'll get. While he's a great offensive player, his greatest value is a gate attraction. I'm not being derogatory about Pete, but this bargaining by free agents hurts baseball. I'll predict—and I've been wrong a lot of times—that in three years major league baseball again will be down to two eight-team leagues. That's when sanity will return to the game. You can't afford to pay out over a period of years more than you're taking in. Do you realize that the 26 clubs in the major leagues are responsible for a quarter-billion dollars in deferred payments because of the contracts players have today? That's a bundle!"[22]

As for Rose, he was now philosophical about the past week's contract hustling and relating how much fun it had all been. As he and Reuven Katz prepared to board the private LearJet for their week of fluff, Pete remarked, "Mr. Katz told me: Get ready for the most fun you ever had in your baseball career. It was fun. It was great fun to meet rich people and, without your having to open your mouth, have them offer you beer distributorships, thoroughbred horses, lifetime security and oodles of money."[23]

Despite his huge contract, Rose was confident that he would receive a warm reception from his new teammates with the Phillies. But in reality, there were mixed emotions among the Phillies about the signing of Rose. Larry Bowa, of course, was excited. During the 1978 season, Bowa had bet Rose a steak dinner on which one them would get the most hits in the season. As it turned out, Rose won, getting 198 hits to Bowa's 192. "Now we can go head to head,"[24] said Bowa. "From now on I won't have to look at the Cincinnati box score every day to see how many hits he got. The beauty of Pete Rose is his knack for bringing out the competitive spirit in others. I think that's what he'll do to all of us. He'll challenge us, bring out the best in us."[25] Catcher Bob Boone, on the other hand, was more cautious, not wanting to over estimate the addition of Rose to the Phillies' lineup. "I think this has engulfed baseball for so long, there's been a tendency to blow it up. We got a real talented player, but it doesn't mean the Phillies will win everything. I don't think it's fair to put that onus on Pete. A lot of things can happen in baseball over a 162-game season."[26]

As for where Rose would play in the Phillies' lineup, the plan was to leave Mike Schmidt at third and move Rose to first base, which had been occupied by Richie Hebner during the previous season. Actually, in 1978,

Hebner had done a fine job at first for the Phillies. In 435 at-bats, he hit .271 with 17 home runs and 71 RBIs while sharing the position with Jose Cardenal. Outfielder Gregg Luzinski was hoping that Hebner would be moved to second base, thereby retaining his power in the lineup. As it turned, out the issue of where Hebner would play with the addition of Rose became moot when in spring training on March 27, 1979, he was traded to the New York Mets along with Jose Moreno for Nino Espinosa.

Christmas was approaching as the news of Rose's signing broke in Philadelphia. The Christmas tree at City Hall was still undecorated, and there were signs still hanging around downtown that welcomed the fans for the Army and Navy football game. For the most part the fans in Philadelphia were satisfied with Rose joining the Phillies. But there were others who considered his flying around the country negotiating for millions with millionaires somewhat crass, and some would have preferred that the Phillies sign Rod Carew. Perhaps Mary Templeton, a widow from Rittenhouse Square whose only means of financial support was her Social Security check, put it best. "The truth? This country's screwed up. You got a grown man playing baseball and making a couple million dollars. Other people are starving. I eat one meal a day and I snack on saltine crackers in between. Pete Rose doesn't mean anything to me. The mailman does."[27]

The Pete Rose sweepstakes had come to an end. He got what he wanted: to be the highest-paid player in professional baseball, and he had signed with the team that he preferred to play for. The proof of the pudding would be: Could he deliver a pennant to the Phillies? At a press conference during the winter meetings in Orlando, Florida, Charlie Hustle attempted to put it all in perspective. "I played with Aaron,"[28] he said. "I played with Mays. I played against Mantle. I played with Koufax, Drysdale, Marichal, Gibson. I played with some great players. It took a long time for me to get to the top of my profession. It's not something you do in two years or five years or 10 years. I think after getting my 3,000th hit and hitting in 44 straight games and playing 16 years in the National League that I've finally become the No. 1 player in my profession, and I just wanted to get paid like it. Whether it's $100,000 or a million dollars or $800,000 or $700,00 dollars. If other guys are getting it, I wanted it too."[29]

Whether or not all the hustling from one city to another was crass is now academic. When Rose set out in late 1978 on his sojourn for cash, it was only the third year that free agency had been in existence. What seemed excessive then is now a common occurrence each year, as players filing for free agency peddle themselves to the highest bidder. The contract that Rose, a 16-year veteran in 1978, got from the Phillies of $3.2 million for four years is chump change when compared to what the market will bear today. Twenty-four years later, in December 2002, free agent Tom Glavine, a 16-year veteran left-hander formerly of the Atlanta Braves, raked in $42.4 million from the New York Mets on a four year contract. Furthermore, in the new millennium not only do free agents from the major leagues travel from city to city seeking the best deal, but players even come from foreign countries to negotiate with major league teams. Such is the case with slugging third baseman Norihiro Nakamura, who, after batting .294 with 42 home runs and 115 RBIs for the Kinestsu Buffaloes in the Japanese Pacific League in 2002, journeyed to America to negotiate with the New York Mets, New York Yankees, Boston Red Sox and Baltimore Orioles. Selling oneself in the free agent market is now as common in baseball as peanuts and Cracker Jacks.

Yet even as the ink was drying on his lucrative contract, Rose was spewing bitterness towards his former team, even becoming so arrogant as to suggest that he had carried the Reds on his back for the past sixteen years. At one point, his former pal Joe Morgan stated that Pete should zip it. The fact of the matter was that the 1979 Cincinnati Reds were still going to be a formable team without Rose, and their lineup was loaded with All Stars and MVPs such as Johnny Bench, Joe Morgan, Tom Seaver, Ken Griffey, Sr., Dave Concepcion and George Foster.

As spring training loomed on the horizon, Tommy Gioiosa now twenty years old had come to Cincinnati on an invitation from Pete and Karolyn Rose as their houseguest. According to Gioiosa, in his interview for *Vanity Fair*, September 2001, on the way home from the race track one evening, Rose asked Gioiosa to get out of bed early the following morning, around 5:30 a.m., and get the newspaper as soon as it arrived and then throw it away. Gioiosa states that he did exactly as he was requested: he retrieved the newspaper and threw it into some bushes, then went back to bed. However, later in the morning, when he came downstairs, he encountered Karolyn yelling at Pete that his attempt to hide the newspaper had been not been successful. Tommy had left his footprints in the snow. The *Cincinnati Enquirer* article that Pete had been attempting to hide from Karolyn named him in a paternity suit by a woman named Terry Rubio from Tampa, Florida, whom Pete had met during spring training in 1977. In fact, it was well known among the Reds that Terry Rubio was Rose's girlfriend and that he had even given her a canary-yellow Triumph sports car. According to Gioiosa, all Pete kept saying to Karolyn was "Don't believe that shit."[30] But the fact of the matter was that Pete had indeed fathered a child by Ms. Rubio in 1978, a girl she called Morgan, and later in the year Rose settled the suit out of court.

Rose wasn't first major league baseball player to father a child outside of his marriage and will not be the last. Even the great Babe Ruth fathered a child by his housekeeper. Pete and Karolyn Rose separated during the 1979 season, and Gioiosa became Rose's roommate. The two moved into a condominium development in Cincinnati called Chateau Lakes.

According to Tommy Gioiosa, Rose had a lot of girlfriends. In his *Vanity Fair* magazine interview, Gioiosa even went as far as to say that as he and Rose became closer friends, he would shuttle Pete's girlfriends back and forth to the airport for him.

Furthermore, Gioiosa states in the article that Rose had taken his Hickok Belt (a prestigious award given to the best athlete in the USA each year, with winners including Otto Graham, O. J. Simpson, Mickey Mantle, Joe Namath, etc.) to Litwin Jewelers and had all the diamonds removed from it so he could make earring sets for various girlfriends, then had fake diamonds inserted in the belt and sold it to a collector for $30,000.

Later in the year, Rose revealed what he liked in women in a interview with *Playboy* magazine, published in its September 1979 issue. "I like class. I don't mean rings and cars, and clothes. I mean just people who you can just tell have class by looking at them. You know, just the way they handle themselves and the way they walk. I like people with personality. I like women with pretty legs. Pretty legs and pretty mouths."

Rose took his philandering ways to Philadelphia with him. George Will, writing in his book *Bunts* relates an incident taken from James Reston, Jr.'s "Collision at Home Plate" where in Rose's first year in Philadelphia, Karolyn Rose saw Pete's Porsche being driven down a local street by one of the Philadelphia Eagles cheerleaders. Subsequently, Karolyn did a fast U-turn and gave chase to the car. When she caught up to the car at a light, she got out of her car and knocked on the window of the Porsche. When the blonde cheerleader rolled down the window, Karolyn without hesitation punched her in the nose. In September 1979 Karolyn Rose would file for divorce. In the settlement she got a Rolls Royce, the $300,000 house and alimony payments for 13 years. Pete got the Porsche, the $175,000 house, his trophies and visiting rights with son Pete Jr. and daughter Fawn. In an article published by GQ in 1989 Pete Jr. stated that what he learned from Pete Sr. was how to "hit the ball where it's pitched."[31] However daughter Fawn stated that Pete Sr. was "the world's worst father."[32] Rose was served with the divorce papers in his hotel room in September while the Phillies were playing in New York. Subsequently, reporters asked him how the divorce would affect his play. "I'd rather go through a divorce hitting .320 than hitting .220,"[33] said Rose. At that point in the season Rose was indeed hitting .320.

While Rose had a bad spring training in 1979, hitting only .194, he was an instant hit with the fans and the city at large in his first year at Philadelphia. He lived in an apartment at 15th and Locust, took the subway to Veterans Stadium, and he had a very good year, with 208 hits and a .331 batting average, second in the National League to batting champion Keith Hernandez of the St. Louis Cardinals, who shared the MVP award for that year with the Pirates' Willie Stargell. In the field, Rose played 159 games at first

Mike Schmidt. (Photo File, Inc.)

base and made only 10 errors, finishing with a brilliant .993 fielding average. His assault on the baseball record book continued, as during the season he became the National League's all-time singles hitter, passing Honus Wagner with 2,427.

However, the addition of Rose did not bring instant success to the

Phillies. In fact, they experienced their worst season since 1974, finishing with a won-lost record of 84–79, fourth in the National League East Division, 14 games behind the division champion cross-state rival Pittsburgh Pirates. The hitting contest that Larry Bowa had predicted with Rose never materialized, as Bowa hit only .241 with 130 hits. Mike Schmidt kept his part of the bargain, hitting 45 home runs with 114 RBIs.

When Pete Rose made his first trip back to Cincinnati as a Philadelphia Phillie, he was still acting as an unofficial ambassador for the Queen City. One of his first orders of business was to introduce Mike Schmidt and other Phillies teammates to the succulent barbecue ribs at the Montgomery Inn. Rose was warmly greeted by the loyal fans he had left behind in Cincinnati. The same could not be said for the team that he left behind, as the Big Red Machine convincingly swept the three-game weekend series from the Phillies. After the Phillies had been mauled by the Reds, Rose told a Cincinnati newspaper sports reporter that he was glad his team was getting out of this place. In 1979, the Cincinnati Reds were still a formidable force without Rose, and they won the National League West Division with a record of 90–71, just squeaking by the Houston Astros by one and a half games before being swept by the Pittsburgh Pirates in the NLCS as the Sister Sledge-inspired team known as "The Family" went on to defeat the Baltimore Orioles in the World Series.

The following year, 1980, the Phillies finally put it all together and won the National League East Division, just getting by the Montreal Expos by one game, with a record of 91–71. While Pete Rose failed to hit .300 for the first time since 1974, finishing with a .282 batting average, he led the league with 42 doubles (one more than batting champion Bill Buckner), and his hustle on the field as well as his leadership in the clubhouse made a huge contribution to the success of the ball club. Nonetheless, the Phillies were carried by National League MVP Mike Schmidt, who had another monster season in 1980, leading the league with 48 home runs and 121 RBIs. Furthermore, it was a home run by Schmidt that won the pivotal game over Montreal in the second to last game of the regular season that clinched the division championship for the Phillies.

The Phillies then defeated the Houston Astros three games to two in the NLCS to win their first pennant in thirty years. Rose hit an even .400 in the NLCS and started the key rally that won game four when he singled in the 10th inning, starting a two-run rally that led to a 5–3 Phillies victory over the Astros.

In 1980, Philadelphia was wild about the Phillies and Pete Rose. On the eve of the World Series, even Dick Vermeil, coach of the Philadelphia Eagles, was high in his praise of the team and Rose. At his weekly press conference, Vermeil stated, "I know nothing about baseball. But I am a Dallas Green [manager], Ruly Carpenter [owner], Pete Rose fan. I like Pete Rose's personality. He could play linebacker for us right now."[34] Suggesting that Rose could play for the Eagles was quite a compliment from Vermeil, considering that the Eagles would go on that season to play in Super Bowl XV in January 1981, losing to the Oakland Raiders 27–10. Rose's late father, Harry Rose, would have reveled in a such a remark from Vermeil.

The Philadelphia Phillies defeated the Kansas City Royals four games to two in the 1980 World Series, giving the franchise its first ever world championship. While Rose was low-key in the clubhouse celebration that followed, he nonetheless proudly rode on the float in the victory parade with his son, Pete Jr., now 15 years old. Pete hit only .261 in the series, but he is probably best remembered for his spectacular catch of a foul ball in game six. With one out, the bases loaded and the Phillies leading 4–1, the Royals' Frank White hit a pop fly foul down the first base line that was pursued by both Phillies catcher Bob Boone and Pete Rose coming in from first base. Boone got to the ball first and settled under it, but suddenly the ball popped out of his catcher's mitt and directly into Rose's first baseman's mitt. Commenting on the play in retrospect, Rose said, "Everyone always asks me about that play. I didn't want to call Boonie off. When it popped up, I just snapped it up. I think the reason I reacted so fast was that I didn't know if Tug McGraw was covering home plate or not."[35]

In an article in the *Philadelphia Inquirer*, December 22, 2002, Bob Boone was quoted as saying that Rose was actually out of position on the famous play when he chased White's foul ball the length of the dugout only to see it pop out of his catcher's into Rose's first baseman's mitt. Furthermore, Boone downplays the impact that Rose had on the Phillies during their championship season in 1980, stating that Rose was just a piece of the puzzle, that the championship was a complete team effort, and that no one player delivered it.

Pete Rose, now 40 years old, entered the 1981 season with 3,557 hits, needing just 74 more to surpass Stan Musial as the National League all-time hits leader. He quickly added three of those hits to his total on April 8 against the Reds and former teammate Tom Seaver. However, the 1981 season was to be one of the wackiest in baseball history, and Pete would have to wait through a 50-day player strike before setting the record.

As the basic agreement that had been signed by the players and owners in 1976 came up for renewal at the end of December, 1980, the owners were demanding more compensation for the loss of players to free agency. To that end, both the players and owners had decided to establish a four-member committee that would study the compensation issue. The committee consisted of Sal Bando and Bob Boone for the players and Harry Dalton and Frank Cashen for the owners. The committee began its study in May 1980. Although the arbitrator in the 1976 decision had not made tenure of any sort a condition of free agency, Marvin Miller suggested a compromise in which free agency would be restricted to players with six years of major league experience and ball clubs losing a player to free agency would be compensated with an additional pick from the annual amateur free agent draft. However, the owners, buoyed by a $50 million strike insurance policy with Lloyd's of London, balked and demanded compensation in the form of a veteran major league ball player from the team that signed a free agent. As the basic agreement expired and the new year came, nothing had been accomplished by the four-member committee. If no agreement was reached by February 10, 1981, the owners were free to put their compensation plan into effect, and by March 1 the players' union could declare their intention to strike.

As things turned out, the owners did put their compensation plan into effect in an attempt to weaken free agency, and the players' union (MLBPA) voted to strike on May 29 if the dispute was not settled by then. After attempts by a federal mediator to settle the dispute, the filing of an unfair labor practices complaint by the players' union, and lastly an injunction, the whole process eventually broke down and the MLBPA announced an immediate strike on June 11. The strike lasted for 50 days, and according to Marvin Miller, when it was settled on July 31, the owners had lost $72 million after insurance payments and the players about $34 million in salaries. The basic agreement was extended to 1984, and the owners' attempt to alter the free agency structure had failed.

The day before the strike began, on June 10, Pete Rose had gotten a single off of Nolan Ryan of the Houston Astros and tied Stan Musial's all-time National League hit mark of 3,630. After Rose got the record-tying, hit he was then struck out the next three times at bat by Ryan. Now he had to wait for a 50-day players' strike to be settled before he would have a chance again to break the record.

But two months later on August 10, 1981, with 60,561 fans jammed into Veterans Stadium, after going 0 for three, Rose led off in the eighth inning and got a single off of St. Louis Cardinal reliever Mark Littell, shattering the National League record for most hits with number 3,631. It was not a classic hit, but a grounder that got by between Cardinals third baseman Ken Oberkfell and shortstop Gary Templeton. Rose, along with Tommy Gioiosa and Pete Jr., had driven all night long to Philadelphia, coming back from the All-Star Game in Cleveland, which was played immediately following the strike. When Rose went up to the plate in the eighth inning, he handed the weighted warm-up ring off his bat to Pete Jr. Rose said that he told Pete Jr., "I want you to watch. I'm going to get a hit."[36] According to Gioiosa who was also in the dugout when Pete got the historic hit off Littell, a Phillies coach began yelling over and over "He done it! He done it! He done it"[37] Fireworks then began to explode high above Veterans Stadium, and 3,631 balloons were released. Stan "The Man" Musial was in the stands to see his record broken and came on to the field to acknowledge Rose's accomplishment as the crowd chanted over and over the familiar Pete, Pete, Pete! Musial told the press, "I talked to our pitchers before the game. I said, let Pete Rose get a hit tonight or I'll get the Polish Mafia after you."[38]

Later in the Phillies' clubhouse, Rose attempted take a call from President Reagan, but the White House was having trouble putting the call through to Veterans Stadium. "Good thing there's not a missile on the way,"[39] joked Rose. "I waited 19 years for this. Maybe he's out there in California watching the Reds and Dodgers."[40] The call eventually got through, and Rose accepted the congratulations of the nation's Commander in Chief.

The fact that there were 60,521 fans in Veterans Stadium on the first day following the end of the players' strike was a tribute to the gate attraction power of Pete Rose. He and he alone was the magnet that drew the fans through the turnstiles that night, when there was a sense of real and open bitterness from many about the strike and many expressed it without hesitation. Joe Permar, a 21-year-old fan from Wilmington, Delaware, stated that night, "I'd as soon get up out of this seat and leave as soon as he gets his hit. I'm here for the hit and that's it."[41] Nineteen-year-old Mike Donohua was even more bitter, vowing to never to return to Veterans Stadium. "I'll come for Pete, but that's it,"[42] he said. "Starting tomorrow, I'm on strike."[43] Mary Ann Smith, a housewife and mother who bought several $4 tickets for the game, was in attendance with her four children and a neighbor's child. She had mixed emotions. She said that she would have come to game without Rose being on the verge of setting a new record, but would not have brought the kids with her. "I broke their hearts when I wouldn't take them the night Pete tied the record,"[44] she said. "This is something special."[45]

When Cal Ripken, Jr. broke Lou Gehrig's consecutive-game record in September 1995, of course it was significant moment in baseball history and a great career milestone for Ripken. However, the significance of the event was overstated by the media. They proclaimed it as a universal healing force that brought fans and major league baseball back together following the 1994 players' strike that wiped out the balance of the season and a World Series. However, from a true historical standpoint, if Ripken's feat is to be taken seriously as a reason for fans to forget and forgive the major league greed, then it is because there was a dress rehearsal for the Ripken love-fest. It took place following the 1981 players' strike, with Pete Rose reminding the press, fans, players, owners and labor leaders alike of the fact that baseball is still a game of dreams. No other single event could have silenced the emotions of the angry frustrated fans in the dog days of August 1981 like Charlie Hustle doing what he had been doing for nineteen years: playing hard and chasing the legends of the game, while children and adults continued to dream along with him. It was indeed a special night, for Pete, for baseball and for America.

With hit number 3,631, there were now only two players in the glorious history of the game that had more career hits than Rose: Henry Aaron, with 3,771, and Ty Cobb, the all-time hits leader with 4,191. Although Rose was now just 560 hits behind Cobb he publicly shrugged off the notion that he could eclipse the Georgia Peach. But did anyone really believe that the thought of being the hit king had not yet entered his mind? Baseball commissioner Bowie Kuhn suggested after the game that night on August 10, 1981, "I've got a feeling there may be 560 more hits in that bat."[46] In the strike-shortened season of 1981, Pete Rose batted .325 and led the National League with 140 hits.

The players' strike had wreaked havoc on the 1981 major league season, so baseball executives had to find a way to salvage the season and generate fan interest. The strike had lasted for 50 days, and baseball realized it was going to take a big hit at the gate. When the strike commenced on June 11, in the National League, the Philadelphia Phillies were leading the St. Louis Cardinals in the East Division by one and a half games, and in the West Division, the Los Angeles Dodgers were a half game in front of the Cincinnati Reds. Consequently, major league baseball devised a complex scheme to continue play that would involve splitting the season into two halves. The team that was leading their division at the time of the strike would be declared the first-half champions. Thus both Philadelphia and Los Angeles were assured of a playoff berth. The second half of the season would begin on August 9, and the pennant race restarted with the winners of both divisions being declared the second-half champions. Now to get to the NLCS or ALCS, the winner of the first half would have to play the winner of the second half in a mini-playoff series. Then both winners of the mini-playoff series would advance to the NLCS or ALCS to play for the National or American League pennant and advance to the World Series.

One can certainly argue that this was a bogus way of determining who should qualify for the playoffs. The ones who got the shaft in this contrived scenario were the Cincinnati Reds, who had the achieved the best record in baseball in 1981 with 66–42 record, but were not eligible for the playoffs. However, in the American League the circumstances were even more bizarre. The Oakland A's in the West Division wound up in the playoffs despite having a losing season with a record of 50–53, while the Texas Rangers, with a record of 57–48, were not eligible. Such a manipulated playoff scenario led New York Times sports columnist Red Smith to refer to the 1981 season as "baseball's dishonest season."[47]

The winners of the second-half season in the National League East were the Montreal Expos and the winners in the West division were the Houston Astros. The Expos defeated the Phillies in the East mini-playoff series three games to two. Pete Rose hit .300, going six for 20. In the West mini-playoff series, the Los Angeles Dodgers defeated the Houston Astros three games to two. Then Los Angeles and Montreal advanced to the NLCS, with the Dodgers prevailing three games to two and subsequently going on to meet the winner of the protracted playoffs from the American League, the New York Yankees, in the World Series. Finally, the Dodgers emerged as world champions, defeating the Yankees in the 1981 World Series four games to two, and baseball's most unusual season had finally come to an end.

In 1982, the Phillies chased and fought off the St. Louis Cardinals all summer long before eventually going into one of their infamous September swoons and come in second, three games behind the Redbirds, for the division championship. On June 21, trailing for the division lead by three and a half games, the Phillies were in St. Louis going head to head with the Cardinals. Although they lost 7–5 that night in a very exciting game, Pete Rose got two hits and tied Henry Aaron for second place on the all-time hits list. In the first inning, Rose hit a ground-ball single to right. After bouncing out in the third, he came up to bat in the sixth to a hearty chorus of boos from the partisan Cardinals fans. After taking the count to 3–1, he lined a clean single to right center for hit number 3,771, tying Henry Aaron for second on the all-time hits list. The ball was given to Rose, and without any fanfare he flipped it to first base coach Deron Johnson for posterity. Following the game, Rose said that he would rather have won the game than gotten the two hits. "As far as I'm concerned, that was just secondary,"[48] said Rose. "We lost the game. It's not that big a thing: I would trade either of those hits for one with guys on first and third."[49]

The next night, Rose made an error in the first inning that led to a 2–0 Cardinals lead. But in the third, he got the Phillies back in the game when he drilled a double off of John Stupor and then slid head first into second with hit number 3,772, passing Henry Aaron and becoming number two on the all-time major league hits list. However, the Cardinals pulled the game out in the eighth, winning 3–2.

Henry Aaron, unlike Stan Musial, wasn't in attendance when Rose surpassed him as the number two hit man in baseball history, but that fact seemed to have no effect on Rose. "He's got things to do,"[50] Rose said. "I'm disappointed my little boy [Pete Jr.] wasn't here more so than Hank. I've got a good relationship with Hank Aaron. Hank and I are buddies. You know Ty Cobb ain't going to be there neither."[51] Overall Rose, now 41 years old, wound up the 1982 season batting .271 with 172 hits. Now he clearly had Ty

Cobb in his sights, being just 322 hits behind the all-time leader's total of 4,191, and suddenly he found himself being compared with Cobb.

Waite Hoyt, the New York Yankee great and Hall of Fame member had pitched against Ty Cobb, and he had been the Reds' radio broadcaster when Pete came up to the big leagues and continued to be his friend. As Pete had grown up listening to Waite's broadcasts of the Reds games, it was a genuine and close friendship between the two.

After Pete passed Henry Aaron on the all-time hit list, Peter Pasacrelli of the *Philadelphia Inquirer* spoke with Hoyt and asked him to compare Cobb and Rose. Waite Hoyt felt that Cobb was a much better hitter than Rose and a better base runner too. While Rose was never a base stealer, he did feel that Rose and Cobb had the same kind of power. However, Hoyt felt that comparisons of players in his generation were unfair. He stated that players of his generation did not pay attention to setting records, but rather focused on what they were accomplishing that particular season. "There are so many vital differences between the game I played and the game played today. And when you get into the area of comparing past players with modern players, you get into an area where there are a lot of untruths. He [Rose] doesn't have great speed. He doesn't sparkle in fielding or throwing or running. He was no Brooks Robinson at third, he was no Charlie Gehringer at second, he was no Willie Mays in the outfield. But you take the whole cloth, and Pete gets the job done. You have to admire what he's been able to do with the abilities he was given. To me, there isn't a question that, if Pete avoids serious injury, he'll equal Cobb's total. And I'll be rooting for him along with everybody else."[52]

Waite Hoyt had known Pete Rose since he came up to big leagues in 1963 and been his friend from the start. Harry Rose, Pete's father, had asked Waite to look out for him, and Hoyt often sat with Pete on Reds team flights. He had seen him pass all the great hitters—Nap Lajoie, Willie Mays, Eddie Collins, Honus Wagner, Tris Speaker, Stan Musial, Hank Aaron—but he would not live to see Rose pass Ty Cobb. Waite Hoyt died on August 25, 1984, in Cincinnati.

Most baseball analysts were now convinced that Rose could catch Cobb in two years, and so was Pete Rose. On the morning after Rose passed Henry Aaron on the all-time hits list and saw only Ty Cobb ahead of him and baseball immortality, Peter Pascarelli of the *Philadelphia Inquirer* brilliantly captured the moment when he wrote on June 23, 1982, "You quickly notice the certainty with which Rose uses the term 'my record. There are no Ifs in the vocabulary of this 41-year-old, going on 21. He is a marvelous merging of talent, extraordinary concentration, durability, dedication and determination colliding to form an accident in nature. With each game, with each hit, he continues to embellish this Walk with the Gods. Thus does the Cobb countdown begin."[53]

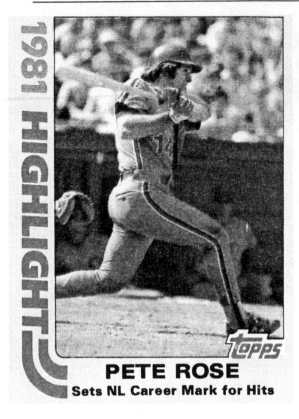

PETE ROSE
Sets NL Career Mark for Hits

Pete Rose, 1982. (The Topps Company, Inc.)

In 1983, the Philadelphia Phillies' roster was filled with so many aging stars that the press often referred to the club as the "Wheeze Kids," making a play on words that described the youthful 1950 National League champion Phillies team the "Whiz Kids." In addition to Pete Rose, who was now 42 years old, also on the roster were former Big Red Machine teammates Joe Morgan, 39, and Tony Perez, 41, along with Ron Reed, 40, Steve Carlton, 38, Tug McGraw, 38, Mike Schmidt, 32, Al Holland, 31, Garry Maddox, 32, Ivan DeJesus, 30, Gary Mathews, 32, John Denny, 30, Bo Diaz, 30 and Ivan DeJesus, 30.

After 85 games, this veteran club under manager Pat Corrales's leadership was only one game over the .500 mark, at 43–42. At that point, Corrales was replaced with Paul Owens, and they went 47–30, including an 11-game winning streak down the stretch in September to finish with a record of 90–72, outdistancing the Pittsburgh Pirates by six games to win the National League East division. The Phillies were led once again by Mike Schmidt, who belted a league-leading 40 home runs, John Denny, whose 19 wins also led the league, and Steve Carlton, who had 15 wins and led the league in strikeouts with 275. It was obvious that age was starting to take its toll on Pete Rose and that he had slipped a bit. He finished the season with the lowest batting average in his 21 years in the major leagues at .245. But he had 121 hits, leaving him just ten hits shy of 4,000 and only 201 hits behind Ty Cobb.

The Phillies then knocked off the Los Angeles Dodgers in the NLCS, three games to one, to win the National League pennant and advance to the 1983 World Series against the Baltimore Orioles. Pete Rose became oldest non-pitcher to ever play in a league championship series, hitting for an average of .375.

In the first game of the 1983 World Series, the Phillies' John Denny and Al Holland combined to hold the Orioles to five hits as Joe Morgan and Garry Maddox hit home runs to give the Phillies a 2–1 victory and a one-game-to-none lead in the Series. Pete Rose went one for four with a one-out single in the ninth.

Prior to the second game of the World Series, an early afternoon news conference was held at which the primary topic appeared to be Pete Rose, as he was the only ballplayer who agreed to participate. Bob Fishel, the assistant to the president of the American League, came to the podium and was bountiful in his praise of Rose. "Pete, I may be an American Leaguer, but you're what the game's all about."[54] Phillies manager Paul Owens then weighed in on the topic of Rose. "He exemplifies class. It's no wonder we all love him—not because of his records, but just to be associated with him."[55] When Owens was asked about the Phillies' intentions of keeping Rose in the 1984 season, he replied, "There has been no decision made ... I think the decision will have to be made by Bill Giles and ownership, because you're talking about a lot of money."[56] When Rose was asked if he thought he would return to the Phillies in 1984, he more or less shrugged off the question, stating he was more concerned about the World Series right now and how he had chosen the Phillies over other teams five years ago because he believed that they had the best chance to go to the World Series. "I wasn't looking for the best offer financially,"[57] said Rose. "If I was I'd have picked Atlanta. Atlanta offered me twice as much as I got in Philadelphia. I wanted to go to an offensive team and a team that had a chance to go to the World Series. I hope to be in Philly next year. If I'm not there, I'll be somewhere else. And if I'm not, I'll swim across the Pacific to Japan. I'd swim across the Pacific to play baseball."[58] No one doubted that Rose would swim across the Pacific to play ball, but at the moment there was serious doubt as to what he was worth to the Phillies' lineup in the World Series against the Orioles, as he went 0 for four in game two. Baltimore won 4–1 and even up the Series at one game apiece.

When the Series moved to Philadelphia for game three, Pete Rose was not in the Phillies' starting lineup. Manager Paul Owens, in a surprise move, had benched Rose in favor of his longtime friend and former Big Red Machine teammate Tony Perez. While the benching of Rose stoked the rumors that he was not coming back to Philadelphia in the next season, Phillies manager Paul Owens stated that it was probably only going to be a one-game sit on the wood for Rose. "I want Pete in there for the right-handers, and he will play against [Orioles starter] Storm Davis on Saturday," said Owens.[59] Actually, Owens was concerned that the Phillies had only gotten eight hits in the first two games and was looking for more power in his lineup, thinking that Perez could possibly hit one out against the left-handed Mike Flanagan. Furthermore, Perez had hit against Flanagan before during his stint with the Boston Red Sox and fared pretty well against him.

Still, it was a huge embarrassment for Rose to be benched, and to be benched in a World Series game. However, he had been benched before. The first time came in June of the 1964 season, his second in the majors, when his batting average dipped to around .200 and Cincinnati Reds manager Fred Hutchinson sat him down in favor of Bobby Klaus. Then during the stretch drive in the 1983 season, he had spent most games on the bench as rookie Len Matuszek was in the lineup against right-handers. Consequently, Rose refused to be questioned by the press except for a pregame interview that had been taped with Howard Cosell of ABC.

Rose told Cosell, "Sure it hurts. And it's embarrassing. This just isn't the way baseball should be played. The two most surprised guys in the ballpark were myself and Tony Perez. I was the one that told him he was playing. That's not the way baseball should be conducted, but it's not the first time it's happened here this year."[60] Regardless of the merits or non-merits of Paul Owens's strategy to bench Rose, it didn't help the Phillies as they lost to the Orioles in game three by the score of 3–2. Tony Perez went one for four in the game. Pete Rose pinch hit in the ninth inning and grounded out. Following the game, Rose dressed quickly and left the clubhouse.

Tony Perez was still in the clubhouse, and the reporters converged on him for a comment on the benching of Rose matter. "I know how he feels," said Perez.[61] "But I cannot do anything about it. I just have to go out there and do my job. That's all I can do. If Pete's in the lineup tomorrow he'll be the same Pete Rose you see for years. He's going to play the same way. When he gets in here, if he sees his name on the lineup, he's going to be as happy as ever. I know him."[62]

When Pete Rose arrived at Veterans Stadium for game four, he did indeed find his name in the lineup and responded with two hits in three at-bats. In the fourth inning he singled to center, moved to third on a single by Schmidt and then scored on a double by Lefebvre. In the fifth inning Rose doubled to center, scoring Denny. Then in the eighth, he walked and moved to second on a pinch-hit single by Perez, but did not advance as Matthews grounded into an inning-ending double play. Despite the rejuvenated play of Pete Rose, the Orioles won the game 5–4 to take a three-games-to-one lead in the Series.

In the fifth game, both Pete Rose and Tony Perez were in the starting lineup—Rose in right field and Perez on first. In addition, their former Big Red Machine teammate Joe Morgan started the game at second. While Rose had two hits to raise his Series average to .313, Scott McGregor shut out the

Phillies 5–0 to wrap up the world championship for the Orioles, four games to one.

It would be Rose's last game in a Phillies uniform. In the ninth inning, Pete had watched the game leaning on the dugout steps with his son Pete Jr. leaning right along with him as they had done so many times before. According to Jayson Stark, writing in the *Philadelphia Inquirer*, as Cal Ripken, Jr. grabbed the line drive off the bat of Garry Maddox to end the Series, Pete Rose grabbed his batting helmet, quickly headed up the ramp to the Phillies' clubhouse, and then denied to reporters that he felt in any way emotional about what was ahead. "I try not to think or worry about things that aren't in my control, so why should I worry about this? I'd say something if I was putting the uniform on for the last time. But I'm not."[63] When another reporter asked Pete about his future, all that he would say was, "Well, I'm going down to Bookbinder's to eat. I'll pick up the tab too."[64]

When Bill Giles was asked about Pete's future in Philadelphia, he stated that the two would get together in the next few days and discuss the situation. "If he says, Bill, I want to come back and just be part of the Phillies, that's a lot different than if he says, Bill, I want to come back and play every day," Giles said.[65] "I think I know what his answer is. He wants the Ty Cobb hit record. He wants to play every day. And I don't know if I can promise him that."[66] The Phillies did not renew Rose's contract. Rose, who would be 43 years old when the 1984 campaign began, did want to be a full-time player, and the Phillies were certain that his .245 batting average in the 1983 season was proof that his bat speed had slowed down.

Mike Schmidt seemed to be eulogizing Pete Rose as he remarked about his leaving the Phillies. "Pete has been a great friend of mine. I've accomplished a lot in Pete's time here. And I think a great deal of it has to do with my professional relationship with him. But time goes on. Life goes on. Careers go on. More people, more factors come in to play, and you can't ignore them."[67] Nineteen years later in 2002, Mike Schmidt was still honoring the bond that he had formed with Rose as he boldly stepped forward and spoke out for his reinstatement to baseball to Bud Selig, the commissioner of Major League Baseball, 13 years following Pete's acceptance of a lifetime ban from the game.

V

The Hit King

In the winter of 1984, Pete Rose was fast approaching his 43rd birthday with a major league total of 3,990 career hits, needing only 202 more hits to surpass Ty Cobb. He had a career batting average of .306 and had been an All-Star at five different positions. But the Philadelphia Phillies had released him, and suddenly he was a free agent with no contract to play baseball. "We hate to lose Pete,"[1] said Phillies president Bill Giles, who had been so instrumental in bringing Rose to Philadelphia in 1979. "But I want to be frank. His bat speed is slowing down."[2] As for a possible Cincinnati homecoming, the Reds showed no interest at all in having Charlie Hustle return.

So Rose, along with his agent Reuven Katz, set out searching through the backwaters of major league baseball seeking a contract. Unlike the fall of 1978, this time around there were no private jets shuttling the pair from team owner to team owner; there were no incentives being waved at them such as a stable full of race horses or beer distributorships. In fact, at times the outlook for securing any contract for Rose looked bleak. Team executives were just unsure what Rose could contribute for what they would have to pay him. Still, there were negotiations with the California Angels and the Seattle Mariners, a 1977 American League expansion team that had not yet had even one winning season. There were even talks with the Yomiuri Giants in Japan about Rose playing there. But eventually, one major league club came to the fore that was willing to consider signing the aging perennial All-Star singles hitter: the Montreal Expos.

John McHale, president of the Montreal Expos, was willing to take a chance on Rose. He told *Cincinnati Post* sports writer Earl Lawson, "I believe there are a lot of good things Pete can do for club. But I just wish I knew the answer to one question. Does he have one more good year left?"[3] Nonetheless Reuven Katz was able to secure a contract from the Expos for Rose that would pay him $500,000 for one year with incentives that could possibly pay him an additional $300,000. The incentives included a games-played clause, extra cash if Rose won the Comeback Player of the Year award, and an attendance clause that would pay Rose additional monies if the Expos drew three million fans through the Olympic Stadium turnstiles in 1984.

The attendance clause seems almost ridiculous today, in view of the fact that the Expos franchise was nearly closed down by Major League Baseball following the 2001 season for lack of fan support and moved a chunk of its home schedule to Puerto Rico for the 2003 season. However, in 1984, the Expos were a talented team with players such as Hall of Fame catcher Gary Carter and hard-hitting Andre Dawson, Tim Raines and Tim Wallach on the roster. Montreal had finished third in the National League East division in 1983, eight games behind Philadelphia. While there was considerable debate among the fans, Montreal press and the Expos' front office on the issue of whether or not the veteran Rose might be capable of providing the leadership necessary to put the team over the top, there was an ace in the hole in Charles Bronfman, Expos chairman of the board.

First, Charles Bronfman was a Pete Rose fan, and second, he liked what Expos and former Phillies batting coach Billy DeMars had to say on the matter. "I think the situation here is exactly the same as it was in Philly when Pete got there,"[4] said DeMars. "I think—knowing Pete Rose and what he can do for a club—that he's the missing link. He's a positive thinker, and we need that on our baseball team."[5]

At a news conference arranged by the Expos for his signing, Rose remarked, "I can't remember the last time I went to spring training not thinking we were going to win, and this time will be no exception. My only wish is that the season would start tomorrow. Baseball is a team game. I am not here to be any kind of cheerleader. My girlfriend is a cheerleader. I am here to provide hits. I want to be treated like Pete Rose the ballplayer, not Pete Rose the 43-year-old. I am not coming here to be a team leader. I want to be ½5th of a league and world champion."[6]

Rose and his wife Karolyn had come to final terms on their divorce agreement in December 1980. The girlfriend to whom Rose referred to in his news conference was Carol Woliung, a former hostess at a now defunct downtown Cincinnati night spot called Sleep-Out-Louie's, where Rose's roommate Tommy Gioiosa had taken a job as a bouncer and bartender following his failed tryout with the Baltimore Orioles that Rose arranged for him in 1982. Sleep-Out-Louie's was located on Second Street, ironically since renamed by the Cincinnati City Council as Pete Rose Way. Carol Woliung was a pretty 5'7" blond, a divorcee, former baton twirler in high school at Lawrenceburg, Indiana, just west of Cincinnati and had also been a Ben-Gal (the Cincinnati Bengals' cheerleading squad). Rose told author Roger Kahn that "I heard she [Carol] had the prettiest bottom in Ohio. Some scouting reports you check out personally."[7]

The Expos started their 1984 schedule in Houston, with Rose getting two hits off Joe Niekro on April 3. On April 10 in Cincinnati, Pete Rose got hit number 3,999 of his career when he tripled off Reds pitcher Mike Smith. The following morning, Pete Rose and Carol Woliung were married in Cincinnati in a small quiet ceremony at the home of his agent, Reuven Katz. On April 13, Pete Rose made his debut before the Montreal Expos home fans, playing against the Philadelphia Phillies. The date also marked the 21st anniversary of his major league debut with the Reds in 1963.

Rose was in the leadoff spot in the Expos' batting order and failed to get a hit in his first at-bat against Phillies starter Jerry Koosman. But with no one out in the fourth and Expos pitcher Charlie Lea on first base, Rose, batting right-handed against the lefty Koosman, hit a 1–1 pitch into the right field corner for a double and hit number 4,000 of his career. As Rose pulled up at second base, the huge opening day Montreal crowd of 48,060 gave him a two-minute standing ovation. One out later, Tim Raines singled to center, driving both Lea and Rose home to give the Expos a 4–1 lead. Then in the seventh, Andre Dawson tripled and was driven home on a double by Gary Carter to give Montreal a 5–1 opening day victory over Philadelphia. Speaking to the press following the game about the tribute the Expos fans had showered upon him, Rose said, "The ovation was special to me because I'm new here. The last time I played here, I got booed. When you have the reaction I got today, you get goose bumps and you want to do something for these people."[8] With 4,000 hits, Rose had now achieved a milestone that only one other player in the history of game had achieved: Ty Cobb, whom he was doggedly pursuing.

The following day, April 14, Rose celebrated his 43rd birthday with hits number 4,001 and 4,002, both singles off former teammate Steve Carlton. But now the hits would start to come a little slower, and it would be three days before hit he got number 4,003 off the New York Mets' Ron Darling. By mid-August, Rose was showing his age. His batting average had slipped to .259, and he was only getting one extra-base hit about every ten games. In fact in 278 at bats he had only produced eight extra base hits and was now reduced to a part-time player by the Expos, who were fading fast in the National League East Division. Frustrated, Rose wanted out of Montreal, and Reuven Katz began to shop around for another team where Rose could play. In late July, Katz first approached the Reds.

A lot of changes had occurred in the Cincinnati Reds' franchise since Pete Rose had left as a free agent following the 1978 season. First and foremost, the era of the Big Red Machine was over. Johnny Bench had retired following the 1983 season, and all the players on those awesome teams were gone now except for Davy Concepcion and the recently reacquired Tony Perez. The Reds were now a team struggling to achieve a .500 record each year and had for the past two years finished dead last in the National League West Division race, with a record of 61–101 in 1982 and 74–88 in 1983.

Changes in ownership and management had occurred, too. Dick Wagner had been fired as general manager in July 1983 and replaced by a recalled Bob Howsam, who had stepped down in 1978. Louis Nippert, the principal owner of the team, had sold his shares to minority owners the Williams brothers (Jim & Bill). The Williams brothers then formed a limited partnership that included Louis Nippert, his wife, Carl Kroch (Kroch & Bertinos), Priscilla Gamble, Frisch's Restaurants, George Strike and Marge Schott, a flamboyant, very outspoken Cincinnati auto dealership owner who was recruited by the Williams brothers.

In mid-August 1984, the Reds were once again struggling with a record of 51–69 under manager Vern Rapp when Katz approached Bob Howsam with the idea of bringing Pete Rose back to Cincinnati as a player-manager. Now it should be pointed out that there are many informed sports writers and authors who actually believe that Marge Schott had something to do with the idea and negotiations to bring Pete back to the Reds, but this is a myth and simply untrue. The fact of the matter is that Bob Howsam thought that Pete Rose would be able to put some fans in the empty Riverfront Stadium seats and that the marketability of his quest for Ty Cobb's all-time hit record was huge. Author Mike Bass, writing in *Marge Schott: Unleashed*, states that Howsam felt "though his playing career was waning, Rose was within reach of Ty Cobb's celebrated record for all-time hits, and Rose wasn't ready to stop trying. Rose said he'd manage, but only if he could play too. Howsam wasn't thrilled with the idea , but acquiesced, figuring if nothing else, that Rose on the field would be a box-office spark for a team in dire need of one."[9] So the deal was done, and on August 16, 1984, Rose was traded by the Montreal Expos to the Cincinnati Reds for infielder Tom Lawless.

On Friday morning, August 17, 1984, the Cincinnati newspapers proclaimed in huge bold headlines on a scale not seen since the end of World War II—PETE'S BACK! Vern Rapp was out as Reds manager and Pete Rose was in as player manager. Rose made his debut that Friday evening as the Reds met the Chicago Cubs at Riverfront Stadium before a crowd of 35,056, fans and Pete pounded out two hits, a single and a double, as the Reds pulled out a 6–4 victory. For Rose, they were career hits number 4,063 and 4,064 and his first hits since August 11. The Reds finished the 1984 season in fifth place, with a record of 70–92. Under Rose they were 19–23. Rose had played in 26 games for the Reds and hit .365. He now had 4,097 career hits and was just 94 hits behind Ty Cobb.

As the 1985 season began, the countdown was on in Cincinnati for Pete Rose to break Ty Cobb's all-time hit mark. About 20 stories up in the Fifth Third Bank building facing Fountain Square, the number of hits Pete needed to reach the coveted 4,191 was displayed with numbers in the windows. Each time Rose got a hit, the number was changed. The *Cincinnati Enquirer* ran a contest offering $4,192 to the person who could come closest to guessing the exact date and time that Rose would break Ty Cobb's record. The entire city was caught up in Rose's quest for baseball immortality, and each hit he got became a reason for a daily dialogue on the matter. The nation was also caught up in the Cobb quest, and legions of photographers and sports writers followed Rose from city to city on a daily basis.

Over the winter, the Reds had been sold to Marge Schott. Furthermore, when the club was still under the control of the Williams brothers, they had allowed general manager Bob Howsam to get out of his contract early and return as a consultant. To replace Howsam on a day-to-day basis, the Williams brothers brought in Bill Bergesch from the New York Yankees to run the club. To bolster the roster and make the team competitive under Rose as player-manager, Dave Parker, a former National League MVP, had been signed as a free agent over the winter in 1983. Now veteran third baseman and All-Star Buddy Bell was added to the roster in July 1985. Rose, Parker, Bell and Ron Oester on the roster gave the Reds a homegrown flavor, as all four players grew up in Cincinnati. Subsequently, with a fine crop of Reds farmhands on the brink of coming up to the majors, like Tom Browning and Eric Davis, while Kal Daniels and Barry Larkin were still being developed in the minors, the team looked like it was going to be in the thick of things in the National League West Division again for quite a while.

As the 1985 season got under way, Rose wasted no time in launching his final assault on Cobb's all-time mark, getting two hits in the Reds' opening day game on April 8 against Montreal. He then proceeded to hit safely in the first six games of the season. Suddenly Rose's magic number displayed high up on the Fifth Third Bank building window read 86. By the end of April, that number had been reduced to 79. On May 5, Rose stroked three singles off the New York Mets' brilliant young right-hander Dwight Gooden, reducing his magic number to 74. On May 20 at Chicago's Wrigley Field, Rose got hit number 4,129 when he hit his first home run since the 1982 season off the Cubs' Scott Sanderson. The following day, he got two singles off of Dennis Eckersley to reduce his magic number to 60. On June 2, Rose got two doubles and a single off three St. Louis Cardinals pitchers, making 53 the number of hits needed to catch Cobb. On July 1, Rose singled off the

Los Angeles Dodgers' Orel Hershiser to reduce his magic number to 37 hits with 87 games to go. It looked like a lock. But there would be only twelve more hits in July, so at the end of the month, the numbers on the windows of the Fifth Third Bank building read 24. But in mid-August, Pete had five hits in two days when on August 17 he got three hits off Houston's Joe Niekro and Frank Dipino and the following day got two more hits off Nolan Ryan and Jeff Calhoun to reduce the magic number to the one he wore on his uniform jersey—14.

The drama really began to build to a high level as the Reds arrived in Chicago on September 6 for a three-game weekend series with Cubs at Wrigley Field. Rose, standing at hit number 4,187, was just four hits behind Ty Cobb's record. Closing in on the record, Rose wanted to break the coveted mark of 4,191 hits in front of the hometown fans in Cincinnati, where the Reds were scheduled to return immediately following the Chicago series on September 10. Regardless, Rose played on Friday, September 6, and got two hits, his second home run of the season off Derek Botelho and a single off rookie Reggie Patterson. He was now just three hits behind Cobb.

On Sunday, September 8, Rose put himself in the lineup against the Cubs. He wasn't going to play on Sunday, and the huge press corps that had been following him actually began to leave Chicago for Cincinnati, where the Reds would open a three-game series with the San Diego Padres on Monday, sure that Rose would tie and break Cobb's record there. Even Pete's wife Carol, his young son Ty and his agent Reuven Katz had returned to Cincinnati to await the historical event. Then Steve Trout, a left-hander who was supposed to be the Cubs' starting pitcher on Sunday, fell off a bicycle while playing with his daughter and hurt his elbow and shoulder. Consequently, he had to be scratched from the lineup. So the Cubs started rookie Reggie Patterson, a right-hander off of whom Rose had gotten hit number 4,189 on Friday, and Rose inserted himself into the lineup.

Rose, batting second in the lineup behind leadoff hitter Eddie Milner, swung at the first pitch he saw from Patterson and drove it into right center field for a single and hit number 4,190. Then in the fifth inning, with the count full, Rose lined a single over the head of Cubs second baseman Ryne Sandberg off Patterson for hit number 4,191, thus tying Ty Cobb's all-time hit mark. The electronic message board attached to the old permanent scoreboard in Wrigley Field began flashing a message "Ty Cobb 4,191" on one line and beneath it "Pete Rose, 4,191." Keith Moreland, the Cubs' right fielder, threw the ball back into the infield and then applauded Rose. All at once, the entire Wrigley Field crowd of 28,269 fans were on their feet, as well as the fans on the rooftops of the apartment buildings across the street behind the outfield fences, applauding Pete as he stood on first base tipping his batting helmet to the crowd. Unlike all the glad-handing spectacle that went on when Mark McGwire hit his 62nd home run to break Roger Maris' mark in 1998 with Sammy Sosa running in from right field to shake his hand, Reggie Patterson stood his ground on the mound and did not come over and shake Rose's hand. Later in the inning, Buddy Bell hit a three-run home run to make the score 5–4 Chicago.

Now that Rose had tied the record, most of the Reds players thought that he would now take himself out of the game. Back in Cincinnati, according to author Mike Bass writing in *Marge Schott Unleashed*, Schott did not know that Rose had inserted himself in the lineup for the Sunday game, and when he got the hit that tied Cobb's record, she received a call at her home from an employee of the team. Marge Schott, as owner, was keenly aware of the box office windfall that she had going on Rose getting his historic hit at home in Riverfront Stadium and was understandably upset. "If that son of a bitch gets that base hit, I'm gonna kill him,"[10] Marge said. "If he gets that base hit in Chicago, he doesn't even need to come back to Cincinnati."[11]

Now it's almost become a national obsession in the media to malign the politically incorrect Marge Schott at the slightest opportunity. However, the writing of Mike Bass in this situation is in question as to its accuracy, for in actuality Marge Schott did not learn about Rose playing in the game through a telephone call to her home, but had gone to the Cincinnati Bengals game that day. "I went to the Bengal game, and I was little late,"[12] said Schott. "I no more than walk in when someone tells me Pete is playing. I almost died. I'm really upset that someone in the Reds organization couldn't call me and let me know."[13] Chicago is an hour behind Cincinnati, and as Schott had a private plane waiting for her at Cincinnati's Lunken Airport, she could have arrived at Wrigley Field in plenty of time to be with Rose on the historic occasion.

As the game progressed into the sixth inning, in the Reds' dugout at Wrigley Field, Tony Perez kept walking by Pete Rose looking at him. "What are you doing, buddy?"[14] said Perez. "What are you doing? What are you going to do?"[15] "I'm trying to get a base hit,"[16] said Rose. Dave Concepcion told Rose, "You better get your batting gloves and go upstairs and watch on TV."[17] Rose replied, "I can't do that."[18] Taking himself out of the game would have been contrary to all that Charlie Hustle had stood for in his career. So, facing the possible wrath of his ball club's owner and possibly disappointing his hometown crowd, Pete Rose saw a chance to win the game and kept himself in the lineup.

With a drizzle starting in Wrigley Field, Rose came up to bat next in the seventh inning to face Lary Sorenson. He took the count to two balls and two strikes, fouled off the next pitch, then grounded out to Cubs shortstop Shawon Dunston. Then the drizzle turned into a hard rain. When Rose came to bat in the ninth inning, the Reds had already tied the game at 5–5

Pete Rose. (Photo File, Inc.)

and the game had already been interrupted by rain for more than two hours. Hard-throwing reliever Lee Smith was on the mound for Chicago as the sun began to set behind the third base side of the field, and there were no lights yet installed in Wrigley Field. With the count two balls and two strikes, Smith struck out Rose. The Cubs failed to score in the bottom of the ninth; then the rain returned and the game had to be called because of darkness. The National League office said that the game counted and was a tie. It would only be replayed if it had a bearing on the outcome of the division race for either team, so for now Rose's hits counted.

Following the game, Rose told *Cincinnati Enquirer* sports reporter Tim Sullivan that he didn't know what to do about putting himself in the lineup that day. "I was real confused. I didn't know what to do. I was in sort of a situation where I didn't want to disappoint everybody. I had 30,000 yelling here and one lady back in Cincinnati, every time I got a hit, kicking her dog"[19] (a reference to Marge Schott's pet Saint Bernard, Schottzie). Perhaps the Reds' team feelings on the matter were best summarized by Rose's long-time friend Tony Perez. "I did not want him to break it. The Cubs fans pulled for him and they see the tie. But the people in Cincinnati deserve to see him break it."[20] Actually, millions would see Rose break the record, as the moment was on national television.

That evening, shortly after 11:00 p.m. when the Cincinnati Reds' flight, United Airlines 352, landed at Greater Cincinnati Northern Kentucky International Airport from Chicago, a small but boisterous crowd assembled to welcome Pete home, chanting the familiar Pete, Pete, Pete!

One fan was wearing a T-shirt that read "Hustling Toward the Record." Another said she had seen Marge Schott at the Bengals game and that she was madder than heck. Rose gave a brief interview, then proceeded toward the baggage claim area as exuberant fans walked along all the way patting him on the back.

As the Reds prepared to open the three-game series with San Diego, with Rose on the brink of breaking Cobb's record, they announced that there were 15,000 tickets still available for the first game on Monday, 16,000 for Tuesday's game and 24,000 for Wednesday's game. Dave Dravecky, a left-hander, was going to be the starting pitcher for San Diego in the first game of the series, so Rose announced that he would not play.

On Tuesday, September 10, Rose was in the lineup as 51,045 enthusiastic fans jammed the stands at Riverfront Stadium. Every time Rose came to bat, they stood up and cheered and chanted his name, Pete, Pete, Pete! In the red seats high up in center field, children unfurled rolls of toilet paper that drifted like confetti down on to the outfield. Even the granddaughter of Ty Cobb, Peggy Cobb Schug, was in the stands, having come from Charlotte, North Carolina to attend the game. In the seventh inning, Ms. Schug visited with Reds owner Marge Schott in her box and reminisced about her grandfather, saying he was undeserving of his villainous reputation. In an article by Howard Wilkinson and John Eckberg printed in the *Cincinnati Enquirer*, Ms. Schug stated that she remembered Cobb as a "gentle man, a caring grandfather who gave batting practice to her brothers and took her to meet other baseball legends like Nap Lajoie."

However, the fans went home disappointed that night, as Pete went 0 for four at the plate and the Padres beat the Reds 3–2. LaMarr Hoyt had stopped Rose on three trips to the plate, getting him to pop out to the short-stop in the first, fly out to left in the fourth and then pop out again to the shortstop in the sixth. Hard-throwing Lance McCullers, who took over for

Hoyt, shut Rose down on a hard line drive to left that was caught in the eighth inning. It was Hoyt's first start since August 18; he had been out with a shoulder injury. "My philosophy was to mix the pitches up,"[21] said Hoyt. "If he was going to get the hit, he was going to have to earn it. Nothing down the middle."[22] For his part Rose, was up front about his hitless performance. "I did something I usually don't do; I swung at a couple of bad pitches, up and in, my first two times up. I swung the bat good one time all night. The last time up in the eighth inning, I hit that ball right on the nose. I was a little disappointed tonight. If you look at the stat sheet, this is only the 12th game since I came back [August 1984] that I haven't got on base by a hit or walk."[23]

So with Rose going hitless and the fans once again clamoring for the chance to see history made, long lines were formed at the Riverfront Stadium ticket office immediately following the game, and 10,000 tickets were sold for the next night's game between the time that Rose made his final appearance at the plate and 12:30 A.M. when the Reds closed the office for the night. With 50,045 fans in the stands for the game, the Reds season attendance total for 1985 had now exceeded 1.5 million, which is believed to be the point where the attendance clause in Rose's contract would kick in. Thus he would receive an additional forty cents per fan for the rest of the season.

One of those fifty-thousand-plus persons, who attended the game and was a guest in Marge Schott's box at Riverfront Stadium that night, was the new baseball commissioner, Peter Ueberroth. Ueberroth had served as president of the Los Angeles 1984 Olympic Organizing Committee, and on October 1, 1984, he had taken over as commissioner from Bowie Kuhn. According to author Mike Bass, writing in *Marge Schott: Unleashed*, the commissioner experienced an unwanted surprise while viewing the game when Schottzie, Schott's behemoth Saint Bernard, urinated on his shoe. However, Rose did not get his historic hit that night, and pressing business awaited the commissioner in New York, so he was unable to stay for Wednesday's game.

Notwithstanding the fact that Rose did not get the historic hit on September 10, the 3–2 loss to Padres also all but eliminated the Reds from the 1985 National League West Division race. The Los Angeles Dodgers swept a doubleheader from the Atlanta Braves leaving the Reds in their dust, nine and a half games behind. At least one player on the Reds, Gary Redus, wasn't happy with Rose's managerial style. Redus, who at the time had 43 stolen bases and was tied for fifth in stolen bases in the National League with Ryne Sandberg, had lost his starting job in left field when Rose moved Nick Esasky there in July and was now splitting playing time in center field with Eddie Milner. "There's a lot of dissatisfaction,"[24] said Redus. "It's too late to even talk to anybody about it. In the last two months, if I've started 10 games, that's more than I've counted. I don't know of anybody that can get their rhythm like that. They keep saying I'm valuable. But I'm not valuable sitting over there on the bench. Maybe I'm not in the plans around here."[25] On December 11, 1985, Redus was traded to the Philadelphia Phillies for Tom Hume and John Denny.

With Rose, Cincinnati and the nation having to wait another night to see history made, it afforded the media another chance to hype the comparisons between the playing conditions of Ty Cobb and Pete Rose: the dead ball of the Cobb era, the night games of the Rose era, transcontinental jet travel vs. railroad sleeper cars, legalized spitballs and the rise of relief pitchers, etc. Tim Sullivan, writing in the *Cincinnati Enquirer* his comparison of the Cobb vs. Rose eras, even entered race into the equation, stating that the inclusion of black and Latin ballplayers into the major leagues had an impact on the quality of the game, and Rose himself agreed. "Just think about this a minute,"[26] Rose said. "I think one of the things that makes hitting a baseball so difficult today than 30, 40, 50 years ago is the number of black outfielders that we have. What I mean is the amount of speed in the outfield. Put an Eric Davis, a Dave Parker, and a Gary Redus out there and try to hit the gap. Or try to hit the gap with Willie McGee and Vince Coleman out there. I go back to the days when Willie Mays and Bobby Bonds were chasing my stuff down."[27]

When morning came on September 11, the city of Cincinnati was again ready for the anticipated celebration that would follow if Rose got the record-breaking hit that night. The police department was poised to deploy additional officers, if necessary, to the area around Riverfront Stadium and on Fountain Square. Mayor Charles Luken had actually scheduled an official celebration on Fountain Square at 11:30 A.M. two days after Rose broke Cobb's record. The delay in scheduling the celebration was due in part to Rose, who didn't want to get up early after playing in a night game and also due to the fact that he was expected to make a round of television appearances on the early morning network news shows, such as *Today* on NBC, *Good Morning America* on ABC, etc., and even tape a *Phil Donahue Show* at Cincinnati's Riverfront Coliseum the morning after the hit. Nonetheless, the city council had passed an ordinance changing the name of 2nd Street to Pete Rose Way, and Mayor Luken said the new street signs would start to go up immediately in an unveiling ceremony at 10:00 A.M. the morning after Pete broke the record.

As for Pete Rose, he started the day with lunch at Flanagan's Landing on 2nd Street and arrived in his Riverfront Stadium office at about 2:30 P.M. After a news conference at 4:00 P.M. and batting practice, at about 6:00 P.M. he headed back to the clubhouse to prepare for the game. When the game started, 47,237 fans had jammed into Riverfront Stadium, and Pete came up to bat against the Padres' Eric Show. At 8:01 P.M., with the count two balls and one strike, Rose stroked a clean single into left field for hit number 4,192, and immediately all hell broke loose in Riverfront Stadium! The Reds' radio network team of Marty Brennaman and Joe Nuxhall drowned out each other's voices as they broadcast the call of the hit. The Goodyear blimp hovered over Riverfront Stadium flashing the news. More than 300 journalist and photographers were on hand, and flashbulbs began to explode like rifle fire at the Battle of Gettysburg. High above Riverfront Stadium in center field, fireworks exploded from the scoreboard, and the huge crowd was now standing and cheering continuously, letting out the emotion that had been building up in them all season long since opening day.

As Rose stood on first base, tears began to stream down his cheeks. Rose was to say later that as he looked up into the lights above the stadium, he saw images of Ty Cobb and his father Harry Rose looking down upon him. Rose grabbed his former teammate and friend, first base coach Tommy Helms, as he sobbed and said, "I don't know what to do."[28] Helms simply replied, "That's OK, boss. You're number one. You deserve it all."[29] Helms then motioned toward the dugout for Rose's son Pete, Jr. [Petey], and he ran out on to the field and embraced his dad as the tears continued to flow. As the Reds' dugout emptied, teammates Tony Perez and Dave Concepcion soon arrived at first base and hoisted Rose on their shoulders. Even Padres pitcher Eric Show, who had sat down on the mound to wait out the pandemonium, got up and came over to first to shake Rose's hand. Then Reds owner Marge Schott arrived and embraced Pete in a tight bear hug, while a red Corvette that she had bought for him was wheeled through a gate in the outfield wall and delivered to Pete at first base. The car bore the license plate number Ohio PR 4192. The celebration went on for seven minutes before play was resumed.

Rose then moved on to second base when Show walked Dave Parker on four straight pitches and eventually scored the first run of the game when Nick Esasky hit into a fielder's choice. In the seventh inning, Rose got hit number 4,193 when he tripled down the left field line and then scored the Reds' second run of the game on a sacrifice by Esasky. When it was over, the Reds had defeated the Padres 2–0, and Rose had scored both runs. The winning pitcher was rookie Tom Browning, who went eight and one-third innings and now had posted a season record of 16–9, needing a little relief help from relievers John Franco in the ninth, who set down Tony Gwynn, and Ted Power, who retired Steve Garvey to end the game.

The night of the "big knock," as Rose liked to refer to the record-breaking hit, was in many ways for him a family reunion. Not only did he profess to see an image of his late father Harry Rose in the stadium lights while standing on first base, sobbing and embracing his 15-year-old son Pete Jr., but his new family—his second wife, 31-year-old Carol, and the couple's 11-month-old son Tyler were also in the stands at Riverfront Stadium. Carol stated, "I was happy looking at everybody. Everybody was so happy."[30] Rose's mother, 70-year-old Laverne Rose Noeth, and his brother David, now 37 years old, were there too.

His former wife, Karolyn, was also in the stadium. She told the press that the sight of seeing Pete hug young Pete Jr. brought tears to her eyes. Karolyn hoped to see young Pete someday play in the major leagues too. Pete Rose, Jr., still known as Petey in 1985, had actually taken batting practice with the Reds' pitchers before the game and shagged fly balls in the outfield. This activity would of course have been forbidden when Dick Wagner was running the ball club. But Petey was now a sophomore in high school and had played American Legion baseball during the summer. In 2001, looking back on the glory of the night that Rose broke Cobb's record, his son Pete Rose, Jr., by then a career minor league player, spoke with CBS reporter Harold Dow in an interview for the program *48 Hours*. "Dad being Dad, Mr. Tough Guy, I'd never seen him cry before. Never really got a hug before or a kiss before. He told me he loved me. I told him I loved him. That was the night, and it was just a special night."

However, the joy of family members in the ballpark that historic evening was counterbalanced by the presence of more ominous persons who represented the dark side of Pete Rose. Tommy Gioiosa, was there and so was a Franklin, Ohio bookie by the name of Ron Peters, who watched the game from a seat along the third base line courtesy of Pete Rose. For the previous two years, it is alleged in the Dowd Report, Gioiosa, Rose's former roommate, had been placing bets for Rose with Peters on college basketball, professional basketball and major league baseball. According to an article published in *Sports Illustrated*, July 3, 1989, Gioiosa and later Peters were permitted by Rose to hang out in the Reds' clubhouse. Peters stated to *Sports Illustrated* that Gioiosa sometimes left tickets for him at the will-call window at Riverfront Stadium, either under his name or Rose's. Subsequently Gioiosa had left tickets for Peters to attend the Reds-Padres game on September 11, 1985, and he witnessed hit number 4,192. Rose's need for money was increasing as his gambling intensified. George Will, writing in his book *Bunts*, makes a reference to James Reston, Jr.'s book *Collision at Home Plate*, where he states, "During the game in which he broke Ty Cobb's career record for most hits, he changed his uniform shirt three times—one shirt for himself, one for the Reds' owner, and one to sell." This obsession of Rose's with the potential economic benefits of memorabilia is corroborated by Tommy Gioiosa in an article published in *Vanity Fair* in September 2001. Gioiosa was in the Reds' clubhouse the evening of September 11, 1985, before the game and states that he watched Rose put on several undershirts instead of just one while dressing for the game. According to Gioiosa, Rose said to him, "I'll sell every one of these motherfuckers."[31]

There was a postgame ceremony for Rose in which Reds owner Marge Schott and Reds radio broadcaster Marty Brennaman presented an engraved silver punch bowl to Rose. The bowl was equipped with a ladle and 12 cups, each engraved with a highlight from Rose's career: April 13, 1963, his first game in the majors; hits number 1, 500, 1,000, 1,500, 2,000, 3,000, 3,500, 3,631, 3,772, 4,000 and 4,192. However, Marge Schott could not resist letting "Schottzie" get in on the ceremony, so the handle of the ladle was engraved to Pete reading, "Woofs and licks, Schottzie."[32]

Then it was into the clubhouse for Rose to receive a congratulatory telephone call from President Ronald Reagan. The following is the text of the telephone call between President Reagan and Pete Rose after the game in which he broke Ty Cobb's major league record for most career hits.

PRESIDENT REAGAN: Is this Pete Rose ... alias Charlie Hustle? This is Ronald Reagan. Listen, I just wanted to say congratulations for breaking one of the most enduring records in sports history. Unless you've done something since I heard the latest, you've made it 4,193. I've been rooting for you, and come to think of it, I used to also root for the fellow who once held that record.

Pete Rose Way, Cincinnati, Ohio.

Rose: Thank you very much for taking time out of your busy schedule to call us.... We really appreciated it, and you missed a good ballgame tonight.

President Reagan: This has established you as one of the all-time greats of the game.... Your new record may be broken, but believe me, your reputation and legacy is secure ... and I think it will be a long time before someone is standing in the spot you're standing in now. I wish the Reds and people of Cincinnati all the best. It's been a pleasure talking with you, and ... Pete, we should do this more often. You know, those of us in the middle of our careers could share tips on how to stay ahead of those younger folks who keep coming up on us from behind.

Rose: If you'd been here tonight, you'd know why we think this is the baseball capital of the world right here in Cincinnati, Ohio.

President Reagan: Congratulations. You really have given a lift to the whole country. God bless you."[33]

As Rose spoke with reporters following the game, he time and time again reflected on what the event would have been like for his father. "My dad would probably have said, 'Nice hitting, but why did you leave the guy on third base with one out?' He'd have patted me on the back and given me five and kicked me in the butt for drinking champagne. Ty Cobb was a tough, tough man. But my dad was a tough, tough, tough, tougher man."[34]

The kid from the west side of Cincinnati had now become the Hit King and positioned himself for baseball immortality. Of the thousands who played the game before him, no one had accomplished what he had in his career, and the fact is that Rose's hit record may be never be broken. Pete Rose had arrived at this monumental level of achievement through his own sheer self-determination and drive. When Rose was 15 years old, he was dropped from an American Legion Team, considered too small to play at that level. His high school baseball coach, Paul Nohr, stated that he was an average player. But regardless of the odds against him, Pete Rose pushed forward determined to make it in professional baseball. The blend of his work ethic, success and common background is the energy that continues to fuel the over-zealous Pete Rose fans in their belief that he can do no wrong. Whatever Pete may have been involved in off the field, be it on the square or otherwise, can be forgiven for what he did on the field. There is a unique relationship between Pete Rose and his fans that is unlike anything seen since the days of Babe Ruth. As with Ruth, the power of Rose's personality overwhelms his fans and hides his personal weaknesses. But it is the fans' very tight embrace of him that actually enables Rose to violate their trust.

Rose finished the 1985 season with 4,204 career hits. He had batted .264 with 107 hits in 119 games. The Reds, under his first full year as manager, finished second in the National League West Division with a record of 89–72, five and a half games behind the Los Angeles Dodgers. Rose's pursuit of Ty Cobb's hit record had lured 1.8 million fans into Riverfront Stadium, making the year a huge box office success for Marge Schott and the other Reds partners.

In 1986, the Reds, under Rose again, finished second in the National League West Division, this time ten games behind the Houston Astros. Rose, now 45 years old, continued to play, even though it was clear to everyone that his bat speed had visibly slowed down. So much, in fact, that at times it looked like he was having trouble hitting the ball out of the infield, and the sports writers were becoming increasingly impatient with his attempts to play. It seemed to everyone that it was time for Pete to retire. But the Hit King was to have one last hurrah. On August 11, he singled four times and doubled to set a National League record with the 10th five-hit game of his career. Then on August 17, Rose struck out against Goose Gossage of the San Diego Padres and never played again.

While Rose did not officially announce his retirement, he told author Roger Kahn in *Pete Rose: My Story* that the reason he stopped playing was that his friend Tony Perez, with whom he had been sharing first base during the 1986 season, was closing in on a record. "Tony was in his last year. He had announced his retirement. He was a couple of home runs behind Orlando Cepeda as the most productive home run hitter of all the Latin players. I wanted him to get the record."[35] Perez wound up in a tie with Cepeda, with 379 career home runs. However, as time passed, the all-time Latin home run king eventually became Sammy Sosa, who hit home run number 500 in his career at the Great American Ball Park in Cincinnati on April 4, 2003 and now is reaching beyond.

There was no grand retirement tour around the league for Pete Rose, no hoopla, no special tributes in the media. One day he just stopped playing. His withdrawal from baseball was a little like the retirement of automobile manufacturing pioneer Henry Ford. After decades of sweat and toil, one morning he got up and just decided not to go to the office. Rose finished with a career batting average of .303 and a total of 4,256 hits. 691 of those hits had come after the age of 40, another major league record. Although Rose was still there as manager of the Reds, he just seemed to fade into the background and out of the game as a player. His sudden disappearance from the game after twenty-four Major League seasons conjures up memories of a statement made some years before by former teammate Johnny Bench, who suggested that when it came time for Rose to retire, they would have to cut the uniform off him. But who was going to do that to Charlie Hustle?

Not Marge Schott, not his teammates, not the press, not his fans. In the end it was Rose who spared all of them the agony as he cut the uniform off himself.

Milestone Hits in the Career of Pete Rose

Number	Date	Hit	Pitcher
1	4/13/63	triple	Bob Friend
100	7/26/63	single	Tony Cloninger
500	9/16/65	single	Al Jackson
1000	6/26/68	single	Dick Selma
1500	8/29/70	single	Carl Morton
2000	6/19/72	single	Ron Bryant
2500	8/17/75	single	Bruce Kison
3000	5/5/78	single	Steve Rodgers
3500	8/15/80	single	Tom Hausman
3631	8/10/81	single	Mark Littell
3772	6/22/82	double	John Stuper
4192	9/11/85	single	Eric Show

Pitchers Giving Up the Most Career Hits to Pete Rose

1.	Phil Niekro	64
2.	Don Sutton	60
3. tie	Juan Marichal	42
	Gaylord Perry	42
4. tie	Joe Niekro	39
	Tom Seaver	39
5. tie	Claude Osteen	38
	Ron Reed	38
6. tie	Bob Gibson	36
	Ferguson Jenkins	36
7.	Larry Dierker	35
8.	Steve Rodgers	32
9.	Steve Carlton	31
10. tie	Clay Kirby	30
	Chris Short	30

Pete Rose Career Hits by Team

Year	Hits	Ave.
CINCINNATI REDS		
1963	170	.273
1964	139	.269
1965	209	.312
1966	205	.313
1967	176	.301
1968	210	.335

Year	Hits	Ave.
1969	218	.348
1970	205	.316
1971	192	.304
1972	198	.307
1973	230	.338
1974	185	.284
1975	210	.317
1976	215	.323
1977	204	.311
1978	198	.302
1984	35	.365
1985	107	.264
1986	52	.219

PHILADELPHIA PHILLIES

1979	208	.331
1980	185	.282
1981	140	.325
1982	172	.271
1983	121	.245

MONTREAL EXPOS

	1984	72	.259
Totals	24 years	4256	.303

Pete Rose Career Statistics and All-Time Rank

Category	Number	All-Time Rank
Games	3,562	1
At-Bats	14,053	1
Hits	4,256	1
Doubles	746	2
Extra-Base Hits	1,041	20
Total Bases	5,752	6
Runs	2,165	5
Walks	1,566	12

VI

Lifetime Banishment from Baseball

The fall of Pete Rose from the grace of Major League Baseball is a murky tale, disjointed, and at times, his accusers contradict the evidence they have brought forth. There is much information regarding his gambling habits, but the smoking gun always seems just a little elusive. In the final analysis, the investigation of Pete Rose leaves unanswered as many serious questions as it answers. Then, of course, there are the legions of Pete Rose fans who choose to view all of the evidence with blinders on, and like Charlie Hustle himself, they do not see any course of action in the matter other than complete denial.

On April 6, 1989, with the investigation of his gambling habits swirling about him while he was still at the helm of the Cincinnati Reds as manager, Rose told the press, "I'm guilty of one thing; I wasn't a very good picker of friends."[1] Indeed, in the end it was his off-the-field associations who led to his demise. But in order to gain an understanding of Pete Rose's steep downhill slide, it is necessary to take the journey through the social wilderness and subculture that he voluntarily entered. We must get to know the people who gained his trust and whom he called his friends when he was on the brink of baseball immortality.

It is alleged that after Pete Rose returned to play for the Cincinnati Reds in August 1984, his habit of placing bets increased dramatically. According to Tommy Gioiosa, in 1985 he "was instructed to find Rose another bookie, one who could handle bets in which $2,000 a game was considered routine."[3] According to the Dowd Report in June of 1984, while Rose was still playing in Montreal, Gold's Gym opened in the Cincinnati suburban community of Forest Park. The principal owner was Michael Fry. Another person involved with Gold's Gym operation was an investor by the name of Don Stenger, who also happened to be a friend of Pete Rose. The Dowd report further states that Stenger then introduced Rose's former roommate Tommy Gioiosa to Fry, and subsequently Gioiosa and Stenger began working out at the gym in September 1984. Pete Rose was now 43 years old and hotly in pursuit of Ty Cobb's all-time hit record. Therefore, he was interested in maximum physical fitness for the task ahead. In November of 1984, Gioiosa and Stenger started to bring Pete Rose to Gold's Gym to work out.

The Dowd Report goes on to state that Gioiosa claimed to have had experience managing health clubs, and after criticizing the Gold's operation on several occasions, he was hired by Michael Fry at $500 a week to manage his gym's day-to-day business activities with the help of Don Stenger and Linda Kettle. Another member of Gold's Gym was James Eveslage, who was the proprietor of the Miami Beach Tanning Salon in Oxford, Ohio and who was also an acquaintance of Don Stenger's. The Dowd Report states that once Tommy Gioiosa asked Don Stenger "if he knew someone who could take bets. Stenger thereupon introduced Gioiosa to Jim Eveslage. Eveslage recalled that Gioiosa approached him and asked if he knew anyone who could take big action for Pete Rose. Gioiosa told Eveslage that he wanted to lay down bets on football for Rose."[2] Eveslage said that he did know such a person and introduced Gioiosa to Ron Peters, a bookmaker from Franklin, Ohio.

It is alleged by Gioiosa in his September 2001 *Vanity Fair* interview that at first he placed bets of $2,000–$5,000 per game with Peters on behalf of Rose on basketball and football, but after a while Rose began to bet on baseball and on various occasions placed wagers directly with Peters. The Dowd Report states that Ron Peters testified that he took bets from Gioiosa and Rose from late 1984 to late 1986, when he stopped accepting bets from Rose. During that period, Peters alleges that Rose bet on professional football, college basketball and Major League Baseball, including games played by the Cincinnati Reds.

Also in 1985, Rose became friends with a person from Brooklyn, New York, by the name of Michael Bertolini. Bertolini was a memorabilia dealer who was in the baseball card show business and became the exclusive photographer for Rose and a few other ballplayers. Subsequently, Bertolini became a business partner of Rose's and the director and producer of his baseball card shows under the name Hit King Marketing. It is alleged in the Dowd Report that Bertolini also became involved with placing bets for Rose

with an unidentified New York bookie from Staten Island, New York, noto-
riously known as simply Val. However, in its August 24, 1989 edition, the
Daily News identified Val as Richard (Val) Troy.

Another person whom Tommy Gioiosa introduced to Pete Rose was
Paul Janszen. Janszen, a barrel salesman who also dealt illegally in anabolic
steroids and regularly worked out at Gold's Gym, was aware of the fact,
according to the Dowd Report, that Gioiosa was a gambler and mule for a
cocaine operation run by Don Stenger and Michael Fry that brought the drug
from Florida to Cincinnati. Janszen was also aware of the fact that Gioiosa
was known to place bets for Rose. Subsequently, Janszen's introduction to
Rose by Gioiosa took place during the 1986 National League playoffs at
Rose's home. Janszen met Ron Peters for the first time near the end of 1986.
Soon after, Janszen and Rose became close friends, and the two traveled
together to baseball cards shows, where it is alleged that Rose asked Janszen
to count the cash that was taken in and put it into paper bags. The Dowd
Report alleges that Janszen estimated that at these various card shows in late
1986, Rose made between $8,000 and $12,000 cash each.

Toward the end of 1986, the friendship between Janszen and Rose
intensified. Janszen's girlfriend, Danita Marcum, also got to know Rose and
his wife Carol as the two couples spent Christmas and New Year's together.
In the Dowd Report, Marcum stated that in addition to placing bets for Rose
of $2,000 per game with Ron Peters in May, June and July 1987, she often
saw large amounts of cash in Rose's home and that she witnessed Gioiosa
and Bertolini placing bets for Rose as well. Then in early January 1987, Rose
and Gioiosa had a falling-out over an incident that took place at Turfway
Race Track, and the friendship between Rose and Janszen intensified again.
Subsequently, Janszen replaced Gioiosa as the intermediary for Rose in placing his bets.

In 1988, the fourth straight year the Reds under Rose finished second
in the National League West Division, this time seven games behind the Los
Angeles Dodgers. On April 30 of that year, Rose shoved umpire Dave Pallone during a dispute at home plate. Consequently he was fined $10,000 and
suspended for thirty days by National League president Bart Giamatti. The
severity of the penalty was unusual and got the attention of everyone. However, Rose refused to protest the penalty, stating that he believed in the
integrity of and importance of the league president. At the same time,
rumors of Rose's alleged betting had begun to circulate in the commissioner's office, and this of course raises the issue of whether there was any
conscious or unconscious reasoning for Giamatti to be so heavy handed in
adjudication of the Rose-Pallone incident.

In 1988, Paul Janszen was under investigation by the FBI for drug
trafficking originating out of Gold's Gym and for making a false statement

on an income tax return. Janszen soon began cooperating with the FBI, and according to *Sports Illustrated* in their July 3, 1989, issue, as part of a plea bargaining arrangement, he set up a cocaine deal in which the FBI arrested Ron Peters. During the subsequent investigation, the name of Pete Rose often came up in his conversations with the investigators. In fact, Janszen told the FBI that he had placed bets for Rose between 1986 and 1987. Janszen was cooperating so well with the FBI that at times he tape-recorded conversations with various suspects on his own undertaking.

While the FBI notified Major League Baseball and began a marginal probe of Rose, it was stated by the investigators that Paul Janszen was not to be included in their investigation until they had concluded their work with him. By January 1989, the FBI was done with Janszen, Michael Fry, former co-owner of Gold's Gym, was about to start serving an eight year prison sentence for cocaine trafficking, and Ron Peters had been indicted. Now Janszen was fair game for the commissioner's office to begin its investigation.

On February 20, 1989, Rose was summoned from the Reds' spring training camp in Plant City, Florida to a meeting with Peter Ueberroth, the commissioner of baseball, along with his soon-to-be successor, commissioner-elect and National League president A. Bartlett Giamatti, and assistant commissioner Fay Vincent at his New York City office. Rose took two lawyers with him, Reuven Katz and his partner Robert Pitcairn. When Rose emerged from the meeting, he spoke to the press. "They wanted my input and advice on a couple of things,"[4] Rose said. "I gave it to them, it took an hour, I left. That was it."[5] However what really was on the commissioner's agenda was a discussion of the gambling habits of Pete Rose. First and foremost on the commissioner's list of questions for Rose was whether he had bet on baseball. According to Rose, Ueberroth asked him, "Do you bet on baseball?"[6] Rose responded, "No, sir. I didn't bet on baseball. The last bet I made was the [1989] Super Bowl."[7] Ueberroth told Rose he wasn't concerned with betting on football: he wanted to know about betting on baseball. Again Rose denied placing any bets on baseball. Ueberroth also asked Rose if he owed any money to bookies, and Rose said that he did not.

The commissioner was also interested in rumors that Rose had recently been the winner of a Pik-Six ticket at Turfway Race Park in Florence, Kentucky, just across the Ohio River from Cincinnati. It was alleged that on January 25, 1989, Rose and Jerry Carroll, owner of Turfway Race Park, had hit for a Pik-Six ticket worth $265,669.20. According to the report submitted by John Dowd to the commissioner of baseball on May 9, 1989, Arnie Metz, a 33-year-old Reds groundskeeper and Rose groupie, had signed for the ticket but did not cash it for two days, when it is alleged that either Rose or Carroll instructed him to do so. Subsequently, Metz delivered the money to

Rose, who gave him $8,000 and then put the remaining money in a satchel and took it with him to the Reds' spring training camp in Florida. For the uninitiated, in a Pik-Six wager the bettor must pick the winners in six consecutive races to win. Rose denied in front of the commissioner on February 20, 1989 that he was one of the partners in the winning ticket. Later Rose told author Roger Kahn, writing in *Pete Rose: My Story*, that "I didn't think that it was any of their damn business whether I bet a Pik-Six or not. Racetrack betting is legal and I just didn't want to get into this." Rose went on to state to Kahn that he was trying to protect Jerry Carroll, the owner of Turfway Race Park. "Two races had already been won and he still let me in on the ticket." However, on March 24, 1989, Kentucky State Racing Commissioner Kyle Robey stated that Turfway Race Park chairman Jerry Carroll had admitted that he and Pete Rose were the actual winners of the January 25 Pik-Six Jackpot.

The January 25, 1989 Pik-Six ticket was not the only one that would surface in the probe of Rose. According to the statements of Tommy Gioiosa in his 2001 *Vanity Fair* interview, he had a sense that as Rose and Paul Janszen became better friends that he was being replaced in his bet-running duties for Rose. On the evening of January 16, 1987, Rose was at Turfway Race Park with several of his cronies, including Janszen. That evening Rose and Janszen were in possession of a sizeable Pik-Six ticket. An agreement had been made between Rose and Janszen on the Pik-Six ticket to split it up according to their shares if it hit, with Rose getting the largest share. Tommy Gioiosa arrived late at the track, and Rose did not want to cut him in on the action. However, Paul Janszen agreed to sell him a portion of his share in the Pik-Six-six ticket to ease the tension between Rose and Gioiosa. The ticket hit for $47,646. Rose then demanded that Gioiosa go to the payout window and cash the ticket. According to Gioiosa, Rose said to him, "You need to show some income. I pay enough to the fucking I.R.S."[8] The Dowd Report states that according to Paul Janszen, Pete Rose owned 75 percent of the winning Pik-Six ticket, with Janszen and Gioiosa splitting the remaining 25 percent. The ticket had cost $2,000, with Rose laying out $1,500 while Janszen and Gioiosa paid $250 each for their shares. When Major League Baseball began to investigate Rose's involvement with gambling in 1989 and he was asked by investigators if he was the winner of the Pik-Six ticket on January 16, 1987, Rose said that he was not and furthermore that Tommy Gioiosa never cashed a winning Pik-Six ticket for him. He further testified that he did not recall even being at Turfway Racetrack on January 16, 1987.

Three days after summoning Rose to New York on February 23, 1989, the commissioner's office hired a Washington, D.C. attorney, John M. Dowd, to begin a formal investigation of Rose and his alleged gambling habits. On February 24, 1989, Paul Janszen, who was now serving six months in a halfway house in Cincinnati for tax fraud, was the first witness to be interviewed by Dowd, with major league security chief Kevin Hallinan present. The Dowd Report states that Paul Janszen had been placing bets for Pete Rose during the period of April through July 1987. Janszen told Dowd that during that time he placed bets of $2,000 per game on various Major League baseball teams, including the Cincinnati Reds, through a person in Florida by the name of Steve Chevashore, who ran bets for the Staten Island bookmaker commonly known as Val and at other times directly with Ron Peters, the bookmaker from Franklin, Ohio. The logistics of placing the wagers, according to Janszen, were that Rose would give him bets in person or on the telephone, and then his girlfriend Danita Marcum would call in the bets to Chevashore, Val or Peters.

At various times Janszen stated that he would use his own money to cover gambling losses for Rose, and within time that amount owed him escalated to $40,000. When Janszen confronted Rose about payment, he was told by Rose to collect the money from Ron Peters, whom Rose alleged owed him $40,000. When Janszen went to collect the $40,000 from Peters, he was told by him that he would not take any more bets from Rose and that Rose owed him $34,000. Nonetheless, Peters gave Janszen $6,000, which was the difference between what Rose alleged that Peters owed him and the amount that Peters alleged that Rose owed to him from gambling losses in 1986.

USA Today, in its June 27, 1989 edition, stated that a week after the FBI contacted Janszen in early 1988 during a drug investigation, he went to see Rose's attorney Rueven Katz and asked him for the money that Rose owed him. Janszen says Katz did not question Rose's debt, but simply told him, "That's it; it's over [for Rose]."[9] The article, by John Bannon, goes on to say that Katz eventually wrote a check in the amount of $10,000 for Janszen. However, Pete Rose maintained that "Paul asked me to loan him some money because he needed a lawyer."[10] In fact, Rose maintained that Janszen owed him $40,000, including a $10,000 loan and a $5,000 bounced check. Rose maintained that the whole investigation of him by Major League baseball began because Janszen "sort of resented the fact that I didn't want to hang around with him any more after I found he was in drugs."[11]

Paul Janszen, in his testimony to John Dowd, admitted that he had tape-recorded conversations in regard to Pete Rose's betting activities on April 4, 1988, with Michael Bertolini and on December 27, 1988, with Steve Chevashore. According to an article by John Erardi and John Eckberg published in the *Cincinnati Enquirer*, June 28, 1989, Rose had a horrendous cold streak in his betting between May 6 and May 11, 1987 in which he lost $49,000 according to the betting records of Janszen. As Rose was failing to make good for his gambling debts, Janszen became concerned and taped a conversation with Mike Bertolini. The following are excerpts from the transcript of the Janszen-Bertolini conversation of April 4, 1988, taped by Janszen and published in the *Cincinnati Enquirer* on June 28, 1989.

JANSZEN: Did you ever get settled up with Pete?

BERTOLINI: About what?

JANSZEN: The money.

BERTOLINI: [Expletive], we're working it out and [expletive], I don't know, the [expletive]. Did you ever?

JANSZEN: He still owes me about 12 grand.

BERTOLINI: So, he paid you about 38?

JANSZEN: Huh?

BERTOLINI: How much, did he pay you anything yet?

JANSZEN: No, well that's all that, what he did was he signed a bunch of autographs for me.

BERTOLINI: I hear you.

JANSZEN: And, you know, plus he wrote some checks that I had cashed that I had sent up to the guy.

BERTOLINI: Yeah.

JANSZEN: So he's into me for about anywhere from, I don't know, once you figure out all the autograph stuff, he probably owes me about, anywhere from like $10,000–$12,000.

BERTOLINI: Yeah, I hear you.

JANSZEN: Did he ever get … wait a minute, he was up to you for how much total?

BERTOLINI: What me or all together?

JANSZEN: No, the guy … the bookies in New York, how much did he….

BERTOLINI: Don't talk like that on the phone; I hate that.

JANSZEN: All right, how much did he owe you, owe them?

BERTOLINI: All together between me and them about two … two and a quarter.

JANSZEN: Jesus Christ.

BERTOLINI: But we're forgetting them; he's just gonna take care of me.

JANSZEN: What do you mean you're forgetting them?

BERTOLINI: Forgetting them. They don't get nothing.

JANSZEN: What are they gonna do to him?

BERTOLINI: I don't know. We're not gonna worry about them.

JANSZEN: Oh my God, Mikey. You're gonna have some people after him.

BERTOLINI: He don't, this is what he's gonna do. I have no control.

JANSZEN: Doesn't he even give a [expletive]?

BERTOLINI: What are they gonna do, Paulie? They made enough off of him. What the [expletive] are they gonna do to him? Like Denny.... Were you with us, yeah, you were with us with Denny McLain, weren't you?

JANSZEN: Yeah.

BERTOLINI: They got enough. You know what I'm saying. It's not like they got 25 and then we started this and now we're gonna screw them out of this. What he owes, they already got that much in previous loss.

JANSZEN: Yeah.

BERTOLINI: Know what I'm saying. Man [expletive], they already raked the guy, [expletive] it, man. I mean look at....

Janszen gave Dowd copies of his personal notebook, in which he recorded bets for Rose during the period of April 8, 1987 through May 13, 1987. The following is excerpted from Paul Janszen's betting records, which allege that he placed the following bets with Steve Chevashore on the Cincinnati Reds to win for Pete Rose between April 8 and April 15, 1987, as reported in the *Cincinnati Enquirer* on June 28, 1989.

Date	Opp.	Starting Pitchers	Reds' Result	Amount W/L	All gms. record	Amount W/L
April 8	Expos	Gullickson-Tibbs	W 7–2	+$2,000	3–1	+$3,800
April 9	OFF				1–3	-$6,600
April 10	Padres	Power-Sdavis	W 6–3	+$2,000	2–2	-$2,000
April 11	Padres	Browning-Show	W 5–1	+$2,000	7–1	+$10,800
April 12	Padres	Hoffman-Whitson	L 5–2	-$3,400	4–4	-$5,600
April 13	Braves	Gullickson-Zsmith	W 7–2	+$2,000	3–3	-$3,000
April 14	Braves	Power-Palmer	W 6–3	+$2,000	2–4	-$6,800
April 15	Braves	Browing-Mahler	L 4–3	-$2,600	3–2	EVEN

A similar set of betting records was presented by Janszen that were alleged to be twenty-four bets that he placed for Rose on the Cincinnati

Reds to win with Val between April 16, 1987 and May 12, 1987. The Dowd Report states that Rose won 228 bets and lost 184 on baseball games during a two-month period in wagers with bookmakers. As for a pattern to his betting habits, the report suggests that Rose preferred the New York Yankees and avoided the Montreal Expos. His greatest success between April 8 and July 5 in his wagers was in betting on the Yankees (8–4), the Toronto Blue Jays (7–3) and the Milwaukee Brewers (6–3). His standard wager was $2,000 a game, which was determined to be insignificant in affecting the odds on a game. According to Mike Roxborough, who at the time was president of Las Vegas Sports Consultants, "He was supposed to be betting $2,000 a game, which is pretty insignificant and could not possibly move the odds on a game."[12]

However, an inconsistency exists in the accusations of John Dowd in regard to Rose's betting pattern. Dowd "claims Rose would not bet when Mario Soto or a second unnamed Reds pitcher was on the mound—a clear sign to the betting world that the Reds may not win that day."[13] However, the betting records of Paul Janszen presented to Dowd in regard to direct betting with Val show that Rose bet on games in which Soto pitched four times between April 21 and May 6, 1987, winning twice and losing twice. Furthermore, according to the betting records of Janszen, on only one occasion when Soto pitched, the game of April 26 against the Astros, which in fact the Reds won 11–3, did Rose not place a bet. Also Janszen gave Dowd copies of what he alleged to be betting sheets in Pete Rose's handwriting that he stated he had obtained from Rose's home. Janszen's girlfriend, Danita Marcum, in her testimony to John Dowd, stated that she recognized the handwriting on the betting sheets as that of Pete Rose.

Spring training was nearing its end when on March 20, 1989, Major League Baseball commissioner Peter Ueberroth issued a formal announcement that his office "has for several months been conducting a full inquiry into serious allegations"[14] about Cincinnati Reds manager Pete Rose. The following day, Rose's former wife Karolyn said that her former husband had refused to admit to a gambling debt and had received a dead fish in the mail. The first real comprehensive news of what was going on in the Rose investigation was reported in *Sports Illustrated* on March 22, 1989. Then *SI*, in their issue of March 27, 1989, in an article written by Craig Neff, stated that Allan Statman, an attorney for Ron Peters, had approached the magazine the previous week in hopes of selling Peter's story alleging that Pete Rose had bet on baseball. Statman told *SI* that Peters would not tell his story to baseball authorities without first selling it to a publication. Subsequently, *SI* declined the offer to buy Peters's story. However, Pete Rose was quoted in the article by Neff as saying, "I'd be willing to bet you, if I was a betting man, that I have never bet on baseball."[15] Also in the article Rose denied he knew Ron Peters. Also on March 27 John Dowd advised commissioner Ueberroth and Commissioner-elect Giamatti that his investigation would require at least several more weeks to complete.

Now all at once, the Pete Rose betting scandal was grist for the continual grinding mills of radio sports talk shows across America, and speculation ran wild. WLW in Cincinnati and WFAN in New York City broadcast endless streams of chatter on the Rose matter throughout their daily programming. Suddenly schoolboys in Iowa knew who Ron Peters was.

On April 1, 1989, A. Bartlett Giamatti formally took office as the sixth commissioner of Major League Baseball, and Ron Peters was awaiting sentencing in Cincinnati after pleading guilty to charges of cocaine trafficking and making false statements on an income tax return. On April 5, 1989, Ron Peters gave a deposition in the Rose matter to John Dowd, at which he agreed to give full and truthful cooperation in exchange for an acknowledgement by the commissioner's office to a U.S. district judge, Carl Rubin in Cincinnati, that he had lent assistance.

If anything, the testimony of Ron Peters was nothing more than icing on the cake for John Dowd in his investigation of Rose. The critical damage to the reputation of Pete Rose had already been done by Paul Janszen. The emphasis of the Peters testimony was that he had accepted bets for Pete Rose through Tommy Gioiosa in 1985 and 1986 and in 1987 through Paul Janszen. Peters's testimony was corroborated by phone records of Rose, Janszen and the Cincinnati Reds that established a pattern of telephone calls prior to the beginning of Reds games, both home and away, during the period of May, June and July 1987. An example of such telephone activity in the Dowd Report takes place on July 1, 1987, when the Reds played the Astros at Riverfront Stadium in Cincinnati. The game was scheduled to start at 7:35 PM. The telephone records in the possession of John Dowd indicated that at 7:07 PM, Paul Janszen called Ron Peters. The call lasted one minute. The Reds won the game 6–4. According to the betting records of Peters, provided to Dowd during the investigation, Rose bet $2,000 each on the Cincinnati Reds, Pittsburgh Pirates, San Diego Padres, Cleveland Indians, Texas Rangers and Minnesota Twins. According to the report, Rose won three and lost three.

Peters's testimony was further corroborated by Michael Fry, who allegedly observed Tommy Gioiosa placing bets for Rose from Gold's Gym while Gioiosa was the manager of the gym and Fry the owner. Lance Humphrey, the daytime manager of Gold's Gym, also testified that Gioiosa remarked to him that he was placing bets for Pete Rose on baseball, basketball and football. According to the Dowd Report, telephone records of Gold's Gym for 1986 list sixty-five telephone calls from Gold's Gym to Ron Peters during the 1986 baseball season when Gioiosa was the manager. Lastly,

Peters's testimony was validated by James Eveslage, who voluntarily told John Dowd that it was he who had arranged for Ron Peters to accept bets from Pete Rose through Tommy Gioiosa.

According to a report in the *Star-Ledger*, June 27, 1989, John Dowd said that the evidence he had collected supported the testimony of Ron Peters, who claimed that he took perhaps more than $1 million in bets on behalf of Pete Rose over a two-year period. On page 214–215 in the summary of the Dowd Report, he states, "It is quite significant that Peters and Janszen were not friends or close associates. At the time of their testimony, Peters possessed a bitter animosity toward Janszen because Janszen assisted the government in catching Peters engaging in activity which led to Peters' ... conviction. Notwithstanding this animosity, Peters corroborates Janszen."[16]

At times the economic relationship between Rose and Peters turned to the absurd. It is alleged that in late 1987 Ron Peters actually owed Pete Rose $50,000 from winning bets. According to an article by Ben L. Kaufman published in the *Cincinnati Enquirer* on June 28, 1989, it was stated that Peters was slow in paying off the debt to Rose and that according to Randy Kaiser, Rose proposed injuring Peters's son to collect the debt. Kaiser revealed this bizarre tale when he was being questioned by Joseph L. Daly, a former FBI agent who was assisting baseball commissioner Giamatti in his investigation of Rose. In late 1987, Kaiser was a passenger in Paul Janszen's Corvette as the two were headed for Turfway Race Park in Florence, Kentucky when Rose called Janszen on the car phone. According to Kaiser, Rose was upset and obsessed with the debt that Peters owed him. "He [Rose] started talking about, you know, how they were going to get their money back, and the thing that Pete thought would be the most effective way to get the money back was to do something to.... Peters' son or kid or whatever and to me, I thought that was pretty upsetting."[17] Kaiser went on to say that later he spoke with Rose and suggested it would be better to get some collateral from Peters, perhaps his car. But Kaiser says that Rose responded, "Well, first of all he's not going to give me anything of his possessions and if I take it, it would be stealing and it could be replaced by insurance. But his kid wasn't replaceable."[18] Kaiser concludes by saying that Rose, in a more rational mood, stated that it bothered him that Peters never had to chase him when he owed him money. Furthermore, Rose remarked that his irrational thought process towards Peters was exacerbated by the fact that Peters had considerable assets, including a business, cars, a home, and that he should liquidate some of them to pay him off.

As for Rose's denial in the Dowd Report and the *Sports Illustrated* article of July 3, 1989, that he did not know Ron Peters, it is alleged by the writers of *SI* article, Jill Lieber and Craig Neff, that Rose had met Peters on at least two occasions, as stated in the Dowd Report. The first time was during a visit by Peters to Gold's Gym in mid-1985, and the second meeting took place in early 1986, when Peters alleges that Rose along with Mike Fry and Tommy Gioiosa, came to visit him at Jonathan's Cafe, his business in Franklin, Ohio, to collect a $37,000 gambling debt that he owed Rose. Furthermore, Peters stated that Rose brought along a black Mizuno bat as a gift for him and autographed it. Peters states in the article that he and Gioiosa went into the men's room, where he paid off the debt in wads of $100 and $50 bills that Gioiosa wanted to put in his socks until he handed him a paper bag in which to carry the money.

On April 6, 1989, Tommy Gioiosa was arrested at his home in New Bedford, Massachusetts, and the following day, stemming from the FBI probe aided by Paul Janszen, he was indicted by a federal Grand Jury on five felony counts for cocaine trafficking out of Gold's Gym and filing a false income tax return that was in part directed at income derived from the Pik-Six ticket he cashed on January 16, 1987, at Turfway Racetrack. In the indictment, it was stated that Gioiosa falsely reported to the IRS, on the necessary tax forms that winners must fill out at the window when winnings are above a certain amount to ensure that tax is immediately withheld, that he was the sole winner of the Pik-Six ticket when in fact it had belonged to someone else. Gioiosa, out of loyalty to Pete Rose, had refused to participate in the investigation by Major League Baseball being directed by John Dowd. This was not first time that Gioiosa had remained loyal to Rose. In 1988, as the FBI began its probe into the gambling and cocaine trafficking allegations of Paul Janszen, Gioiosa was contacted by the FBI and asked what he knew about Pete Rose. All that Gioiosa would say to the investigators about Rose was that he's a "great baseball player."[19]

One by one, the persons identified by Paul Janszen in the cocaine ring operating out of Gold's Gym had their day in court. On March 8, 1989, Michael Fry was sentenced to ten years in prison for possession with intent to distribute cocaine and one count of filing a false income tax return. According to Fry in his testimony with John Dowd, Rose had sold Don Stenger his $100,000 BMW for $75,000 in cash to pay a gambling debt. However, the Dowd Report states that Rose recalled the price as $50,000 because he had blown out the engine after a couple of years. On March 24, 1989, Don Stenger was sentenced to four years in prison for conspiracy to distribute cocaine and tax evasion, and Linda Kettle was sentenced to four years in prison for one count of conspiracy to distribute cocaine.

In his testimony with baseball investigators, Paul Janszen had also attempted to implicate Pete Rose in the cocaine trafficking ring at Gold's Gym. According to an article in the *Cincinnati Enquirer* on June 28, 1989, Janszen claimed that Rose once asked him to set up a cocaine ring. John Dowd quoted Janszen as saying, "Rose said he had a certificate of deposit for

$75,000 that was maturing in a couple of weeks and he could use that money to buy kilos and keep it in his house, as nobody would come in his house."[20] It should be pointed out that Pete Rose has never been charged with any crime involving the use of or distribution of illegal substances. Furthermore, these allegations by Janszen have never been corroborated by anyone else. Of all the people John Dowd interviewed or got sworn testimony from in his investigation of Rose, Paul Janszen was the only one who alleges that Pete Rose wanted to buy into a cocaine operation. Michael Fry, who was interviewed by baseball investigators on April 11, 1989, stated Rose was not aware of the fact that he was dealing in drugs. Don Stenger went on to tell baseball investigators that if "Tommy Gioiosa had not been friendly with him [Stenger], Paul Janszen, Ron Peters, and Mike Fry, then Pete Rose would never have met any of these people."[21]

As mid–April approached, the Rose story was in full swing around the country. CBS was reporting on Rose, alleging that he regularly bet with Paul Janszen on the Reds to win. In Providence, Rhode Island, a newspaper told police that Pete Rose invited Joseph Cambra, a convicted bookmaker, to stay at the Reds' spring training hotel.

On April 18, commissioner Bart Giamatti sent a letter to U.S. District Court Judge Carl Rubin in Cincinnati asking for leniency for Ron Peters. The letter would prove to be a colossal blunder by Giamatti, as Rose's attorneys would seize upon it as proof that Giamatti had already passed judgement on Rose before hearing his side of the story. Giamatti's letter identified Peters as Rose's principal bookmaker and said in part, "he has been candid, forthright and truthful with baseball investigators and provided critical sworn testimony about Mr. Rose and his assoicates."[22] Rubin, who was about to sentence Ron Peters, was outraged. Judge Rubin was and remains a popular figure in Cincinnati himself. In the 1960s he appeared on a weekly television talk show broadcast on WCPO-TV and is a Reds fan. The roots of Rose's popularity go deep in the Cincinnati community, and Judge Rubin was outraged and publicly accused Commissioner Giamatti of "entering into what I think is … a vendetta against Pete Rose."[23] Robert C. Brichler, an assistant U.S. Attorney, told Judge Rubin that Rose was also being investigated by a grand jury on tax matters. He further stated that Peters has told Federal investigators that "he took bets over a period of two years from Mr. Rose that could very well amount to in excess of a million dollars."[24] On April 27, 1989, Judge Rubin disqualified himself from Peter's case.

Ron Peters was sentenced to two years on charges of drug trafficking and tax fraud. He began serving his sentence on July 17, 1989. Ironically, at about the same time Peters was being sentenced, Paul Janszen was being released from a halfway house by federal authorities. Meanwhile, one of Rose's attorneys, Reuven Katz, suggested that Commissioner Giamatti should disqualify himself from the Rose matter because of the letter he had sent to Judge Rubin.

On April 21, 1989, it was Pete Rose's opportunity to set the record straight with baseball as he met with John Dowd. The meeting took place in the cafeteria of a Catholic convent in Dayton, Ohio. One of Rose's legal team, attorney Roger Makley, had selected the site to protect Pete from the media. His statements would be included in a 358-page deposition, but he was aloof and not very cooperative. In his deposition Rose denied under oath that he ever bet on Major League Baseball or associated with anyone who placed bets on his behalf, including Paul Janszen or Danita Marcum. However, Rose did admit that he had placed bets on other sports activities with Tommy Gioiosa. But he denied knowing any bookmakers from Ohio or New York. Likewise, Rose denied knowing Ron Peters or of ever having Tommy Gioiosa collect $37,000 in gambling winnings from Peters in a back room at Johnathan's Cafe in Franklin, Ohio. He also denied ever being delinquent in his gambling debts or borrowing money from his associates to pay gambling debts. During the deposition, John Dowd and the other investigators played the entire tape of the April 4, 1988, telephone conversation between Paul Janszen and Michael Bertolini for Rose. Rose listened intensely to the tape and then remarked that it "didn't mean did-ly-squat to me."[25] Rose's reaction to the tape was that Bertolini was making up things to say to Janszen and he described it as "the blind leading the blind."[26] Rose was adamant is stating, "I owe nobody nothing ... I'm going to say this one more time. I don't owe anybody a dime. New York, New England, New Mexico. A dime. Nothing."[27]

As for the most recent accusation that had come to the fore, that he knowingly associated with convicted bookmaker Joseph Cambra during the Reds' spring training camp, Rose stated that he had met Cambra in West Palm Beach, Florida, when he was a player for the Montreal Expos in 1984, but never knew that he was a bookmaker or that he had been convicted of bookmaking until about two weeks before being there in Dayton giving his deposition to John Dowd. Rose did, however, admit to Dowd in his deposition that he had been the winner in the 1989 Pik-Six ticket controversy, but when asked about why he denied this fact in his meeting with former baseball commissioner Ueberroth on February 20, 1989, Rose responded that he did not recall making such a statement.

According to the Dowd Report, Rose also stated that he did not recognize the handwriting on three betting sheets found in his home. However, on March 16, 1989, Rose had voluntarily had given handwriting exemplars to Richard E. Casey, a retired FBI agent hired by Major League Baseball. Casey also was provided with known samples of Rose's writing from 1987. The *Star-Ledger* reported on June 27, 1989, that it was the conclusion of Casey that

Rose was the writer on the sheets with entries for April 9, 10 and 11 with the exception of three fractional entries 8½, 9½ and 9½ appearing in the lower right-hand margin of the document.

Rose continued to maintain in his deposition that the $10,000 check that Janszen obtained from Reuven Katz in March 1988 was not a payment for gambling debts, but rather a loan to Janszen to assist him in hiring an attorney. The check did indeed bear a notation "for loan";[28] however, Janszen testified that Katz said, "We can just make it look like a loan."[29] Nonetheless, Janszen maintained that Katz never asked him to sign a promissory note. Rose stated that Janszen called Katz, not Rose. In his testimony on the matter, Rose stated, "Katz called him and told him Janszen wanted his $20,000. Rose told Katz he would loan Janszen half that amount because he did not know if Janszen had enough money to pay him back $20,000."[30] Rose went on to accuse Janszen of trying to blackmail him and ruin his reputation in Cincinnati and then summarized his opinion of the individuals who had been accusing him of betting on baseball. "Those guys [Bertolini, Peters, Fry, Stenger and Janszen] could have been a quintet in the last three months. Because they're all singing. They're singing a lot. They have to sing or they'll be in Sing Sing."[31]

Less than a week after Rose gave his deposition to John Dowd, an Atlantic City casino, Tropworld, cancelled a June date for a baseball card show promoted by and starring Pete Rose. On May 3, 1989, a federal grand jury seated in Cincinnati began hearing evidence concerning Rose on income tax matters.

On May 9, 1989, John Dowd presented his 225-page report, accompanied by seven volumes of exhibits, to the commissioner of baseball. The Dowd Report detailed 412 wagers on baseball allegedly made by Rose between April 8 and July 5, 1987, including 52 wagers on the Cincinnati Reds. Evidence presented in the report included the betting slips alleged to be in Rose's own handwriting, along with telephone and bank records. Upon receiving the report, Commissioner Giamatti said that he would study it thoroughly. However, the commissioner wasted no time in his perusal of the material, as the very next day he announced that he had concluded his study. Subsequently, on May 11, 1989, the commissioner provided a copy of the report to Rose and his attorney, then scheduled a hearing for Rose on May 25, 1989. On May 19, 1989, Rose acknowledged the fact that he had read the report and requested that an extension for his hearing be granted until June 26, 1989. On May 22, Commissioner Giamatti granted the postponement.

Meanwhile, Major League Baseball stated that it was keeping the Dowd Report under tight security, but somehow a freelance writer got hold of a copy and began to peddle it to news organizations. All at once, the content of the Dowd Report, warts and all, was out in the open, and the controversy grew even larger. Despite the swirl of speculation and the numerous innuendoes generated by the report, the Cincinnati Reds under Rose were hanging right in there and making a run at it in the pennant race. On June 5 the Reds were in first place, three percentage points ahead of the Giants in the National League West Division. Reporters were now numerous in the Reds' clubhouse for every game, and also there was a new group of visitors in the Reds clubhouse: lawyers standing by Rose as he answered questions from the press.

The press was speculating that Dave Bristol would be a possible successor to Rose should he be fired or resign. Bristol had returned to the Reds in 1989 as coach on Rose's staff and was present each day as the multitude of reporters converged on Rose and asked the obvious questions. According to Bristol, Rose had his chance to come clean on the gambling issue right there and then. "I was coaching with him that year in 1989,"[31] said Bristol. "I asked the same questions as the reporters, if he was not guilty, he needed to lay it out. However, when they asked Pete about whether or not he bet on baseball, he just let his lawyers speak. If he wasn't guilty why did he take the suspension?"[32]

As for Reds majority owner Marge Schott, she was disappointed but in no mood to fire Rose. She feared the backlash of the diehard legions of Rose fans and even more the possibility of the entire city of Cincinnati coming after her head in a display of public discontent not seen since the arrest of Marie Antoinette during the French Revolution. How could she fire a guy who had a street named for him running right in front of the stadium? Also, at the time the media began to break the story of Rose's shady associations and gambling habits, the Reds were in first place. Therefore firing Rose didn't seem like a viable strategic option either.

Bill Bergesch had been fired as the Reds' general manager by Schott following the 1987 season and replaced by Murray Cook. Therefore, as Rose was Schott's manager, Cook attempted to get Schott involved with the investigation, but to no avail. Unlike Charles Comiskey, the owner of the Chicago White Sox, who immediately sent telegrams to "Shoeless" Joe Jackson and seven other members of the team suspending them on September 28, 1920, the day after a grand jury in Chicago began investigating his players for allegedly throwing the 1919 World Series, Schott wanted to distance herself from the controversy. Cook told Schott, "You can't stick your head in the sand and pretend that nothing happened."[33] "She wanted to hide,"[34] said Cook. "She wanted to separate herself from it."[35]

Then on June 19, 1989, Charlie Hustle decided to fight back against the charges being made against him. Rose's attorneys, Reuven Katz and Roger Makley, went to the Hamilton County Common Pleas Court in Cincinnati and filed suit against Major League Baseball and the commissioner seeking to permanently halt all proceedings leading to the June 26 scheduled hearing with Giamatti. In addition, the Cincinnati Reds were also named in the suit as preventive measure to keep Marge Schott from suddenly firing Rose.

In his suit, Rose stated that Commissioner Giamatti could not be impartial in his case and asked the court to bar the commissioner from deciding his fate in the gambling allegations made against him. In the court papers filed by Rose's attorneys, it was charged that "Baseball Commissioner A. Bartlett Giamatti is 'biased and prejudiced' and the commissioner's investigation into Pete Rose's gambling is a 'hatchet job.'"[36] Katz said in the statement "that Giamatti already decided that the accusations against Pete were true before he or his investigators even heard evidence from Pete Rose."[37] Furthermore Rose's lawsuit contended that the information in the Dowd Report was biased and gathered from two convicted felons (Ron Peters and Paul Janszen). The suit also contended that the Dowd Report ignored numerous witnesses such as Michael Fry, who testified that Rose did not bet on baseball.

In addition, the suit claimed that Paul Janszen passed a lie-detector test after failing his first polygraph. In a letter to John Dowd on May 15, Robert Makley accused Dowd of misrepresenting the credibility of Janszen's second lie detector test. "You rationalized his failure to pass by saying that it happened because the examiner upset Janszen. You provide no other information as to what he did to upset him and you then describe how Janszen volunteered to undergo a second examination with 'one of the foremost polygraphers in the United States.' Presumably the first polygrapher was something less than that. You then conclude that, in fact, Janszen had been telling the truth all along. Since Janszen has passed one polygrapher examination and failed another, maybe we should go for the best two out of three."[38]

At 9:30 AM on June 20, the parties got together in the chambers of Judge Norbert A. Nadel of the Hamilton County Common Pleas Court in Cincinnati, and the judge set the date for the hearing on Rose's request for June 22. Judge Nadel also issued a restraining order blocking Rose's hearing before Giamatti on June 26. Now it comes as a no-brainer that Judge Nadel was playing to the house in the Rose matter. Judge Nadel served in a judiciary post that was an elected office, and furthermore he was due to be up for re-election in 1990 in front of a block of partisan Rose voters in greater Cincinnati. Also Nadel had accepted more than $1,500 in contributions during previous campaigns from lawyers in two of the law firms that were representing Rose. In fact, on June 29, 1989, the *Cincinnati Enquirer* reported that during his campaigns for the bench in 1982 and 1984, Nadel had accepted 26 separate contributions from lawyers in the law firms that were representing Rose in the matter before him.

On June 22, during the hearing before Judge Nadel, baseball investigator John Dowd stated that he had evidence that Rose bet on major league baseball games, including games played by the Cincinnati Reds in 1985, 1986 and 1987 seasons, that included telephone records and betting slips in Rose's handwriting, further indicating that he bet on baseball games. One of the witnesses called by Rose's lawyers was former chief counsel to the Senate Watergate committee, Sam Dash. Dash attacked the investigation of Rose led by John Dowd as flawed and one-sided. Rose's attorneys focused on a portion of the Dowd's deposition with Ron Peters taken on April 5, where an alleged deal was made.

"Q. Now on behalf of the Commissioner we have an understanding, do we not?

A. Yes sir.

Q. And you correct me if I'm wrong, but in exchange for your full and truthful cooperation with the Commissioner, the Commissioner has agreed to bring to the attention of the [U.S.] District Judge in Cincinnati the fact that you were of assistance to us and that we believe that you have been honest and complete in your cooperation. Is that the understanding?

A. Yes, it is."[39]

The lead attorney for Major League Baseball, Louis Hoynes, in his closing argument stressed the importance of enforcing Major League Baseball's Rule 21 (d) which he pointed out is posted in every major league team clubhouse.

On a June 26, a Sunday no less, Judge Nadel ruled that Bart Giamatti had "prejudged" Rose and issued a temporary restraining order preventing both the Cincinnati Reds and Major League Baseball from disciplining Rose for 14 days. Subsequently Rose's hearing with Commissioner Giamatti was put on hold until July 6. That next day, Judge Nadel, although he had personal regrets, was forced by the orders of the Ohio Supreme Court to release the findings of Major League Baseball in the Rose matter to the press. All at once, eight volumes of allegations against Pete Rose that would commonly become known as the Dowd Report were in the public domain, and suddenly the sordid private world of Pete Rose was in the street for everybody and anyone who had 35 cents to buy a newspaper to see. There it all was that had been speculated about and debated for weeks in black and white, pages and pages of testimony from Ron Peters and Paul Janszen, copies of cancelled checks paid to gamblers to cover debts, transcripts of telephone conversations between Paul Janszen and Mike Bertolini, as well as the betting slips alleged to be in Rose's own handwriting, all complete with detailed analysis by journalists from every state in the union.

The ruling of Judge Nadel had stunned baseball and threatened to undermine its authority to adjudicate internal matters. As the legal wrangling heated up, it was now Giamatti's turn to fight back and recoup his jurisdiction in the Rose matter. Subsequently, Giamatti's attorneys asked an Ohio appellate court to lift the restraining order preventing him from conducting his hearing on the Rose matter. In a 220-page request to have the restraining order lifted by the court, Major League Baseball argued, "For the past several weeks, the charges against Pete Rose have focused enormous public attention on gambling and the possible corruption of the game. Now that Pete Rose has aired these charges by bringing suit, it has become critical for the commissioner's office to act promptly to maintain public confidence in the integrity of the game. If every action of the commissioner to investigate and determine matters affecting the integrity of the game were to be subject to court intervention and delay, the commissioner's ability to safeguard the integrity of the game would be destroyed. The action of the court below threatens the very reputation of Major League Baseball and deprives the commissioner of the power to protect the integrity of the game."[40]

However, on June 28, a three-judge panel consisting of Rupert A. Doan, Harry T. Klusmeier and Lee H. Hilderbrandt of the Ohio First District Court of Appeals based in Cincinnati refused to lift the temporary restraining order that had been issued by Judge Nadel. Therefore unless the Ohio Supreme Court became convinced by Major League Baseball that the Rose should face Giamatti in the hearing originally scheduled for June 26, the next step in the process was for Giamatti to appear before Judge Nadel on July 6 and hear arguments from Rose's lawyer's that he should be blocked permanently from conducting a hearing on the matter on the grounds that he had already prejudged the issue surrounding Rose. Following the ruling by the Ohio First District Court of Appeals, Louis Hoynes, the attorney representing Bart Giamatti, stated, "It continues to be our contention that the temporary restraining order was improperly granted and that the trial court had no authority to interfere with the ongoing processes of the commissioner."[41]

As the legal wrangling continued, the popularity of Pete Rose remained high, and not just in hometown Cincinnati. A *Time*/CNN poll showed that out of 504 people questioned only 30 percent felt that Rose should be suspended from baseball for life if the aqccusations made against him were proven to be true. Forty percent of those polled felt that only a one-year suspension would be warranted, and 20 percent were against any suspension.

On July 3, Giamatti's lawyers moved to transfer Rose's suit to federal court in Cincinnati. However, because of Rose's popularity in Cincinnati, the United States District Court transferred the case to the United States District Court in Columbus under Judge John D. Holschuh, Sr. Meanwhile, on July 4, Rose took time to appear at a baseball card show in Valley Forge, Pennsylvania, where he signed 1,100 autographs at $15 each. On July 5, Rose's attorneys filed a motion in federal court to keep the case in state court. Keeping the case, in a state court jurisdiction was particularly important to Rose. So far the state court had been sympathetic to his case, and if it moved to the federal jurisdiction, then Rose could find himself in for a very long and extremely expensive battle with Major League Baseball. In the motion filed by Rose's attorneys, they asked Judge Holschuh to send the case back to the state court on the grounds of lack of diversity of citizenship. However, the dispute was indeed between citizens of different states—Rose of Cincinnati, Giamatti of New York. Subsequently, Bart Giamatti agreed to take no further action in the Rose matter unit the federal court made a ruling. On July 6, Judge Holschuh stated that he would put off making a decision for at least two weeks. Then the wheels of justice ground almost to a halt as Judge Holschuh delayed the decision again on July 20, when he told both sides that he wouldn't make a decision before July 31.

Now at this point, it appeared that Pete Rose, whose salary for the season was $500,000, had the most protected job in the United States outside perhaps of some radical tenured university professor. Rose was protected from Marge Schott firing him and protected from Bart Giamatti throwing him out of the game. In fact, whether Rose realized it or not, he was so protected by the court at that moment that he could have placed bets at will with bookmakers without having to face disciplinary charges from the commissioner of baseball. As the legal process dragged on through the summer, some of the major league club owners were becoming critical of Giamatti. A distinct few owners expressed a belief that it would have been more expedient for Giamatti to first suspend Rose, then hold a hearing if he appealed the suspension. It was felt that Giamatti would have had greater control on the process in the case. But Giamatti expressed a belief that his actions were designed to show fairness to Rose by not taking preemptive action. Ironically Giamatti's fairness was now at the head of the list of Rose's grievances being considered by the court.

As the summer and the legal haggling moved along, the Rose siege was starting to take a toll on the Reds in the pennant race. On June 5 the Reds were in first place. They were still holding on to first place on June 10 with a record of 35–24; then Rose filed his suit on June 19, and by July 23 they had sunk all the way down to fifth place. By July 27, they suffered their 32nd loss in 42 games since June 10. By late July, the Rose affair had cost both sides legal fees approaching $2 million dollars, and there was no sign of when it would all be over. Would there be a permanent injunction, no injunction,

what court would wind up with the case, an appellate court in Ohio or possibly the United States Supreme Court? On and on it went, being dragged
through the legal abyss. During the summer of 1989, the Rose case con-
sumed the sports pages unlike anything since the scandal of the 1919 World
Series broke in September, 1920.

However, despite the Rose controversy, 1989 had been a spectacular
season for Major League Baseball. But the Rose story overshadowed the fact
that Kevin Mitchell and Will Clark had led the San Francisco Giants past both
the Reds and Dodgers into first place in the National League West Division,
with Mitchell, at least for a while, chasing Babe Ruth as he headed for an
MVP season. The Chicago Cubs, under manager Don Zimmer, were making a strong run for the National League East Division championship, and
the Philadelphia Phillies were heading for the basement in the East as Mike
Schmidt decided it was time to retire. In the American League, the Sky-
Dome opened in Toronto and the Blue Jays went neck and neck with the
Baltimore Orioles in the East Division race, while in the west the Oakland
A's, who had lost slugger Jose Canseco for half the season, were still out dis-
tancing the Kansas City Royals, who were led by the strong efforts of Bo
Jackson and Cy Young award winner Bret Saberhagen. Also the California
Angels featured a pitcher, Jim Abbott, who was born with only one hand.
When Giamatti became commissioner, Bill White replaced him as president
of the National League and became the first African-American to hold such
a high administrative position in sports history.

While Bart Giamatti, the new commissioner of baseball, had started
his reign on April 1, almost from the first day on the job he had been bogged
down with the Rose investigation. Deputy baseball commissioner Fay Vincent, remarking about the first months of Giamatti's stint as commissioner,
said in late July, "It hasn't occupied the dominant part of our time and energy,
but it has been a significant part of our first four months. There's no question when it's over, we will notice it's gone."[42]

Most of the owners, notwithstanding Marge Schott, felt that the longer
the Rose affair dragged on the more irrevocable damage was done to baseball's image. Nonetheless, they believed that Giamatti was the proper person to have jurisdiction in the Rose matter. "Bart Giamatti is a man of great
conscience and honesty,"[43] said Fred Wilpon, owner of the Mets. "Pete Rose
would get a fair hearing from Bart Giamatti. If something happened subsequent to Bart hearing it, Pete Rose would have the right to go to court,
but Bart is the man who should hear the matter."[43] John McMullen, owner
of the Houston Astros, said he believed "that Rose's legal efforts have been
an abuse of the legal system."[44]

Then on July 31, U.S. District Judge John Holschuh, in a 47-page opinion, gave baseball and Giamatti its first victory when he ruled that the Rose's

case should be heard in federal court, not state court as wanted by Rose. Judge Holschuh ruled "that the controversy in this case is between plaintiff Rose and defendant Giamatti; that they are the real parties in interest in this case; that the Cincinnati Reds and Major League Baseball are, at best, nominal parties in this controversy; that consequently, the citizenship of the Cincinnati Reds and Major League Baseball may be disregarded for diversity purposes."[45] In short, Judge Holschuh was ruling that no one in major league baseball, including the 26 teams, had any control over Giamatti's investigation of Rose or on any of the possible disciplinary action against him. Nonetheless, Judge Holschuh extended until August 14 the agreement made by lawyers from both sides that protected Rose from suspension by the Reds or Giamatti.

Now the legal maneuvering of both sides kicked into high gear. In addition, baseball kept up its intense investigation under John Dowd. At that time, Dowd was attempting to gain new information from Richard Troy, the Staten Island resident known as "Val" who had been arrested in October 1988 and indicted in January 1989 on bookmaking charges. On August 7, Bart Giamatti, trying to get the Rose case once again before him, set a hearing date for Rose on August 17. Quickly Rose's platoon of lawyers filed another suit to block the hearing scheduled for August 14 in federal court, revealing that Giamatti has set August 17 as a date for a discipline hearing for Rose. Subsequently Judge Holschuh ruled in favor of Rose on August 11, stating that Giamatti could not hold a disciplinary hearing on Rose until the court ruled on Rose's appeal.

On August 8, Rose asked the United States Court of Appeals for the sixth district in Cincinnati for permission to appeal the decision of Judge Holschuh. Now it was being considered that the legal maneuvering of the parties could drag on into 1990. Then on August 14, Major League Baseball asked the United States Court of Appeals to deny Rose's case returning to state court by asserting that a dispute between Rose, a local Cincinnati hero and Giamatti, a New York City citizen deserved a federal forum. The reply by the Giamatti lawyers to the latest appeal by Rose stated that his purpose in appealing the ruling of Judge Holschuh, "is transparent. He seeks to avoid joining issue on the merits indefinitely while continuing to frustrate the Commissioner's efforts to resolve the troubling gambling charges against the plaintiff that strike at Baseball's integrity. The Court must reaffirm that Section 1292 (b) is not to be used as vehicle for gamesmanship."[46]

With the legal winds now howling about him, Pete Rose continued to manage the Cincinnati Reds with the same intensity that he had shown as a player. With a lifetime ban from baseball possibly only days away, he became embroiled in yet another near controversy on the field. On the evening of August 16, the Reds lost to the Chicago Cubs 5–2 in 12 innings. The last out in the game saw Ron Oester called out on strikes. Oester immediately flung his bat and began to argue the call with home plate umpire Bill Hohn; then first base umpire Joe West became involved in the argument and twice pushed Oester. At that point, manager Pete Rose stepped between the two and lightly pushed West in the chest with his forearm. Rose maintained that he was acting as a peacemaker. In the Reds' clubhouse, Rose told the press, "I'm not an expert in shoving umpires. I did it one time in my life, and I paid dearly for it—both in days and money."[47] Rose, of course, was referring to the Dave Pallone incident when he shoved the umpire and received a $10,000 fine and 30-day suspension from then National League president Bart Giamatti. The current National League president, Bill White, reviewed the tapes of the incident and took unannounced action, most probably on Oester.

On August 17, the United States Court of Appeals for the sixth district in Cincinnati rejected Rose's petition to return his case to state court, and the outlook started to look very bleak for him. The next day, on August 18, Judge Holschuh set August 28 as the start of the hearing in federal court on Rose's request for a preliminary injunction that would continue to block his appearance before Giamatti. But it was over for Pete Rose. Giamatti had him in a corner, and it was only a matter of time before he had to face the inevitable. Consequently, negotiations began between the parties.

On Monday, August 21, Rose, in his last game as Cincinnati Reds manager, saw his team beat the Chicago Cubs 6–5 in 10 innings at Wrigley Field. Then on Tuesday, August 22, Rose became a father for the fourth time as his second wife Carol gave birth to a daughter, Cara Shay, at Jewish Hospital in Cincinnati.

On August 23, an agreement was reached between Rose and Giamatti that would permit the matter between the two to be resolved without a hearing. It was agreed that the commissioner would not make any determination that Rose had bet on any Major League Baseball game. In exchange, Rose would have to accept a lifetime ban, being declared permanently ineligible in accordance with Major League Rule 21 and placed on the Ineligible List. The agreement, however, did not preclude Rose the right under Major League rule 15 (c) to apply for reinstatement. It would be noted in the agreement that by signing it, Rose was not making an admission or denial of the allegations that he had bet on any Major League Baseball game. Finally, there was to be no gag order in the agreement, and both Rose and Giamatti were free to make any public statement they deemed necessary as long as it did not contradict the terms of the agreement. The agreement was signed by Pete Rose and Reuven Katz as his witness and by Bart Giamatti and Fay Vincent as his witness.

Then, knowing that his career in baseball had crashed and burned, facing a lifetime ban, it was business as usual for Pete Rose. He flew to Minneapolis and appeared on the Warner Cable Network's Sports Collections show, hawking autographed Pete Rose baseballs for $39 apiece, bats for $229 and autographed jerseys for $399. Following the show, he did not speak to reporters, and at 12:40 AM he boarded a private jet for Cincinnati.

A. Bartlett Giamatti. (National Baseball Hall of Fame Library, Cooperstown, N.Y.

As the sun rose behind the stands of Riverfront Stadium on that fateful day of August 24, 1989, there was no joy in Mudville as the storied career of Charlie Hustle came to an abrupt and dusty end in one more head-first slide into infamy. At 9:00 a.m. in Manhattan, with millions of Americans watching their televisions in a stunned silence, Major League Baseball commissioner Bart Giamatti held a news conference and issued the following statement that said, in part, "The banishment for life of Pete Rose from baseball is the sad end of a sorry episode. One of the game's greatest players has engaged in a variety of acts which have stained the game, and he must now live with the consequences of those acts. By choosing not to proffer any testimony or evidence contrary to the evidence and information contained in the report of the special counsel to the commissioner, Mr. Rose has accepted baseball's ultimate sanction, lifetime ineligibility.

"This sorry episode began last February when baseball received firm allegations that Mr. Rose bet on baseball games and on the Reds' games. Such grave charges could not and must never be ignored. Accordingly, I engaged and Mr. [Peter] Ueberroth—then commissioner—appointed John Dowd as special counsel to investigate these and any other allegations that might arise and to pursue the truth wherever it took him. I believe then and believe now that such a process, whereby an experienced professional inquires on behalf of the commissioner as the commissioner's agent, is fair and appropriate. To pretend that serious charges of any kind can be responsibly examined by a commissioner alone fails to recognize the necessity to bring professionalism and fairness to any examination and the complexity a private entity encounters when, without judicial or legal powers, it pursues allegations in the complex world.

"That Mr. Rose and his counsel chose to pursue a course in the courts rather than appear at hearings scheduled for May 25 and June 26, and then chose to come forward with a stated desire to settle the matter, is now well known to all. My purpose in recounting the process and the procedures animating that process is to make two points that the American public deserves to know:

"First, that the integrity of the game cannot be defended except by a process that itself embodies integrity and fairness; "Second, should any other occasion arise where charges are made or acts are said to be committed that are contrary to the interests of the game or that undermine the integrity of baseball, I fully intend to use such a process and procedure to get to the truth and, if need be, to root out offending behavior. I intend to use, in short, every lawful and ethical means to defend and protect the game.

"The matter of Mr. Rose is now closed. It will be debated and discussed. Let no one think that it did not hurt baseball. That hurt will pass, however, as the great glory of the game asserts itself and a resilient institution goes forward. Let it also be clear that no individual is superior to the game."[48]

Informally Giamatti stated that Rose could apply to the baseball commissioner for reinstatement in one year. But he went on to emphasize that the application comes with no guarantee that it would be granted. Giamatti further stated that Rose had agreed not to contest the decision banning him for life or the procedures used by the commissioner's office when filing for reinstatement. But Giamatti emphasized, "There is no deal for reinstatement. He [Rose] has been fired by me."[49]

At 10:00 AM at Riverfront Stadium in Cincinnati, Pete Rose held a news conference. Clenching his hands and fighting back tears for the second time in his career, Rose told the assembled media, "I made some mistakes, and I am being punished for those mistakes. As you can imagine, this is a sad day. Regardless of what the commissioner said, I did not bet on baseball. I did not bet on the Reds. It's something I told the commissioner in February and it's something I've said to you [the media] for four months."[50] Rose went on to say that he was not a habitual gambler and would not undergo rehabilitation for a gambling problem. However, when asked by a reporter, "If you didn't bet on baseball, why did you accept this penalty?"[51] Rose became silent, stepped back from the podium, and his lawyer Reuven Katz stepped forward. According to *Cincinnati Post* reporter Mike Bass, at times Rose became defensive during his news conference and at other times confrontational, sarcastic and witty. A reporter asked, "Pete, if you're willing to tell your side of the story, where and when will you do that?"[52] Rose's response was, "That's to be determined in the near future. Give me your card, and I'll call you first."[53] With that said, Rose left the room.

On the same day that Rose was banished from baseball, the trial of Tommy Gioiosa began in federal court. A jury was seated, and as opening arguments began, U.S. District Judge S. Arthur Spiegel warned the jurors, "Pete Rose's shadow is going to be involved in this case. I want to make sure all of you can decide this case on evidence."[54] At that time, nine persons involved in the cocaine peddling and sports gambling ring had already been convicted, went to prison or were offered shortened sentences through plea bargaining. Gioiosa was offered no such deal and was facing up to 33 years behind bars. One of those persons already convicted was Paul Janszen who would testify against Gioiosa.

Among the arguments prosecutors raised against Gioiosa was that he had personally became a tax dodge for another gambler trying to avoid paying taxes. Of course, this was the infamous Pik-Six ticket at Turfway Race Park on which Gioiosa claimed $50,000 in winnings. However, Paul Janszen claimed that Gioiosa owned 25 percent of the Pik-Six ticket and that Pete Rose owned the rest. Assistant U.S. Attorney William Hunt told the jury that "The ticket was really bought by Pete Rose. Mr. Gioiosa falsified the tax form and he did so in a conspiracy with other people. Let's face it, Mr. Rose's tax bracket in 1987 was substantially different than Mr. Gioiosa's."[55]

On September 12, 1989, Tommy Gioiosa was found guilty in federal court on three of the five counts against him, and on February 1, 1990, was sentenced to five years in prison. He would be released in 1992; nonetheless Gioiosa would do his time in prison while remaining as silent on his relationship with Pete Rose as J. Gordon Liddy did on Watergate. It would, in fact, be twelve more years before Gioiosa gave a tell-it-all interview with *Vanity Fair* magazine in September, 2001.

On August 24 in Columbus, Ohio Judge Holschuh was informed of the news of the agreement made by Rose and Giamatti, and the case was officially closed at 9:10 AM, while in Cincinnati a federal grand jury continued its investigation of Rose's tax returns.

The public opinion on Rose varied. Sparky Anderson, who was now manager of the Detroit Tigers, offered his thoughts. "I feel sick about it. He still is the greatest competitor I have ever been around or will be around.

People don't realize that things are going through your body at times like that which are unbelievable. And he stood there and took it like a man. He is still incredible."[56] Many others, such as former Reds third baseman Buddy Bell, Reds general manager Murray Cook and former Phillies shortstop Larry Bowa, just did not want to talk about it. The good people of Cincinnati were split in their reaction to the settlement. Some felt Rose was railroaded by Giamatti, that it had all been nothing more than a witch hunt, and others felt his own greed drove him to new lows. Nonetheless, the majority of people in Cincinnati were already starting to forgive their favorite son. However, Marge Schott was noncommittal on her feelings in the matter of Rose. Behind closed doors she had referred to Rose as "that son of a bitch"[57] and disliked his taking the spotlight from her. Most observers speculated that Marge was relived by Giamatti's action, which did what she didn't have the guts to do.

Paul Janszen, who had set the whole investigation of Rose in motion, watched both the commissioner's news conference and Rose's news conference on television at home with his fiancée, then later spoke with Sarah Sturmon of the *Cincinnati Post*. "Last night I felt really good because I thought Pete was going to finally admit he bet on baseball and the Reds,"[58] said Janszen. "But after the press conference today, I have a feeling of sadness because even today he denies he has a gambling problem. Until he can face he has these problems, he is never going to start on the road to recovery. From now until the day I die I will always say, if asked, that Pete Rose did bet on major league baseball and bet on the Cincinnati Reds."[59]

While one Rose was going out of baseball, another Rose, Pete Jr., was just starting his career with the Baltimore Orioles' AA affiliate in Frederick, Maryland. With the fallout of the gambling scandal involving his father swirling about him, the fans waved dollar bills at Pete Jr. as he came up to bat. But soon the fans insults would became more mellow in tone, as they simply muttered, "He'll never be as good as the old man."

Nine days following the banishment of Rose, on September 1, commissioner Bart Giamatti suffered a heart attack and died. Giamatti was 51 years old. He was succeeded as commissioner by deputy commissioner Fay Vincent. Former Cleveland Indian great Bob Feller states, "Bart Giamatti was the best commissioner of baseball ever and I have known all of them."[60] With Rose called out by the commissioner, Tommy Helms was appointed to manage the Reds for the remainder of the 1989 season, and the ball club lumbered along, finishing fifth in the National League West Division with a record of 75–87 (14–21 under Helms).

The 1989 World Series between the San Francisco Giants and Oakland Athletics would be dedicated in Giamatti's honor. However, as game three was about to begin on October 17, the World Series was abruptly halted at

5:04 PM when a devastating earthquake hit the Bay Area. While there was massive destruction of property in the Bay Area and several dozen casualties occurred, no one was fatally injured at Candlestick Park. Eventually the series was resumed, and on October 28 the Athletics completed a four-game sweep of the Giants.

Around the time of the World Series, U.S. Postal inspectors seized a sports betting book being operated by Mike Bertolini. In the seizure, the inspectors found betting slips with the fingerprints of Pete Rose on them. In a subsequent trial, Bertolini pleaded guilty to conspiracy to commit federal tax fraud.

Just maybe prize fighter Billy Conn was wrong when he said, "How soon they forget." In an article published in the *Cincinnati Enquirer* on August 22, 1999, Tom Groeschen wrote that ten days after Rose was banished from baseball in 1989, a Harris Poll was released that stated 84 percent of the baseball fans in the survey were convinced that Rose had bet on baseball and 68 percent believed he had bet on the Reds. But regardless, 71 percent said he deserved to be in the Hall of Fame.

VII

Charlie Hustled Off to Prison

As the winter snows melted away in the spring of 1990, Tommy Gioiosa, Paul Janszen and Ron Peters, all former friends and alleged gambling associates of Pete Rose, had been prosecuted and convicted. Gioiosa was serving a five-year term in a federal prison in Pennsylvania on charges of cocaine trafficking and tax fraud. Janszen had pleaded guilty to tax evasion. He was released from custody after completing four months of a six-month sentence in a halfway house. Peters was convicted on drug and tax evasion charges and was serving a two-year sentence at a federal prison in Terre Haute, Indiana. Now the long arm of the law was reaching out for Pete Rose.

The Dowd Report, with its primary intent of exposing Rose's alleged gambling on baseball also exposed him to prosecution by the Internal Revenue Service. There were allegations in the Dowd Report about large amounts of cash that Rose had earned at baseball card shows, and according to Paul Janszen, Rose wanted to be paid in cash at the shows because "cash money did not have to be claimed."[1] According to the Dowd Report, following one card show Rose asked Janszen to put the money in a brown paper bag. "Janszen estimated that Rose made between $8,000 and $12,000 in cash on each card show. Yet there are no deposits from cards shows identified in Pete Rose's financial records."[2] Then, of course, there was the Pik-Six fiasco as well. It would be alleged by federal prosecutors that Rose had won $137,000 in ten Pik-Six races at various race tracks in the Cincinnati metropolitan area between 1984 and 1987. All of these allegations led to a thorough investigation beginning in May 1989 by a grand jury.

On February 21, 1990, Roger Makley, acting as attorney for Pete Rose, stated that the Internal Revenue Service was conducting an exhaustive investigation of Rose's income. Makley also stated that there were no negotiations planned for an out-of-court settlement. Nonetheless, only a month later, on March 20, as the evidence against Rose continued to mount, the *Cincinnati Post* was reporting that Rose and his lawyers had indeed reached an agreement with federal prosecutors whereby Rose would not have to face charges of income tax evasion, but would plead guilty to a lesser charge. Subsequently, on April 16, without hesitation Rose signed an agreement, pleading guilty to two counts of filing false income tax returns for 1985 and 1987. In return, federal prosecutors dropped charges that Rose failed to report $25,132.90 in gambling winnings in 1985 and 1987. He was then scheduled to appear on April 19 before U.S. District Court Judge Arthur Spiegel to enter a plea of guilty while facing a possible sentence of up to six years in prison and a $500,000 fine.

Charges filed by U.S. District Attorney D. Michael Crites and the plea agreement signed by Rose were unsealed on April 19. The content was published in the *Cincinnati Enquirer* on April 20, and it stated that in 1985 Pete Rose had reported to the IRS $33,500 in earnings from autographs, appearances and memorabilia sales and no income from gambling activity. However, it was determined that in 1985 he had earned an additional $95,168 from appearances and $11,309 from gambling. Subsequently, in 1987, Rose had reported $18,000 in earnings from autographs, appearances and memorabilia sales and no income from gambling. However, it was determined that in 1987 Rose had earned an additional $171,552 from appearances and sales and $13,823 from gambling. Therefore, under the plea agreement, Rose was going to plead guilty of underpaying his federal taxes by $162,000. The formal charges involved only the years of 1985 and 1987; however, the plea agreement referred to the years 1984 through 1987. In that period, Rose reported a total taxable income of $4.6 million and paid more than $2 million in taxes. While the plea agreement required that Rose file accurate tax returns before facing Judge Spiegel for sentencing, there was nothing in the agreement that exempted him from back taxes, interest and IRS civil penalties. Consequently, Rose found it prudent to quickly pay $366,000 in back taxes and penalties owed to the Internal Revenue Service before sentencing. Also, Rose had begun private counseling sessions with Dr. James Randolph Hillard, head of psychiatry at the University of Cincinnati, about his gambling habits which he now publicly declared to be the root of his problems.

When the news of Rose's plea agreement reached Paul Janszen, he made the following statement to the press: "Everybody else involved in this case, including myself, did some type of time. Pete is charged with two counts of what I was charged with. I'm a one-count felon. He's a two-count felon. The tax he evaded is 30 times the tax I evaded. Leona Helmsley got some time, Jim Baker got some time. Should a .303 lifetime hitter get some time? Should he get less time than a .220 lifetime hitter? The only time he's honest is when he's already been caught. And then he has an excuse for why he's lied."[3]

Marge Schott, the principal owner of the Reds, had no comment on the Rose matter, nor would baseball commissioner Fay Vincent offer any statement. However, former Big Red Machine teammate Ken Griffey, Sr., stated, "I care about Pete as a friend. I hate to see it.... I feel bad this whole thing has happened."[4] The current third baseman for the Reds, Chris Sabo, had mixed feelings about Rose's predicament. Sabo had come up from the minor leagues to play for Rose, and the two had genuine admiration for each other as ballplayers. In fact, it was Rose who had given Sabo his nickname "Spuds," alleging that his facial features resembled "Spuds McKenzie," the dog featured in the Budweiser beer commercials at that time. "I'm so sorry it had to happen, but you've got to pay your taxes,"[5] said Sabo. "It's unfortunate. It's been a bad year for Pete. I hope this is the last thing that happens to him and he can go on with his life."[6]

On Thursday morning, July 19, 1990 at 9:40 AM, Roger Makley held a tight grip on the left arm of Pete Rose while leading him through the crosswalk at Fifth and Main Streets in downtown Cincinnati and into the federal courthouse. It appeared as if Makley was a father assisting his young son while crossing a busy street on the first day of school more than an attorney heading to court with a baseball legend client about to be sentenced for filing false income tax returns. Rose, dressed very sharply in a blue pinstripe suit with a red tie and white shirt, had a bewildered look about him as he gingerly climbed the steps into the federal building. Rose had recently suffered a leg injury and following his sentencing was scheduled for outpatient surgery.

Upstairs in the federal building, at least twenty people had been waiting in the hall for the bailiff to open the doors to the courtroom since 7:45 AM. Shortly before 10:00 AM when Rose, flanked by his two of his three attorneys, Reuven Katz and Roger Makley, along with his wife Carol, arrived, there were 180 people, including the media and Rose's friend, restaurateur Jeff Ruby, jammed into a courtroom equipped with 150 seats. The attorney representing the United States government in the case, William E. Hunt, had arrived in the courtroom as well.

Rose was seated at the defendant's table with his attorneys. He folded his hands and just stared straight ahead. At 9:59 AM, the Honorable S. Arthur Spiegel entered the courtroom. All in attendance were commanded to rise as the judge took his seat on the bench. Judge Spiegel was a federal judge, an appointed judge nominated by a U.S. President and confirmed by Congress, and not subject to re-election as had been the case with Commons Pleas Court Judge Norbert Nadel a year before. Consequently, Judge Spiegel was immune to the shenanigans of public opinion of which Judge Nadel was in such fear and was all business in the proceedings. Furthermore, Judge Spiegel had been the judge in both the federal cases of Tommy Gioiosa and Ron Peters and subsequently sentenced both to prison terms. The following are excerpts from the transcript of the proceedings that day before Judge Spiegel:

JUDGE SPIEGEL: Inasmuch as we have a long docket this morning, Mr. Rose's case will be taken first, following which there will be a brief recess. We'll then resume with the balance of the docket.

    Now, since the court is now in session, no one is going to be permitted to leave the courtroom until the recess. Following the sentencing, Mr. Rose and his family and his lawyers will leave the courtroom first, and after they've left, then everyone will be free to leave.

    I recognize that many of the reporters present here this morning are dealing with deadlines, and in order to accommodate you, copies of any comments that I may make and the sentence I intend to—I impose today in skeleton form will be available to you in my chambers immediately following the sentencing. I just ask that you go about obtaining the copies from my staff in an ordinary fashion.

    I would like to remind everyone that no recording devices are supposed to be in the courtroom nor is there any photography. I have arranged for you to have your cellular phones out in the hallway so you can use them following the sentencing.

    One final comment for the artists: If any of you are using watercolors, please do not shake your brushes on our rug.

    We're ready to proceed with the case of the United States of America versus Peter Edward Rose, Criminal 1-90-44. Would you step forward, Mr. Makley?

MR. MAKLEY: Thank you, Your honor.

JUDGE SPIEGEL: Mr. Rose, are you in pain because of your leg?

MR. ROSE: No, sir; I'm okay.

JUDGE SPIEGEL: Stand back there. If you are, you're welcome to sit down if you would rather not stand. Mr. Makley and Mr. Pitcairn.

MR. MAKLEY: Yes, Your Honor.

JUDGE SPIEGEL: Have you gentleman had an opportunity to review the presentence investigation in these proceedings with Mr. Rose?

MR. MAKLEY: Yes, we have, Your Honor.

JUDGE SPIEGEL: And as a result of your discussion, do you wish to challenge any of the facts in the presentence report?

MR. MAKLEY: No, Your Honor.

JUDGE SPIEGEL: You know of any reason why sentence should not be imposed on the defendant at this time?

MR. MAKLEY: I do not, Your Honor.

JUDGE SPIEGEL: Do you wish to make a statement on behalf of the defendant or present any information in mitigation of punishment?

MR. MAKLEY: Your Honor, we, as you know, have submitted a comprehensive sentencing memorandum setting forth all of the information we wish the court to know and to take into consideration in imposing sentence in this case. And beyond what's in that report, I have nothing further to say. Mr. Rose would like to address the court.

JUDGE SPIEGEL: Fine. Mr. Rose, have you had an opportunity to review the presentence investigation with your lawyers?

MR. ROSE: Yes, sir.

JUDGE SPIEGEL: And do you have any comments you would like to make or do you wish to challenge any of the facts in the report?

MR. ROSE: No, sir.

JUDGE SPIEGEL: You wish to make any statement on your behalf in mitigation of punishment?[7]

At this point Rose and his attorneys conferred privately.

JUDGE SPIEGEL: You may do so, sir.

MR. ROSE: Yes, sir.

JUDGE SPIEGEL: You may do so now if you would like.[8]

As Rose stood up and began to speak his voice broke, but he forged right ahead.

MR. ROSE: Your honor, I would like to say that I am very sorry. I am very shameful to be here today in front of you.

I think I'm perceived as a very aggressive, arrogant type of individual, but I want people to know that I do have emotion, I do have feelings, and I can be hurt like everybody else, and I hope no one has to go through what I went through the last year and a half. I lost my dignity. I lost my self-respect. I lost a lot of dear fans and almost some very dear friends.

I have to take this opportunity to thank my wife for giving me so much moral support during this ordeal. It had to be very tough on her when your five-year old son would come home from school and tell her that his daddy is a jailbird.

I really have no excuses because it's all my fault, and all I can say is, I hope somewhere, somehow in the future I'm going to try to make it up to everybody that I disappointed and let down. Thank you very much.

JUDGE SPIEGEL: Thank you, Mr. Rose. Do you know, Mr. Rose, of any reason why sentence should not be imposed on you at this time in these proceedings?

MR. ROSE: No, sir.

JUDGE SPIEGEL: Mr. Hunt, do you know of any reason why sentence should not be imposed at this time?

MR. HUNT: No, Your Honor.

JUDGE SPIEGEL: Does the United States wish to make a statement on behalf of the government, or do you wish to offer anything in regard to this case?

MR. HUNT: We have nothing to offer, Your Honor. We would ask the court impose a sentence within the ranges established by the sentencing guidelines and the presentence report that's been quite completely done in this case.

JUDGE SPIEGEL: Thank you. Mr. Hunt.

In deciding what to do in this case, I have read everything that's been furnished to the court, including the defendant's very complete sentencing memorandum and attachments, the many letters I have received from the public, which have been made available to Mr. Rose's lawyers as well as to the United States Counsel and the Probation Department and, of course, the presentence report prepared by the Probation Department.

I have a number of comments before imposing sentence.

Foremost, you must recognize that there are two people here today: Pete Rose the living legend, the all time hit leader, and the idol of millions; and Pete Rose, the individual, who appears today convicted of two counts of cheating on his taxes.

Today we're not dealing with the legend. History and the tincture of time will decide his place among the all-time greats of baseball.

With regard to Pete Rose, the individual, he has broken the law, he's admitted his guilt, and he stands ready to pay the penalty. Under our system of law and sense of fairness, when he's completed his sentence, he will have paid his debt to society and should be accepted by society as rehabilitated. Only time will tell whether he is to restored to the position of honor for his accomplishments on the ball fields of America.

Neither are we here today to consider whether Pete Rose was treated fairly by the baseball commissioner, whether the Dowd Report was an objective and balanced report of his activities, whether Pete Rose gambled on baseball, or whether he should have been banished from baseball.

We're here today to impose a sentence on a man whose life has been an inspiration to millions of people because of his exploits on the ball diamond and his determination to succeed in his chosen profession. We hope that he understands that the sentence we impose is fair and necessary under the circumstances, and that he will make the most of the opportunities presented to him while confined and under supervision so that he can regain confidence in himself, continue his rehabilitation, continue to help others and, therefore, return to society with a clean slate, having paid his debt.

Mr. Rose has pleaded guilty to two counts in the information: one count relating to a false tax return filed for the year 1985, and the other count relating to the false tax return filed for the year 1987. Because these two counts cover two separate time periods, they are governed by two different sentencing systems.[9]

At this point Judge Spiegel went on to explain how the sentencing process works in a case such as this, hence the judge determines the maximum length of sentence and the Parole Commission how long the defendant will actually have to serve. In addition, the judge must take into consideration the guidelines for sentencing established by Congress as well as the defendant's personal characteristics and the nature of the offense, while considering the need for respect for the law, the protection of society, rehabilitation, etc.

JUDGE SPIEGEL: After carefully considering all of these factors, I have concluded that Mr. Rose must serve some time in a prison setting for his crime in order to maintain respect for the law and as a deterrent to others who might consider cheating on their taxes. Although I do not think that society needs to be protected from Mr. Rose, since he is on the road of rehabilitating himself, our law requires that when one commits a crime, he must be punished and the punishment must be fair. Recognizing that Mr. Rose is a well-known figure, it might be a temptation to make an example of him by imposing a heavy sentence. On the other hand, because he has suffered so much in the past year, in his career and financially, there, there might be a temptation to go light. I have attempted to weigh all of these considerations in determining Mr. Rose's sentence in an effort to be fair to the defendant and to fulfill the court's duty to society.

Mr. Rose's sentence will include incarceration at a Federal Correctional Institution and a halfway house, supervised release and community service, and fine to cover the cost of prosecution, confinement, and supervision. We are also fashioning his sentence to recognize the fact that during his career he has been unselfish, helping others, particularly children, both on and off the ball diamond. Hopefully Mr. Rose will help the adult prisoners where he'll be confined. The sentence will also require Mr. Rose to return to his roots in the inner city during his supervised release in order to help children there make something of themselves and to encourage them to work to succeed in their goals with the same determination and dedication that he did in his own life. We particularly want him to show these children that in spite of the mistakes he has made, he can learn and profit from them and become a more humble and better person from the experience. Mr. Rose's lawyers have pointed out in the sentencing memorandum to the court that his hard work led him to "unprecedented heights," and I'm quoting, and "even his mistakes can serve as an example that no one is immune from personal problems nor above the law." We believe his enormous desire to succeed can be harnessed to help children in the inner city. The children with whom Mr. Rose will be working need a role model with whom they can identify in order to make the most of their chances in life. Pete Rose can provide the necessary inspiration, if he is half the person I think he is.[10]

Judge Spiegel then proceeded to the sentencing and imposed sentence on the second count first.

JUDGE SPIEGEL: The sentence of the court on Count 2 is that Peter Edward Rose be committed to the custody of the Attorney General of the United States, or his authorized representative, for imprisonment for a period of five months to followed by a term of supervised release of one year with one of the conditions of supervised release being that Mr. Rose be confined in a community treatment center or halfway house for a period of three months immediately following his release from imprisonment. Other conditions of supervised release are: that the defendant abide by the standard conditions of supervised release adopted by the United States District Court for the Southern District of Ohio; that the defendant be prohibited from possessing a firearm or any other dangerous weapon during the term of supervised release; that the defendant provide the Probation Officer access to any requested financial information; that the defendant continue to receive psychiatric treatment for his admitted gambling addiction throughout the term of supervised release or until released by his psychiatrist in conjunction with the approval of his Probation Officer; and that the defendant pay any local and state income taxes owed due to the defendant's involvement in the matter before the court today, and Mr. Rose will furnish the Probation Department with written documentation with regard to this matter; and that the defendant perform 1000 hours of community service to be monitored by his Probation Officer at the rate of 20 hours per week during one-year supervised release term.

Now, it is the further sentence of this court that the defendant is fined the sum of $50,000 on Count 2. The purpose of the fine is to cover the cost of confinement, halfway house time, supervised release, and cost to Mr. Rose's investigation and prosecution, and the defendant shall pay a special assessment of $50 on Count 1.

Therefore, the sentence in total is that Peter Edward Rose will be confined to an institution of the Bureau of Prisons for a period of five months. It is recommended of this court that Mr. Rose be designated to serve his sentence at the Ashland Kentucky Correctional Institution camp. Following five months of imprisonment, Mr. Rose will be required to serve three months in a community treatment center or halfway house here in Cincinnati as a condition of supervised release. Supervised release will last one year under the conditions previously noted, and there is a fine of $50,000 to be paid immediately, and a total assessment, special assessment, of $100. That competes the sentence.[11]

Judge Spiegel then advised Rose of his right to appeal the sentence within ten days, then proceeded to grant a stay of imprisonment until August 10, 1990, so that Rose could have surgery on his knee. Subsequently, Rose was instructed to report to the prison designated by the Bureau of Prisons at 12:00 noon on August 10 to begin serving his five-month sentence and was released on his own recognizance.

Suddenly the Hit King was a tax cheat and a convicted felon. Following his sentencing, Rose, along with his wife Carol and restaurateur friend Jeff Ruby, went back to his lavish home in the upscale Cincinnati suburban community of Indian Hill and cried. A reporter asked Ruby how the Roses were doing, "Neither one is doing very well,"[12] said Ruby. "He [Rose] spent a lot of time up in his room crying. He's been beat up pretty good. This is probably the first time he's cried since he broke Ty Cobb's record. It was a different kind of cry this time. He's not doing too well."[13]

The reaction on the Reds team was varied. Reds owner Marge Schott just shook her head when she heard of the sentencing. Third baseman Chris Sabo stated, "I figured he'd get some time because that's what everyone's been saying. Pete probably will get through it better than anybody. He's a survivor and he'll survive."[14] Relief pitcher Ron Dibble felt that Rose's conviction was old news. "It was gambling last year; now it's taxes. This has no bearing on what we do. What you do off the field is your own business. I don't like to see anybody go to jail, but it's not like he's going to Attica State Prison."[15] Meanwhile the Cincinnati City Council stood fast on not changing the name of "Pete Rose Way" back to Second Street. Regardless of his conviction, Rose was still a hero to most people in Cincinnati. Mayor Charles Luken said, "We may have acted too quickly in naming the street for Pete Rose, but I think we would be making a mistake if we acted quickly to take the name off."[16]

As to how the guilty plea would affect Pete Rose's chance of gaining entry to the Hall of Fame, most writers polled said that filing false tax returns was not enough to keep him out of the Hall. Hal Brodley, a baseball writer for *USA Today* at the time of Rose's sentencing, said, "It's a big deal. I don't want to say it's not.... But over the years there have been a lot of players who have had problems with drugs or whatever that have been inducted. He [Rose] is not the first."[17] *New York Times* columnist Dave Anderson said, "I've always said I'd vote for him. I will still vote for him. This is just another chink in his armor that wasn't there before."[18]

Rose had three weeks of freedom left in which to take care of his personal business and get his ailing right knee attended to. On August 10, no later than noon, he was to report to prison to begin serving his sentence. Judge Spiegel had recommended that Rose be sent to the Federal Correction Institute at Ashland, Kentucky. However, the prison assignment was really up to the Bureau of Prisons. When *Cincinnati Enquirer* reporter Christine Wolfe contacted James Van Over, the executive assistant at the Federal Correction Institute at Ashland, he stated that he had received no notice that Rose would be coming to Ashland.

The fact of the matter was that Rose was going to do his time at the notorious United States Prison at Marion, Illinois. Marion, the modern Alcatraz of the federal prison system, is situated in a remote section of southern Illinois. The prison complex actually comprises two facilities, one a high-level security prison for males and an adjacent minimum-security prison camp for males. The prison camp was the facility designated for Rose's incarceration. While Rose would be the most famous inmate at Marion until 1992 when New York mob boss John Gotti would arrive to begin serving his life sentence in the high-level security unit that houses some of the nation's most violent prisoners, the prison was already home to such notorious rogues as John Walker Jr., who had sold U.S. Navy secrets to the Soviet Union, and Carlos Lehder, a Colombian drug smuggler who was serving a 135-year sentence.

On a sunny day at Cooperstown, New York, on August 6, 1990, just a few days before Rose was scheduled to begin his prison term at Marion, his former Big Red Machine teammate Joe Morgan was inducted into the National Baseball Hall of Fame.

Morgan had been keeping a special diary of the induction ceremonies for publication in the *Cincinnati Post*. Subsequently, on August 7, the day after his induction into the Hall, Morgan wrote the following in the *Post*. "I forgot to say a lot of things in my speech. I was going to introduce more people. And I wanted to make a pledge that I would uphold the dignity and honor of the Hall of Fame. I was going to say a few things about Pete Rose, but I decided not to. I was concerned someone out there would boo, and I didn't want to cause that, not with Jim Palmer coming up next. So I just mentioned his name with some of the other people I had thanked. There are better times for that. I didn't want to risk hurting the mood of some people there, including the commissioner Fay Vincent. I heard he was quoted in the papers around the country the other day and was pretty tough on Pete in terms of the Hall of Fame. It will be hard for Pete to overcome that."[19]

Rose was still recovering from his knee surgery when his incarceration date was at hand. Nonetheless, to avoid all the hoopla and media hysteria, he decided to report to Marion two days early. So on Wednesday, August 8, Rose, together with his wife Carol and the wife of his friend Jeff Ruby, slipped quietly out of Cincinnati and drove 300 miles to just outside Marion, Illinois, where he arranged for government officials to pick him up and then drive him the final nine miles to the prison. For the next five months, Pete Rose, whose jersey number had been 14 with the Reds, Phillies and Expos, would simply become inmate number 01832-061 at Marion. The warden, John Clark, stated that the prison would respect Rose's wishes to not speak with reporters and that guards would not be permitted to ask him for an autograph. He would work as a welder in the prison machine shop and serve his sentence routinely and uneventfully. "The toughest part of being in prison,"[20] said Rose, "was when my wife and little boy visited and then having to watch him lean out of the car window waving goodbye as they drove away."[21]

The dormitory at the Marion prison camp in which Rose slept had a large-screen color TV. It was surely heart-wrenching for Rose to watch the Reds, essentially the same team that he had managed only a year ago, play in the World Series while he was incarcerated. The Reds had hired Lou Piniella as manager in 1990, and bolstered by a trio of hard-throwing relief aces, Rob Dibble, Norm Charlton and Randy Myers, "The Nasty Boys," the team won its first nine games of the season, then went wire to wire to win the National League West Division title. They then advanced to the NLCS and defeated the Pittsburgh Pirates four games to two. Going into the World Series, the Oakland A's featuring the "Bash Brothers," Jose Canseco and Mark McGwire, who had hit 76 home runs between them during the 1990 season were heavy favorites. But the Reds swept the Series four games to none.

On January 7, 1991, Rose was released from Marion and returned to Cincinnati, where he served an additional three months in Talbert House, a halfway house facility located in Mt. Auburn, an urban neighborhood located near downtown Cincinnati, while he continued to perform the necessary 1000 hours of community service that was part of his sentence. Following his prison term in Marion, Rose's popularity remained high. With the permission of his parole officer he made many public appearances, signed autographs and appeared at various baseball card shows. At the completion of his sentence and community service, Rose moved to Florida, where he felt that there would be less intense scrutiny of his day-to-day activities by the media.

It had been part of his agreement in 1989 with then commissioner Bart Giamatti that he could seek reinstatement to baseball after one year, but for some reason Rose declined to do so and in fact did not apply for reinstatement until September 1997. However, while Rose was still serving his post-prison time at Talbert House, the board of directors of the Hall of Fame took preemptive action to make it difficult for him to gain entrance to the Hall. In a 12–0 vote in February 1991, the Board of Directors amended the bylaws so as to deem anyone on baseball's ineligible list to also to be ineligible for enshrinement in the Hall of Fame. Consequently, the baseball writers with voting privileges were now blocked from voting for Rose on the annual Hall of Fame ballot. The Hall of Fame officials denied that the change in bylaws was directed at Pete Rose, and baseball commissioner Fay Vincent also denied that he had been the catalyst in the rule change. Nonetheless, fair or not, it now appeared that Charlie Hustle's fate was once again placed in the hands of the commissioner of baseball.

VIII

Life in Exile

When Pete Rose went into exile, he went quietly. Rose moved to Boca Raton, Florida, licensed his name for the opening of a restaurant, and hawked memorabilia in his gift shop. For a while his fans moved on and concentrated on the game again. However, a significant number of Rose and Reds fans were left with displaced anger. They wanted in some way to blame Pete, but deep in their hearts he clung tight. The commissioner who sent him into exile was dead, while his former friends and accusers had all disappeared like the thieves in the night that they perhaps were. Consequently, the National Baseball Hall of Fame became a target for the displeasure of Rose fans. With seething discontent, Pete Rose's diehard fans at first refused to visit or support the Hall of Fame in any manner. However, gradually, over the ensuing years, as former Big Red Machine players such as Johnny Bench, Joe Morgan, manager Sparky Anderson and Tony Perez entered the Hall, the tide of anger among the Rose fans subsided, and they began to return to Cooperstown en masse.

In August 1994, Rose fans, with all major league fans in general, were given a new object for their wrath when they were caught in the middle of monumental riff between the players and owners. The major league players, making millions of dollars a year in salaries, had walked out on strike, thereby canceling one of the most exciting major league seasons in decades. The strike also canceled the World Series for the first time since 1904, while the complacent club owners, fanatisizing about breaking the players' union, did nothing to prevent it. By the time the new millennium arrived, it seemed

Pete Rose Ballpark Collectibles, Cooperstown, N.Y.

as if the Rose ban might not have ever happened at all and that it was really just a matter of time before Pete would join his contemporaries in the hallowed hall at Cooperstown.

Meanwhile, Pete Rose went on with his life. Life was good to him in exile. He was making a very decent living doing commercials for Maaco, appearing at card shows and on the Home Shopping Network, and being a spokesperson for the World Wrestling Federation. Rose carefully built his memorabilia business, taking care to keep the prices for his signed balls, jerseys, bats and pictures lower than his contemporaries. Then, of course, there were the restaurant and gift shop in Boca Raton to act as a cash cow. In fact,

Pete now had licensed his name for two restaurants. Eventually, he moved to California, and his young daughter by his second marriage, Cara, took up acting. He continued to gamble, too. Despite his casino appearances, he stood fast that he was not a casino-type gambler. But intermittently he slipped back into his hometown of Cincinnati and together with Arnie Metz and others played the horses at River Downs Race Track. The Rose contingent would gather in the clubhouse, and as in years past, Pete would pick the horses and Arnie would place the bets and cash the winning tickets.

Arnie Metz was a typical kid growing up in a typical Cincinnati neighborhood of Fairview Heights. He attended St. Monica grade school and Roger Bacon High School and loved baseball. Like most young guys his age growing up in Cincinnati in the 1960s and 1970s, he idolized hometown hero Pete Rose. However, when Metz became a groundskeeper at Riverfront Stadium, he was able to actualize his dreams by meeting and developing a superficial friendship with Rose. It mattered very little to Metz that his relationship with Rose was asymmetrical, as he was blinded by his devotion to his idol.

Although Rose now had a new family and was content, he truly loved his first son and he continued to agonize over the plight of Pete Jr. while he languished in the minor leagues. The early scouting report on Pete Jr. had been "Decent glove, but no stick." It almost seems impossible that a guy named Pete Rose, Jr., would not be able to hit a baseball. After starting his professional career with the Baltimore Orioles' farm chain after being picked in the 12th round of the 1988 amateur draft, Pete Jr. was traded to the Chicago White Sox for Joe Borowski, a pitcher. Pete Jr. played a year in the White Sox chain with their Class A affiliate in Sarasota, Florida, in 1991, then moved on to the Cleveland Indians organization, where between 1992 and 1994 he played for their farm teams in Columbus, Ohio, and Kinston, North Carolina. Returning to the White Sox organization in 1995, Pete Jr. played for five different teams before becoming a free agent at the end of the 1996 season, when the hometown Cincinnati Reds signed him.

Following the 1996 season, Pete Jr. began to change his approach to the game. Over the winter he had bulked up, and he stopped attempting to copy his father's style of slapping singles and started to hit with power. The Reds assigned him to their AA team in Chattanooga, where with his new physique and hitting style he began to finally show some promise, hitting .308 with 25 home runs in 112 games. After a stellar performance at Chattanooga, he was promoted to the Reds' AAA affiliate in Indianapolis, where he played 12 games before getting a call up to the big leagues.

To many observers, the Reds were just putting on a publicity gimmick by bringing Pete Rose, Jr., up to the Reds. However, the reality was that there was very heavy pressure from the Reds fans and Cincinnati media alike to bring young Rose up. The Reds were going nowhere in 1997. At Labor Day they had a season won-lost record of 59–75 and had already changed managers from Ray Knight to Jack McKeon at midseason. So the question that was being asked by the Pete Rose, starved fans of Cincinnati was, could it hurt any to give his son a chance to play? Earlier in the year, the Reds had brought up Eduardo Perez, the son of Tony Perez, who had grown up side by side with Pete Jr. Young Perez would hit .257 with 16 home runs in 108 games that season for the Reds.

Pete Rose, Jr., made his big league debut on September 1, 1997, in an interleague game against the Kansas City Royals before 31,920 fans at Cinergy Field. The Royals beat the Reds 7–4. Pete Rose, Sr., was in the stands at Cinergy Field that day; so was his mother, Karolyn Rose, who had bought 180 tickets for the games. "Let me tell you; I cried,"[1] said Karolyn Rose. "Oh my God, it was like—This is what he's longed for; this kid's so happy."[2] Young Rose wore his father's number, 14, as he trotted out to assume the third base position for the Reds. As was his custom in almost every minor league game that he had played in, he took his spike and scrawled the number 4,256 in the dirt, his father's career hit total. As he came up to bat for the first time to thunderous applause, using a black Mizuno bat his father had given him twelve years ago, he struck out. However, in his next plate appearance in the fourth inning, he used a Barry Larkin model bat. After taking two pitches for balls from Royals pitcher Kevin Appier, fouling off three, then taking ball three, Pete Jr. lined a single off the glove of the KC first baseman Jeff King for a hit. In the stands, Pete Rose, the Hit King, stood up and cheered Pete Jr., the same kid who had been there at first base with him after he had broken Ty Cobb's record twelve years before. Pete Jr.'s big day ended with one hit, two strikeouts, and a walk. Pete Rose, Jr., played in 11 games for the Reds in 1997, hitting .143 with two hits in 11 at-bats, while striking out nine times. According to Pete Jr., his big day in the major leagues was "everything and more. The nine years of bus rides, bad food and bad fans, it was all worth it."[3] Following his cup of coffee with the Reds, it was back to the minors for Pete Jr., with stops at Nashville and Indianapolis.

On May 20, 1998, Pete Rose, Jr., while playing for the AAA Indianapolis Indians (a Reds farm team) became part of baseball history in his own right. Playing in a game against Pawtucket in the fifth inning, Pete Jr. led off with a home run. Later in the inning, Jason Williams hit a three-run home run. As the fifth inning continued, Glenn Murray hit a grand slam, and then the scoring in the inning was completed when Guillermo Garcia hit a two-run round-tripper. The Indians won the game 11–4, with four players hitting home runs to complete the cycle, a feat never done before in professional baseball.

In June the Reds sent Rose Jr. down to Double-A Chattanooga, but later that month he signed with a Pittsburgh Pirates AAA team, the Nashville Sounds. However, the Pittsburgh Pirates soon released Rose Jr. and his tour of the minor leagues in America continued. He finished up the 1998 season with the independent New Jersey Jackals of the Northeast League, where he hit a respectable .300 with 15 home runs and 53 RBIs in 81 games at Yogi Berra Stadium in Little Falls, New Jersey.

As young Rose continued to chase the elusive dream of following in his famous father's spikes, no one was sympathetic to his minor league odyssey. He was on his own. Typical of the attitude of most of the media was that expressed by Harvey Araton of the *New York Times*, who wrote in 1998, "Other than 4,254 major league hits, we should understand there is not much difference between father and son. They are stubborn souls, with stocky builds, and familiar bulldog faces. But by most accounts, baseball's career hit king, who was banished nearly nine years ago for gambling, hardly knows the man he and his ex-wife once called Petey. For having his father's name, but not his attention, as he struggled to make it on his own, sympathy for Pete Rose, Jr., comes easily enough. But the fact of the matter is that players with less celebrated names would not have survived six years in Class A ball, often not hitting their weight. The reality is that lineage was as much as a factor in Rose's career-defining moment as his surprising 25 home runs last season in Class AA."[4]

Nonetheless, in spring training 2000, Pete Rose, Sr., got Philadelphia Phillies manager Terry Francona to give his son a shot at making the big club. However, he was eventually sent to the AA Reading Phillies, where he signed a $30,000 contract. By 2002, Pete Rose, Jr., now 32 years old, was still pursuing the dream of making a major league roster. Then on May 10, 2002, in his 14th season in professional ball, he was released by the Cincinnati Reds' AA farm team in Chattanooga after hitting .226 in nine games. He was offered a chance to coach in the Reds' minor league system but turned it down. Pete Jr. wound up the 2002 season playing for the Winnipeg Golden Eyes, where he wore jersey number 3 and hit .344 with eight home runs and 53 RBIs in 56 games. According to Pete Rose, Sr., his son will continue to pursue the elusive dream indefinitely. "It's just mind-boggling to me that no one will give him a chance to play in the big leagues. There can't be 750 players in this world better than Pete Rose the second. I'm totally convinced of that. He's going to play baseball until they tell him, 'You're not going to play any more—you can't play.'"[5]

In December 2002, *Sports Illustrated* was speculating that Pete Rose, Jr., might hang it up after all and in 2003 become a manager in the newly formed U.S. Professional Softball League, whose commissioner is his father's friend and former Philadelphia Phillies teammate Hall of Fame member Mike

Pete Rose, Jr., with the Cincinnati Reds. (Photo File, Inc.)

Schmidt. However, for Pete Rose, Jr., being a ballplayer is the only thing he ever wanted. "I'm a baseball player; it's in my blood,"[6] says Rose Jr. "That's the only thing I've ever wanted to do. I've always wanted to be just like Dad."[7]

As was part of his agreement with Bart Giamatti, Rose applied for reinstatement to Major League Baseball in September 1997. But his application languished on the desk of current commissioner Bud Selig. Rose alleged that he was being treated like a leper by the commissioner's office and felt used in that Major League Baseball only had contact with him when it felt there was something to gain economically from the association. He stated that the commissioner's office would not even return his telephone calls.

But time and public opinion were on the side of the Hit King. The defining moment for reconsideration of the Pete Rose's reinstatement to the eligible list of Major League Baseball came on the evening of October 24, 1999, at Turner Field in Atlanta prior to the second game of the World Series. In balloting for the 30-player All-Century Team, 25 players had been picked by the fans, and five players were picked by a panel of baseball experts and executives. Rose had been selected by the fans as member of the All-Century Team. Feeling some corporate pressure, commissioner Bud Selig relented and permitted Rose to participate in the ceremonies along with other living members such as Ted Williams, Stan Musial, Sandy Koufax, Cal Ripken, Jr., Willie Mays and others. When announcerVin Scully called Rose's name, the fans gave him a 55-second rousing ovation, even louder and longer than that given to local hero Henry Aaron. Consequently, the nation and Bud Selig alike took notice.

Many believe that this brief moment when Pete Rose once again basked in the stadium lights of fan adulation might have passed on into oblivion if it had not been for NBC correspondent Jim Gray, who, following the official ceremonies for the All-Century Team, allegedly did an ambush interview of Rose as a disgusted national television audience watched. As Rose and the other All-Century Team players were leaving the field, Gray approached Rose and began an over-enthusiastic attempt to extract a confession from him on his alleged betting on baseball. Rose was gracious, yet firm as he sidestepped Gray's attempts as a shocked national prime-time television audience looked on. The intrusive actions of Gray appeared out of bounds to the millions of viewers, and his shotgun approach to electronic journalism set off a groundswell of sympathy for the Hit King and reopened the question throughout America of whether or not he had been treated fairly by Major League Baseball when he agreed to the lifetime ban he signed with Bart Giamatti in 1989. The following day, Gray became the topic of discussion at coffee breaks across America and on radio talk shows as well, while being castigated in the press and by millions of fans through other media forms.

Typical of the outpouring of support for Rose was that expressed by B. Lord Martinez, editor of the *Augusta Chronicle.* "In response to Jim Gray's NBC-TV interview of Pete Rose, this was the most tasteless excuse of an interview I have ever seen. If Mr. Rose did bet on baseball or anything else such as the sun coming up, this was not the forum to air it. Mr. Rose is, without a doubt, one of baseball's greatest players. He always played the game with heart of a lion, thus the nickname Charlie Hustle. Would Mr. Gray ask President Bill Clinton as harsh and pressing questions as he did Mr. Rose? I think not. Mr. Gray is a coward and would like to make his mark in history. He can take a walk and take Joe Morgan and Tim McCarver with him."[8]

Pete Rose, Jr., with the Reading Phillies. (Photograph by David M. Schofield.)

Gray was adamant in defense of his interview tactics and did not apologize for his style. Furthermore, he defended his actions by stating that Rose had been asked the very same questions by other reporters in a news conference less than an hour before he approached him. But Jim Gray had done what all of Pete Rose's expensive lawyers had failed to do: He had brought the question of fairness to the fore of public opinion and in some respects made Rose a martyr. Now the genie was out of the bottle, and Bud Selig knew that at some point he was going to have to deal with the dreaded Pete Rose question.

In 1999, Rose intimated that he might file suit against Major League Baseball to end his lifetime ban. "You can't keep a guy from making a living,"[9] said Rose. "It's not the American way."[10] In Cooperstown he began to exert pressure on the Hall of Fame when he opened Pete Rose's Ballpark

Collectibles on Main Street, just a few blocks away from the Hall of Fame, and began making appearances during the Hall of Fame weekend. The shop is operated by Andrew Vilacky, and the venture is part business and part political. Visitors can buy Pete Rose autographed memorabilia while signing a petition for his entry into the Hall of Fame. Meanwhile, with the growing popularity of the internet, it was now possible to sign an online petition for Rose to be admitted to the Hall of Fame. In October 1999, an Associated Press poll showed that by 2–1 margin, most fans believed that Rose's lifetime ban from baseball should be lifted. Suddenly Charlie Hustle was making a comeback.

However, Bud Selig, now sensitized by the groundswell of support for Rose he had witnessed at the All-Century Team ceremonies, continued to stonewall Rose and deny him permission to participate in significant events such as the celebrations organized by the Cincinnati Reds to honor the 1975 team and Philadelphia Phillies to honor the 1980 team, both world champions that Rose had played with. In the Cincinnati ceremony that took place in June 2000, each member of the 1975 Big Red Machine was introduced and then took his place on the field. When Rose's name was announced, Barry Larkin, who was the Reds' All-Star shortstop, went onto the field and placed a single red rose on the third base bag to the thunderous cheers of the huge crowd at Cinergy Field. It all seemed so ludicrous as the crowd once again chanted the familiar Pete! Pete! Pete! somehow hoping that if they chanted loud and long enough, the spirit of their exiled hero would suddenly appear and tip his cap. Meanwhile, video clips provided by Reds president John Allen played on the stadium screen, showing highlights of Rose's career as radio play-by-play announcer Marty Brennaman emphatically stated to the listening audience, "No. 14 should be here and isn't."[11]

The void left in the ceremonies once again gave license for sports writers and reporters to vent their frustration with Bud Selig, a commissioner whom they felt was blatantly sidestepping baseball's roots and traditions as he advanced his agenda, attempting to mold baseball into an image that he alone had of it, rather than one that the masses could identify with. Such was the case with John Delcos, who wrote in the *Home News Tribune*, "Banned or not—and this is what drives Selig crazy—is that for all Rose's transgressions, he still stirs passion among baseball followers. Selig has consistently proven either a disregard or ignorance for baseball history in most every decision he's made—and that history is why the commissioner should be trying to reach a truce with Rose rather than not return his calls. If Selig believes Rose should not be employed by a team until he apologizes for the embarrassment his gambling caused the game and admits and seeks treatment for a gambling addiction—and he's right in that demand—that's fine. However, in the interest of fairness, Selig should allow Rose his rightful place in baseball history, and that's the Hall of Fame and to be remembered by fans who appreciated how he played the game."[12]

Regardless of the opinions of the fans and press, a few weeks later Selig locked Rose out of another celebration in Philadelphia to honor the world champion 1980 Phillies. When Phillies announcer Harry Kalas announced Rose's, name the Veterans Stadium crowd of 37,292 immediately gave Rose a standing ovation and once again broke into the now legendary chant Pete! Pete! Pete! as former manager Dallas Green held Rose's No. 14 Phillies jersey above his head and waved it at the chanting crowd. Green then neatly folded the jersey and placed it on first base. "The commissioner said Rose can't be here and we have to abide by that,"[13] said Green. "This is about a team, though, not about Pete Rose. He was part of this team and he should be here."[14]

A single rose placed on third base, a folded jersey placed on first base, these are the kinds of tributes that baseball teams make to a dead man. But Pete Rose was 59 years old, alive and well. It was all surreal and absurd. The fact of the matter was that the nation's love affair with Pete Rose would simply not go away. The commissioner could not will it to go away, and the fans would not let it go away. In some respects, these continued trite snubs of Pete Rose by Major League Baseball and the commissioner raise the question of whether the ban of Rose is about more than just gambling.

Some authors have attempted to intellectualize the Pete Rose dilemma. In 1997 James Reston's book *Collision at Home Plate: The Lives of Pete Rose and Bart Giamatti* was published. In an otherwise well-written book that captures the lives of both men in extraordinary detail, Reston attempts to make the case that a clash of cultures between Rose the river rat and Giamatti the Ivy Leaguer was a deciding dynamic in their confrontation over baseball ethics as they hammered out their 1988 agreement. In 1998, George Will attempted to reinforce Reston's thesis in his book *Bunts*. But the fact of the matter is that there was not any more of a class difference playing a part in the commissioner's actions in 1988 than there was between Shoeless Joe Jackson and Judge Kenesaw Mountain Landis in 1920 or Leo Durocher and A. B. "Happy" Chandler in 1947. Stratification never played a part in the banishment of Rose; nonetheless, the harshness of the penalty begs the question of why others who have periodically soiled baseball's good name have gotten lesser penalties.

July 23, 2000, was a big day for Cincinnati Reds fans in Cooperstown, New York. Not only were former manager Sparky Anderson and Big Red Machine team leader Tony Perez being inducted into the Hall of Fame, but so was longtime Reds broadcaster Marty Brennaman. However, the winds of the Pete Rose controversy swept into the celebration. On July 22, the evening before his induction, Brennaman was approached by former Reds catcher Johnny Bench, who said he was acting on behalf of fellow Hall of Fame members Bob Feller and Ralph Kiner. Bench asked Brennaman to forgo any mention of Pete Rose in his acceptance speech the next day, as it would offend the sensitivities of Feller and Kiner and both might walk out. However, Gaylord Perry, a Hall of Fame pitcher himself, told Brennaman to say what he wanted. Brennaman became very angry with Bench and his intermediary cloak-and-dagger tactics. "He made me so mad,"[15] Brennaman said. "He said, 'You might have some people walk out.' It ruined my night."[16]

The next day at the ceremonies, with a large contingent of Cincinnati fans on hand, as Bud Selig was introduced he was peppered with the familiar chants of Pete! Pete! Pete! while 47 members of the Hall of Fame seated on the stage looked on. Marty Brennaman received his award from Ralph Kiner then began his speech. Speaking about the Big Red Machine, he thanked "those from that team that should be in the Hall of Fame, but aren't. Bob Howsam, who built two world championship organizations in St. Louis and Cincinnati. Davey Concepcion, who was the preeminent shortstop of his time. And yes, by God, Peter Edward Rose."[17] As Brennaman mentioned Rose, the assembled crowd broke into loud cheers. However, no one walked out. While Sparky Anderson did not mention Rose in his acceptance speech, Tony Perez did. He referred to Pete Rose as "my brother in Cincinnati." Looking back in retrospect on the incident at Cooperstown, Bob Feller's position was quite clear. "If loud-mouth Brennaman wanted to make a fool of himself, it was his First Amendment right."[19]

The furor kicked off by the pressure Johnny Bench had attempted to put on Brennaman to modify his speech at Cooperstown returned home to Cincinnati with them. As a result, Bench resigned from a radio show he had been co-hosting with Brennaman on WLW-AM. While Brennaman was on the air doing the show on Wednesday, July 26, the ever-vacillating Joe Morgan called in, spoke with Bench's replacement Bill Cunningham, and offered to mediate the tiff between Brennaman and Bench. "Everybody knows I care about Pete Rose,"[20] Morgan said. "I also care about John [Bench]. A lot of people take some of the things John says about Pete the wrong way."[21]

While Brennaman was amenable to working things out with Bench, Pete Rose was still shaking his head at the whole episode that began in Cooperstown. "At first, I was surprised when I heard what [Bench] did,"[22] said Rose. "But nothing he does surprises me. Honestly, I don't understand his constant problem with me. All I do is praise him everywhere I go."[23] The fact of the matter is that Johnny Bench had indeed been demonstrating some animosity toward Rose for some time prior to the Cooperstown incident. Most analysts feel that it had more to do with a failed business venture between Bench and Rose in the early 1970s than Rose's alleged gambling or banishment from baseball.

In September 2001, the ghost of Tommy Gioiosa returned to haunt Rose. Out of jail and putting his life back in order while living in Florida, Gioiosa broke the twelve-year silence on his friendship with Rose when he gave an interview to Buzz Bissinger that was published in *Vanity Fair* magazine. Gioiosa claims he decided to do the article because Pete never reciprocated the loyalty that he had shown him. He stated that he was hurt by the fact that Rose never offered a thank you for his efforts in attempting to protect him. "For the past 11 years, people have thrown me in with the same guys who cut a deal to bring Pete down,"[24] Gioiosa said. "I didn't cut a deal. I was looking for a friend and he was nowhere."[25]

In the article Gioiosa painted Rose in a most unbecoming way, making several startling accusations. Among the many accusations made by Gioiosa was that when visiting the Reds' clubhouse after Rose had become player-manager of the Reds, Rose showed him a corked bat that he used in games while in pursuit of Ty Cobb's record. Gioiosa says that when he asked what would happen if the bat broke in a game, Rose told him, "There'd be fucking cork all over the place."[26] However, Gioiosa further stated that Rose assured him that he would never use the corked bat in a game against a pitcher who would cause a bat to break. Gioiosa also stated in the article that in the condominium that he once shared with Rose, Pete hid $10,000 in bundles of cash behind a ceiling panel in the basement. He also alleged that Rose taught him how to forge his signature on memorabilia and discussed with him the possibility of buying a few kilos of cocaine. Gioiosa says that Rose had a CD maturing and discussed with him investing the money in cocaine. In regard to the alleged cocaine discussion with Rose, Buzz Bissinger says that Gioiosa paraphrased his conversation in his interview with him to "use that money and buy the kilos and I'll [Rose] keep them in my house because nobody would have the balls to come in my house."[27]

The cocaine allegations made by Gioiosa were moot, as the statute of limitations had expired for any federal or state prosecution, but that didn't prevent Rose from responding to them. "I've been accused of everything, but I've never been accused of being a cocaine dealer and a drug dealer,"[28] said Rose. "All I can tell you is, they better have credible evidence if they start writing that kind of stuff. He's [Gioiosa] got to be so embarrassed. I treated him like a son, and for him to do this all these years later, it's unbelievable."[29]

While this might seem like pretty strong stuff, it didn't stint the resurgence of popularity for Charlie Hustle one bit. As a matter of fact, the *Vanity Fair* article was viewed by most Rose fans as being about as credible as a *National Enquirer* article on little green men from outer space. Warren Greene, Rose's business agent, told the *Cincinnati Enquirer* that Gioiosa's remarks in the article "are one-sided and refer to events more than a decade old, and that Mr. Gioiosa, a convicted felon, cannot be considered credible."[30]

On March 31, 2003, the Cincinnati Reds opened a new $330 million taxpayer-funded stadium called the Great American Ball Park adjacent to Cinergy Field. In the fall of 2002, while the new stadium was still under construction, plans were being made by the Reds' management to play their last home game in Cinergy Field on Sunday, September 22. For a swan song to the glorious 32-year history of the ballpark formerly known as Riverfront Stadium, which had seen 64.7 million baseball fans go through its turnstiles while hosting 2,572 games, five World Series, seven NLCS and two All-Star Games, the Reds invited back many of the former players who had played on the stadium's artificial turf.

Prior to the game, Reds coach Ray Knight placed a single red rose behind home plate to honor Pete Rose. It was not surprising that the crowd of 40,964 went crazy, chanting the ever familiar Pete! Pete! Pete! Ironically, it was Knight who had replaced Rose at third base for the Reds in 1979 after he had signed as a free agent with the Philadelphia Phillies.

In the final game at Cinergy Field, the Reds lost to the Phillies 4–3 with Aaron Boone hitting the last home run in the grand old ballpark. When Todd Walker hit a routine ground ball for the final out to bring down the last curtain on the stadium, immediately three tuxedo-clad members of the Reds' grounds crew went out onto the field and dug up home plate so that it could be transported next door to the new Great American Ball Park.

For those fans remaining in the stands, it was now time for a nostalgic trip down memory lane. A video history of significant moments in the history of the ballpark was shown on the center field screen. Then Marty Brennaman, the Reds' Hall of Fame radio announcer, began to introduce Reds players from years past, who lined up down the base lines. There were players from the 1990 world champion Reds such as Tom Browning, Todd Benzinger, Eric Davis, Rob Dibble, Danny Jackson, Hal Morris, Joe Oliver, Paul O'Neill, as well as Jose Rijo and Barry Larkin, who were still active on the Reds roster. There were many players from the Big Red Machine era introduced too, such as Johnny Bench, Jack Billingham, Pedro Borbon, Dave Concepcion, Clay Carroll, Rawly Eastwick, George Foster, Cesar Geronimo, Ken Griffey, Sr., Don Gullett, Tommy Helms, Will McEnaney and Tony Perez. Former Reds managers Sparky Anderson, John McNamara and Russ Nixon were there too. In all, 52 former Reds players were introduced, but there was no Pete Rose. Once again Bud Selig had banned Rose from the ceremonies. To honor Pete Rose, former pitcher Tom Browning who had played for him when he managed the club, spray-painted his number on the mound as the other former Reds players looked on.

Rose was in town; he had watched the closing ceremonies at the Cinergy Field/Riverfront Stadium on television, and then there was a dinner planned to honor him that evening at the Waterfront, a popular Cincinnati restaurant. But it seemed absurd for Pete Rose to have been watching on television, locked out by the commissioner from the closing ceremonies of a ballpark, the street in front of which bears his name, rather than being in it among the fans, press and players sharing the many memories that he had been a huge part of. Perhaps Rose's feelings that major league baseball treated him like a leper did indeed have some merit after all. The closing of Cinergy Field was an event about baseball history, not the integrity of the game. The ceremonies were scheduled for after the last pitch of the last official league game ever to be played in the facility. How Bud Selig could have arrived at the conclusion that by barring Rose from participation in the event he was protecting the sanctity of the game is beyond reason. The action taken by Bud Selig in the closing ceremonies at Cinergy Field did nothing but demonstrate a harsh reality that he is not capable of discerning between what is reality and what is symbolic when it comes to dealing with matters concerning the administration of the lifetime ban from major league baseball of Peter Edward Rose. Furthermore, it appears that rather than taking time to make clear, well thought-out decisions on such matters, more often than not Selig will submit to his penchant for making knee-jerk reactions in matters concerning Rose.

In a tribute to the end of Cinergy Field/Riverfront Stadium, the *Cincinnati Enquirer* printed a special collector's section on Sunday, September 22, 2002. In the section, the *Enquirer* listed the 100 most memorable moments in the history of the ballpark. There was the dramatic home run by Johnny Bench in the fifth game of the 1972 NLCS against Pittsburgh. There was the controversy over the play at the plate of Carlton Fisk possibly interfering with Ed Armbrister in game three of the 1975 World Series. There was Pete Rose crashing into Ray Fosse at home plate in the 1970 All-Star Game and Hank Aaron's 714th home run, tying Babe Ruth in 1974, among others. But the moment that was listed as the number one memory in the history of the stadium was that of Pete Rose breaking Ty Cobb's all-time hit record on September 11, 1985. In fact, three of the top ten memories on the stadium list were Pete Rose moments. *Cincinnati Enquirer* sports columnist John Erardi wrote in the September 22, 2002, edition of the paper, "As somebody once wrote, from dust we came and to dust we shall return. The difference between Pete Rose and the rest of us is the dust he raised in between."

However, Pete Rose would yet have his night in the old ballpark. For some time prior to the Reds' last game played at Cinergy Field, Hamilton County, which was the owner of the facility, had been negotiating with Rose's business agent Warren Greene and his company Dreams, Inc. to hold a softball game in the stadium. As the game would have nothing to do with major league baseball, the coast was clear for Pete Rose to participate. Subsequently, the game was scheduled for Monday, September 23, 2002, at Cinergy Field, the day following the Reds' final game there. While the softball game was promoted as a sort of an unofficial fairwell to Cinergy Field/Riverfront Stadium, it was in reality a very slick, calculated marketing opportunity for Warren Greene to promote his number one client, Pete Rose. However, no one seemed to care about the subterfuge in the promotion. Hey, Pete Rose was going to be back at Riverfront Stadium one last time, and this was just fine with his many legions of fans.

In all, 41,092 fans turned out for the event, 128 more than were there for the Reds' final game the day before. Only the draw of Pete Rose could sell out a major league stadium for a softball game. In reality, there had been no other sports event like it since 1960, when professional wrestlers Lou Thesz and "Nature Boy" Buddy Rodgers packed 40,000 fans into Chicago's Comiskey Park for a "ham and egger" heavyweight championship match. But such was the drawing power of the Hit King in his hometown. In Cincinnati, it made no difference to the fans if a 61-year-old, overweight and out-of-condition Pete Rose was going to play in a comedic softball game; it was after all still Pete, and the town still loved him. A typical response of the fans arriving at the stadium was that of Esther Mintz of the Cincinnati suburb of Covedale. "I can't believe I'm seeing this. He is special. We love him and always will."[31]

The game was organized so that a group of former Big Red Machine players, officially called the Reds Legends, would play against a team of former major league All-Stars, officially called the Major Leaguers. Playing for the Reds were Pete Rose, Johnny Bench, Caesar Geronimo, Ken Griffey, Sr., George Foster, Joe Morgan, Tony Perez and others. Playing for the All-stars were Mike Schmidt, Steve Carlton, Steve Garvey, Dave Parker, Ryne Sandberg and others.

The cost of a ticket to the event was $30, which meant that the gate alone grossed $1,232,760. What Rose's cut of the profits for the evening were is not known. Each fan entering the stadium was given a Pete Rose bobblehead doll as a souvenir. Pete the promoter was quick to point out that his bobblehead doll was unique too. "The reason my bobblehead doll is a good bobblehead doll, I'll tell you why, there's only one reason why. It's because I don't have a hat on,"[32] Pete said. Prior to the game, Pete Rose signed autographs in one of the stadium ticket booths. A long line of fans stretched around the stadium plaza for a chance to get the Hit King to sign the official program for the event, which cost $5. Rose signed autographs for 45 minutes; however, the policy was no program, no autograph. When it was time for the game, Rose had to be escorted from the ticket booth to the field by seven members of the Cincinnati Police force.

During the introduction of the players, when Rose's name was called, the flashbulbs began popping and the fans gave him a thunderous three-minute standing ovation. The crowd had delayed this moment for a day, and while it wasn't the seven-minute ovation they gave Rose upon his hit number 4,192, it was still pretty obvious to even an uninitiate that this guy was something very special to the fans. Standing between former Reds owner Marge Schott, who also received a 20-second ovation from the fans, and George Foster, the crowd continued to roar as Foster raised Rose's left arm in the air. Rose then introduced his young daughter Chea, and she sang the National Anthem.

In the game, the Reds Legends were trounced by the Major Leaguers, 19–6. But the highlight of the game was provided by none other than Pete Rose. In the sixth inning, after going 0 for two, Rose got a hit down the third base line past Mike Schmidt. Joe Morgan followed with a hit, and Pete took second. He then tagged up on a fly ball and took off for third, diving head first into the bag ahead of the tag by Mike Schmidt. The crowd was ecstatic; it didn't make any difference if Pete had slid into third or actually fell into third. This was the reason they came: to see Charlie Hustle one more time as they remembered him, playing the game full tilt. Former Reds manager Dave Bristol saw highlights of the game on ESPN and was greatly amused. "I saw Pete play in that softball game on TV last night that they had at Riverfront. Man, he looked like he could barely run down to first base. I couldn't believe it,"[33] said Bristol. "What is he now, 61 or something?"[34]

In actuality, the whole affair that night at Cinergy Field turned into a Pete Rose love-fest. Marge Schott, who as an owner use to refer to Rose as "that son of a bitch," was absolutely mushy about Pete, hugging him and telling the press how much she loved him. Perhaps Schott had mellowed somewhat after having her own personal troubles with the commissioner's office and could now identify with Rose's circumstances much better. Also, George Foster was given an award during the introductions and used the opportunity to get on the public address system and say, "Let's all get together and put Pete Rose into the Hall of Fame."[35] But the most shocking of events was still to come. Johnny Bench and Pete Rose used the occasion of the softball event to publicly bury the hatchet. Rose stated that he and Bench had always had a cordial relationship until his problems with the commissioner became public. In regard to Bench's actions at the Hall of Fame ceremonies in 2000 where he warned Marty Brennaman not to say anything in his acceptance speech about Rose, Pete remarked, "Johnny's a big boy. He's entitled to his opinion."[36] Bench said he and Rose "have always had a relationship, and we've never not gotten along. What happens with baseball is their choice, and that's what people have to understand. And he understands that. We all would like things to be different, but they aren't.

Pete would go to war for me, and I would go to war for him."[37] With all this said and done, it is still debatable whether or not Johnny Bench is simply jumping on the Pete Rose bandwagon and how long the peace between Bench and Rose will really last. Perhaps if the Reds' manager's job became available with Rose back on the eligibility list, it would be a good acid test of their relationship.

But regardless of all of the commercial aspects of the event, it was quite the evening at Cinegry Field. It was part business, part nostalgia, and an awful lot of fun. It seemed like the only thing missing was for the public address announcer to proclaim: "Ladies and gentleman, Elvis has left the building." Howard Wilkinson wrote in the *Cincinnati Enquirer* the following morning, "Wreck it, implode it, sell the seats and the sod. No one will mind now, because Pete Rose has come home. It was all the 41,000-plus fans who filled Cinergy Field Monday night for a 'Farewell to Cinergy' wanted to see."

The next morning, the highlights of the event at Cinergy were being broadcast around the world by ESPN. Subsequently, a call was placed to the office of Rose's business agent, Warren Greene, in Florida. Candy, an administrative assistant, took the call and stated that Mr. Greene was still in Cincinnati. However, she stated that "all morning long the phones in the office have been flooded with media requests for appearances and interviews with Pete."[38] It was quite obvious that Pete Rose, despite being exiled by the commissioner's office, was still one of the biggest draws in baseball.

It seemed for once that the commissioner's office was taking notice of the growing resurgence of popularity surrounding Rose. Bud Selig gave his consent for him to appear in San Francisco on Wednesday evening, October 23, prior to game four of the 2002 World Series between the Giants and Anaheim Angels in a commercial event sponsored by MasterCard to honor baseball's most memorable moments. "The fans voted for the most memorable moment. This is really a fans' vote, and I certainly am not going to get in the way of that,"[39] said Selig. As usual, Rose got a huge ovation from the fans in San Francisco, accompanied by the always present chant of Pete! Pete! Pete! But now, all at once, it was being rumored that perhaps Bud Selig, with the passage of time and the ever present popularity of Pete Rose, was starting to change his mind on reinstatement.

IX

Hall of Fame or Hall of Shame

Major League Baseball Rule 21(d.) states that any player who bets on a game shall be declared ineligible for one year and any player who bets on his own team shall be declared permanently ineligible. "I think my dad got screwed,"[1] says Pete Rose, Jr., referring to the lifetime banishment of his father from baseball. Pete Jr. says that his dad once looked him straight in the eyes and told him the gospel truth of the matter about his alleged gambling on baseball, but refuses to divulge the content of that discussion. "What's the Hall of Fame for? It's for baseball players,"[2] adds Rose Jr.

Herein Rose the younger raises a paramount question. Is election to the National Baseball Hall of Fame about baseball or is it about morality? If the answer is the latter, then there are a lot of tarnished plaques hanging in Cooperstown. Whether or not we want to admit it, gambling, vice, sex, alcohol and substance abuse, and racism have always been part and parcel of the game of baseball since its inception. In fact, some of the game's immortal stars have been involved in controversy throughout the game's history, including Ty Cobb, Tris Speaker, Eddie Collins, Ray Schalk, Leo Durocher, Babe Ruth, Mickey Mantle and even Joe DiMaggio, among others. Yet two of the game's biggest stars, Shoeless Joe Jackson and Pete Rose, seem to be excluded from the Hall of Fame for perceived wrongdoings that all others have been forgiven by the past and present lords of baseball.

When asked what their position is on the exclusion of Pete Rose, the National Baseball Hall of Fame offered the following response. "Please understand that the Hall of Fame is not and never has been involved in electing candidates for enshrinement. The Baseball Writers' Association of America and the Veterans' Committee are the only bodies that elect eligible candidates to the Hall of Fame. In order for Pete Rose to be considered for election to the Hall of Fame, he must first apply for reinstatement to the office of the commissioner of Major League Baseball, which he has done. If he is reinstated by Major League Baseball, his election would be in the hands of the Baseball Writers' Association of America (BBWAA), the caucus responsible for electing recently retired ballplayers. Hence the Hall of Fame has no role in his attempt to regain eligibility or earn election to Cooperstown. Regardless of his status, it's important not to understate Mr. Rose's generosity toward the Hall of Fame, as evidence by the 20 or so artifacts he has donated to us from his playing days. As one of baseball's all-time greatest players, his career is well documented in the museum, which strives to accurately depict the vast history of our great game. The museum portrays the careers of all players to make a significant contribution to the game, both Hall of Famers and those players not fortunate enough to earn election to Cooperstown."[3]

As the Hall of Fame states, the first step for Pete Rose in gaining entry is for him to apply for reinstatement to the eligible list with Major League Baseball. Rose agreed with the commissioner's office to a lifelong ban from baseball for gambling in 1989 with the provision that he could apply for reinstatement after one year. To this end, Rose hired an attorney Robert Makley and did just that in 1997. However, the commissioner's office until very recently would not even return his telephone calls. In fact, there seemed to be bad blood between commissioner Bud Selig and Pete Rose. An example of such is from an interview that Selig gave to New York City sports talk radio station WFAN in 2000 when Selig stated categorically on the *Imus in the Morning Show*, that "Pete Rose will never be reinstated while I am commissioner of baseball."[4] Rose stated in a documentary on Fox cable network's *Beyond the Glory* in July 2001 that the commissioner's office has a vendetta against him. "They can't stand the fact that I'm still alive. They wish I was dead."[5]

Rule 3E of the Rules for Election to the National Baseball Hall of Fame states, "Any player on baseball's ineligible list shall not be an eligible candidate." Assuming that Rose somehow could miraculously gain reinstatement, his next hurdle would be election to the Hall of Fame by the Baseball Writers' Association of America (BBWAA), which is authorized to hold an election every year for the purpose of electing members to the Hall of Fame from the ranks of retired baseball players. Here Rose would find some very stiff opposition too. Unfortunately, in late 2002, Rose lost a huge supporter for his entry into the Hall of Fame. Former *Macon Telegraph* sports editor Harley Bowers, who passed away in December 2002, was a voting member of the BBWAA and supported Rose. Speaking from his Macon, Georgia home in September 2002, Bowers stated, "I think he's being mistreated. He should have been on the ballot years ago. He's been punished enough. However, if I voted for Pete Rose, they would cancel my ballot."[6] In fact, Rule 4B of the Rules for Election states, "Write-in votes are not permitted."

It is possible that there are many more voting members of the BBWAA who would like to vote for Rose, but most remain mum on the topic at present. Even if Pete were placed on the eligible list and then did not find enough support for election to the Hall of Fame by BBWAA, he would eventually wind up on the eligible list of the National Baseball Hall of Fame Committee on Baseball Veterans, where he would find stiff opposition as well. The rules for election of the so-called Veterans' Committee were changed in 2001, and it is currently made up of 90 members that include all members of the Hall of Fame voted in by the BBWAA (61), the living recipients of the J. G. Taylor Spink Award (12), the living recipients of the Ford C. Frick Award (14) and the members of the former Veterans' Committee whose terms have not yet expired (2). The new term for appointment to the Veterans Committee is for life. Beginning in 2003, election for players takes place every two years and election of umpires, mangers and executives every four years. For any reader who is interested in more detailed information on this subject, the complete list of rules for election to the Hall of Fame can be found on the museum's website (www.baseballhall-offame.org).

Regardless of whether the former 15-member Veterans' Committee was still in place or the new 90-member Veterans' Committee in existence now voted on Rose, he would still need to receive at least 75 percent of the ballots cast in his favor to be elected. That might be a hard sell, as there are those whom one might think support Rose for election who absolutely do not, and there are others who constantly change their support for him, depending on which way the wind is blowing. One such example of vacillating support is Rose's former Big Red Machine teammate, current ESPN baseball broadcaster and Hall of Fame member Joe Morgan. In an interview in *Playboy* magazine in 1999, Morgan was asked if he thought that Pete Rose belongs in the Hall of Fame. Morgan replied: "Pete and I were the two closest guys on the team. I lockered next to him for nine years. There's never been anyone I ever played with or against that played the way he did. He played every single game like it was the seventh game of the World Series. I didn't play it that way. There were days when you're just not all there. I never saw him when he wasn't all there. But I'm also on the board of directors of the Hall of Fame [Veterans' Committee]. My duty as a board member is to uphold the integrity of the game. I take that seriously, and from that standpoint Pete did not deserve to be in. Personally, I believe he needed to be punished for what he did, and he has been punished. If Pete Rose were to stand up in front of America and say, 'I made a mistake and I'm sorry,' then I would say yes. But until he does, I'm sorry."[7]

However, Morgan isn't the only former supporter who has turned on Rose. Former teammates and Hall of Fame members Johnny Bench and Frank Robinson have done likewise. During the summer of 2000, a growing animosity between Bench and longtime Reds radio broadcaster Marty Brennaman was revealed just prior to the Hall of Fame induction ceremonies that year. It was feared that Brennaman, who was in Cooperstown to receive the Ford C. Frick Award for broadcasting excellence, might make a pitch for Pete Rose's inducting into the Hall of Fame during his acceptance speech and consequently offend some of the Hall of Fame members in attendance. Bench, wanting to save the highly popular broadcaster from some potential embarrassment, approached Brennaman prior to the Sunday ceremonies and told him to temper any remarks he was going to make about Pete Rose in his speech because Hall of Fame members Bob Feller, Ralph Kiner and Frank Robinson would walk off the stage if it appeared to them that Brennaman was campaigning for Rose.

What blatant hypocrisy exists in the minds of commissioner Bud Selig and a select number of voting members of the Hall of Fame alike. One can hardly imagine the naivete of the commissioner and these voting members regarding the sordid history of baseball. How can they, in reasonable con-scientisusness, apply one set of standards for morality to Pete Rose, while others who are immortalized in the Hall of Fame are given a pass for behavior no less offensive? While the argument is made that admitting Pete Rose to the Hall of Fame will compromise the integrity of the game, the fact is that every day that passes with Pete Rose waiting for reinstatement to baseball compromises the integrity of the game. It is impossible to have a double standard of morality for the heroes of Cooperstown without having the whole process look just a little phony. If Rose is continued to be denied eligibility for the Hall of Fame, then the board of directors needs to reexamine the history of those whom it has already sanctimoniously immortalized in Cooperstown, apply the same standards to those enshrined, and determine if there is a tarnished plaque or two that needs to be taken down. In fact, one might suggest to the pusillanimous current commissioner of baseball, Bud Selig, and a select number of the living members of the Hall of Fame who sit with such ignoble piety in judgement on Pete Rose, such as Joe Morgan, Johnny Bench, Frank Robinson, Ralph Kiner, Bob Feller and others, that a good place to embark on a crusade to sanitize the character of the membership in the Hall of Fame would be with an examination of members with questionable events in their background. Perhaps they could start such an inquiry with Ty Cobb.

Immediately after the last scheduled game of the 1926 American League season, both Ty Cobb, player-manager of the Detroit Tigers, and Tris Speaker, player-manager of the Cleveland Indians, abruptly resigned. John McGraw of the New York Giants, delighted that Cobb might be available, moved quickly to negotiate with Cobb about taking over the position of assistant manager previously held by Hughie Jennings. Barney Drefuss, president of the Pittsburgh Pirates, wanted to negotiate with Speaker about being an assistant to his new manager Donie Bush. However, before either man could reach Cobb or Speaker, baseball commissioner Judge Kenesaw Mountain Landis interceded and sternly told both McGraw and Drefuss to back off immediately. Something was up.

On Wednesday morning, December 22, 1926, the story broke in the press. Ty Cobb and Tris Speaker had been implicated in a betting scandal. Organized baseball, still reeling from the fallout of the alleged fix in the 1919 World Series between the Chicago White Sox and Cincinnati Reds, was beside itself. Baseball had worked diligently to clean itself up and restore the public trust following the 1919 scandal. Eight alleged perpetrators on the White Sox in the 1919 World Series scandal, including Shoeless Joe Jackson, had received lifetime bans from baseball. The major leagues reorganized administratively and appointed a full-time independent commissioner with broad sweeping authority and discretion to keep the game clean, but now here were two of its biggest stars staring down the barrel of a shotgun full of scandal, and once again baseball was looked at with a jaundiced eye by the general public.

An allegation was made by former Detroit Tigers pitcher Hubert Benjamin "Dutch" Leonard that player-managers Ty Cobb and Tris Speaker had conspired to fix the last game of the 1919 American League season so that the Tigers could win the third-place share of the 1919 World Series money. Despite the fact that the Tigers actually finished fourth in the 1919 pennant race, the allegation was taken seriously. Furthermore, Leonard alleged that former Cleveland pitcher "Smoky" Joe Wood had placed bets on baseball games for both Cobb and Speaker. Subsequently, in October 1926, baseball commissioner Judge Kenesaw Mountain Landis traveled to the home of Dutch Leonard in California and took his testimony on the matter. Leonard stated that he, Cobb, Speaker and Wood had met under the grandstand at Detroit's Navin Field on September 24, 1919, and agreed that Detroit would win the game the following day on September 25, 1919, thus allowing the Tigers to clinch third place in the American League pennant race. According to Leonard, "After the first game between Detroit and Cleveland, September 24, Cobb, Speaker, Wood and I happened to meet under the stand and of course the talk was about baseball, and that we [Detroit] wanted to finish third. Speaker said, 'Don't worry about tomorrow's game. We have got second place cinched and you will win tomorrow.'[8]

Tris Speaker. (Photo File, Inc.)

"Everybody agreed that if it was going to be a setup, we might as well get some money on it. Then we talked about getting the money down on the game. Cobb said he would send West down to us [Fred West was a private police officer at Navin Field and was aquatinted with the bookmakers]. I was to put up $1,500, Cobb $2,000 and Wood and Speaker $1,000 each. During the talk under the stand about the next day's game, Speaker said he would go in and pitch himself if necessary. There was not very much talk and we did not stay there very long. There were just the four of us, and no other player was in on it. When I met Wood the next spring [1920], I said to him: "What do you think, Cobb wrote me that he did not get any money up on that game,' and Wood said: 'He told me the same thing.'[9]

Leonard backed up his allegation by turning over to the American League office two letters, one written by Cobb, the other by Wood, which corroborated his story. However, it should be pointed out that Leonard, who had been released by the Tigers after the 1925 season, was, at the time of the presentation of the letters to the commissioner's office, pressing a claim against the Tigers. It is believed that Leonard was paid the sum of $20,000 to turn the letters over to the American League office. Furthermore, Leonard would not come to Chicago and face Cobb at the commissioner's hearing. The reason offered by Leonard was that "they bump people off once in awhile around there [Chicago]."[10] Leonard also told Landis that his business in California would not permit him to leave.

The game in question, between the Detroit Tigers and Cleveland Indians, was played on Thursday, September 25, 1919, and was won by the Tigers 9–5. The box score from the game is presented below.

CLEVELAND	AB	R	H	Outs	DETROIT	AB	R	H	Outs
Graney lF	5	1	3	1	Bush SS	5	2	3	2
Lunte SS	4	1	1	2	Young 2B	4	0	2	4
Speaker CF	5	2	3	6	Cobb CF	4	0	2	4
Harris 1B	5	0	3	11	Veach lF	5	2	1	1
Gardner 3B	3	0	0	0	Heilmann 1B	4	1	3	8
Wambsganss 2B	3	0	1	2	Shorten RF	4	1	2	2
Smith RF	4	0	1	0	Jones 2B	4	0	2	3
O'Neil C	3	1	2	2	Ainsmith C	3	2	2	1
Meyers P	4	0	1	0	Boland P	2	1	1	2
Totals	36	5	15	24	Totals	35	9	18	27

	1	2	3	4	5	6	7	8	9	R
Cleveland	0	0	2	0	1	1	1	0	0	5
Detroit	2	2	0	0	2	1	0	2	x	9

Errors—Cleveland 3 (Lunte 2, Harris) Detroit none.
Two base hits; Harris, Heilman, Graney; three base hits, Speaker 2; Boland,
Struck out Meyers 1, Sacrifice hits, Young, Ainsmith, Lunte, Boland, Gardner,
Stolen bases, Bush, Cobb 2, Bases on balls, off Boland 2, Double play. Bush, Young
and Heilman,
Left on bases, Detroit 5, Cleveland 3, Wild pitch Boland, Time 1:56, umpires Nallis
and Owens.

The amount of money involved in the betting scandal was actually
$600 bet by Dutch Leonard and $420 by Smoky Joe Wood on the Tigers to
win. According to Commissioner Landis, during the hearing on the matter
there was nothing in the testimony to indicate that either Cobb or Speaker
had actually bet on the game, but he indicated that both Cobb and Speaker
had knowledge of the bets being placed. That would corroborate Dutch
Leonard's allegation that prior to the game Cobb had actually planned to
bet $2,000, Leonard $1,500 and Wood and Speaker $1,000 each.

On November 27, 1926, Commissioner Landis convened a hearing into
the matter at his Chicago offices. Subsequently, Cobb, Speaker, Leonard and
Wood were called to testify. Smoky Joe Wood pitched for the Boston Red
Sox from 1908–1915 and for the Cleveland Indians in 1917 and from 1919–1920.
His career record was 116–57. However, in 1912 he had a record of 34–5. At
the hearing, Judge Landis asked Joe Wood to tell him about the bet. "The
day before the game," Wood answered, "Leonard came to me and said that
Boland was going to pitch against us and that in baseball the last few games
of the season, with nothing at stake with a ball club, it eases up. He asked
me if I wanted to go in on a bet. I told him I did not care to put up as much
money as the $2,500 he suggested, but a friend of mine from Cleveland said

he was willing to take a third of it. The day before the game he told me West [Cobb's go-between] would be at the hotel. West came up the next morning and said the best he could get was 10–7. Detroit was the favorite. We decided to lay the money. In a little while, West came back to the hotel and said all he could get was $600 against $420, but that he could get more up at five to two. We talked that over and decided not to bet at these odds."[11]

Wood denied in his testimony before Landis that he had any conversation with Cobb at the ballpark on September 24 or 25 about betting on the game. He also denied that he ever had a conversation with Speaker about betting on the game in question. However, Wood did state that he spoke to Cobb following the game on September 25 and that Cobb asked him, "How much money did you bet on this game today?"[12] "I asked him why?"[13] Cobb answered, "Leonard asked."[14] Wood then testified that, thinking it was none of Cobb's business, he gave him a superficial answer as to the actual amount he had wagered on the game.

Ty Cobb, in his testimony before Landis on the matter, asserted that he had never bet a cent on an American League baseball game. While he admitted that his letter to Leonard made references to a betting proposal, Cobb categorically denied that he was part of a plot to fix the game between Cleveland and Detroit on September 25, 1919. However, he also stated that the reference in his letter to a bet was in his opinion a legitimate wager not unlike those commonly entered into by baseball players. Furthermore, he stated that besides his own ethics of not betting on games in his own league, it was a common occurrence for players to bet on their own teams and that he sometimes had knowledge of such bets, just as he had knowledge of team owners betting on horse races or on baseball games.

It was reported that Cobb told Landis with a quiver in his voice, "I have been in baseball for twenty-two years. I have played the game as hard and square and clean as any man did. All I thought of was to win every year, every month, every day, every hour. My conscience is clear. I will rest my case with the American fans and will match my record in baseball against that of anybody connected with the game."

"Leonard got $20,000 for those two letters, I understand from the American League officials. I think, too, that he tried to sell them to the newspapers on the Pacific Coast. If Leonard had anything on me, do you think that I would have released him in 1925? I always was friendly with him, but I had to let him go for the good of the club. If I had feared anything or had anything to fear, is it reasonable that I should gain his ill will by getting waivers on him?"[15]

Cobb admitted that he did indeed write the letter that Leonard had turned over to American League officials and that he knew about the bet on the game when Leonard came to him and asked for someone that they could trust to place the bet. Cobb admitted that he recommended West for the job. Landis then questioned Cobb on his knowledge of the bet that was placed on the game.

LANDIS: When did you hear that a bet was to be put on the game?

COBB: Leonard came to me and wanted to know who would be a man they could trust. I pointed out West.

LANDIS: What did you understand Leonard to mean?

COBB: I figured that he wanted to bet on the game.

LANDIS: Have you had any conversation with him before about betting on ballgames?

COBB: No sir.

LANDIS: Did you have any conversation with Wood about this bet?

COBB: I did not have any conversation with Wood about this bet. Not until I asked him about the amount of money that was bet.

LANDIS: Did you have any conversation with Speaker about the game?

COBB: None whatever.

LANDIS: Did you bet on the game?

COBB: Positively did not.

LANDIS: Did you have any conversation with anybody about your betting on the game?

COBB: I did not.[16]

Judge Landis then asked Cobb to explain his letter to Leonard.

Subsequently Cobb stated, "It is apparent that in a way, I tried to veil the betting end of it as a business proposition. I wanted to convey information he had asked for. I stated to him just what Wood had told me. The amount of $2,000 to $1,400 quoted was entirely different to the information Wood conveyed to Leonard in his letter, which would indicate that I was not in on the betting proposition, and that Wood merely put me off by giving me the wrong information and a factious amount. In the letter I state the information given to me by Wood was that there was no money bet. If I was in on the proposition, Wood certainly would have given me the true information. I was merely giving Leonard the information that Wood had given me. That information was that Wood had not got up a cent. It was 2 o'clock and the other side refused to deal with him."[17]

Landis concluded Cobb's testimony by asking him what he had meant in his letter about the phrase, "We completely fell down?"

Cobb responded, "That is just in keeping with the veiled manner in which I tried to give Leonard the information he had asked for."[18]

The following are transcripts of the letters provided to the American League office by Hubert B. [Dutch] Leonard that were made public by the commissioner of baseball, Judge Landis, following his inquiry into the matter.

Smoky Joe Wood's letter to Dutch Leonard:

Cleveland, Ohio, Friday
Dear Friend Dutch:
Enclosed please find certified check for sixteen hundred and thirty dollars ($1,630.00).
The only bet West could get down was $600 against $420 (10–7). Cobb did not get up a cent. He told us that and I believed him. Could have put up some at 5 to 2 on Detroit, but did not as that would make us put up $1,000 to win $400.
We won $420. I gave West $30 leaving $300, or $130 for each of us. Would not have cashed your check at all, but West thought he could get it up to 10–7, and I was going to put it all up at those odds. We would have won $1,750 for the $2,500 if we could have placed it.
If we ever have another chance like this we will know enough to try to get down early.
Let me hear from you Dutch. With all good wishes to Mrs. Leonard and yourself, I am,
Joe Wood[19]

Ty Cobb's letter to Dutch Leonard:

Augusta, Ga., Oct. 23, 1919
Dear Dutch:
Well old boy, guess you are out in old California by this time and enjoying life.
I arrived home and found Mrs. Cobb only fair, but the baby girl was fine and at times Mrs. Cobb is very well, but I have been very busy getting acquainted with my family and have not tried to do any correspondence, hence my delay.
Wood and myself were considerably disappointed in our business proposition as we had $2,000 to put into it and the other side quoted us $1,400, and when we finally secured that much money it was about 2 o'clock and they refused to deal with us, as they had men in Chicago to take up the matter with and they had no time so we completely fell down and of course we felt badly over it.
Everything was open to Wood and he can tell you about when we get together. It was quite a responsibility and I don't care for it again, I can assure you.
Well I hope you found everything in fine shape at home and all your troubles will be little ones. I made this year's share of world's series in cotton since I came home and expect to make more.

I thought the White Sox should have won, but I am satisfied they were too over confident. Well, old scout, drop me a line when you can. We have had dandy fishing since I arrived home.

With kindest regards to Mrs. Leonard, I remain.

Sincerely,

Ty[20]

Tris Speaker testified before Landis that he had no knowledge of the betting scenario suggested by Leonard and did not participate in any under-the-grandstand talk about fixing the game. He also indicated that he had knowledge of Leonard attempting to implicate him through the aforementioned letter as far back as July. "Mr. Johnson [Ban Johnson, president of the American League] came to Cleveland and told me that Leonard had some such letter from Wood. He asked me if I knew anything about it and I said no. Then I asked Wood about it. I had never heard of it before."[21]

Speaker pointed out to Landis that he had used his regular lineup in the September 25, 1919, game and that he himself had gotten three hits, two of them triples in the game. Furthermore he pointed out that Cleveland was

Ty Cobb. (Photo File, Inc.)

in the game until the eighth inning, when Detroit scored two runs to take
a four-run lead. "If I had known anything about the game being fixed, or if
I had money placed on the game, I certainly would not have been out there
making that kind of record, and I would not have permitted Wood to have
remained out of the game."[22] Speaker later called Leonard a Judas and
pointed out to the press that he was not mentioned in either letter by Wood
or Cobb.

On January 27, 1927, commissioner Judge Kenesaw Mountain Landis
cleared both Ty Cobb and Tris Speaker of all charges that would have made
them ineligible for participation in baseball. Consequently both Cobb and
Speaker were given permission to rescind their resignations and return to
the reserve lists of the Detroit Tigers and Cleveland Indians. In a press release
handed out by Leslie O'Connor, secretary to the commissioner, Landis
stated: "This is the Cobb-Speaker case, these players have not been found
guilty of fixing a ballgame. By no decent system of justice could such finding
be made. Therefore, they were not placed on the ineligible list. As they
desire to rescind their withdrawal from baseball, the releases which the
Detroit and Cleveland clubs granted at their requests in the circumstances
detailed above are cancelled and these players' names are restored to the
reserve lists of those clubs."[23]

As for Dutch Leonard and Smoky Joe Wood, it made no difference if
Landis cleared them or not. Both were out of baseball and retired. Leonard
was waived out of the Pacific Coast League in 1925 and working on his ranch
in California, while Wood was the baseball coach at Yale University.

Perhaps Speaker was not guilty. The evidence is not very compelling
against him, and as he stated in his testimony to Landis, he was not mentioned in either letter to Dutch Leonard by Joe Wood or Ty Cobb. But for
Commissioner Landis to give Cobb a pass on the matter undermined his
own pious edict issued following the 1919 World Series that is posted in every
major league clubhouse until this very day.

"Regardless of the verdict of juries, no player that throws a ball game,
no player that entertains proposals or promises to throw a game, no player
that sits in a conference with a bunch a crooked players and gamblers where
the ways and means of throwing games are discussed, and does not promptly
tell his club about it, will ever play professional baseball."

One thing is for sure: Neither Cobb or Speaker was invited to rejoin
his former club following the ruling. The owner of the Detroit Tigers immediately sent out telegrams to the other American League owners offering
Cobb to any club that wanted to take him, thereby breaking a twenty-two-
year relationship between Cobb and the Tigers. He was signed for the 1927
season by Connie Mack and played the last two years of his career with the
Philadelphia Athletics. Speaker signed with the Washington Senators for the

1927 season and then joined Cobb with the Athletics for the last year of his career in 1928.

The disparity in the justice handed out in the Ty Cobb case in 1927 as opposed to the justice delivered in the Pete Rose case of 1989 by the commissioner's office is appalling. First of all if ever there was a smoking gun to implicate Cobb in knowing that a game was a possible fix and furthermore that he may have had a betting interest in the outcome, it is in his own handwriting in the letter he sent to Dutch Leonard on October 23, 1919. The question that this evidence raises when compared to the commissioner's investigation in 1988 and 1989 of whether or not Pete Rose bet on baseball is whether Cobb's letter to Leonard is any less incriminating evidence than the alleged betting sheets with Pete Rose's own handwriting on them displayed in Section IV of the Dowd Report.

The Cobb incident of 1919 becomes absolutely hideous as compared to the Rose affair when it is considered that Cobb testified in front of Commissioner Landis that he never bet on American League games, but it was common knowledge that sometimes players bet on their own teams and he sometimes was aware of it. How is this any different from the conclusion that was reached in the Dowd Report that "No evidence was discovered that Rose bet against the Cincinnati Reds?"[24] It is the assertion of Rose that he had never bet on baseball, period, American, National or whatever league. In his own words, he told a *Sports Illustrated* writer, "I'd be willing to bet you, if I were a betting man, that I never bet on baseball."

Tyrus Raymond Cobb stated in the investigation that he played every day, month, year and hour to win. Would anyone deny the fact that Peter Edward Rose ever played to any less degree of intensity in the record 3,562 games in his career? The evidence seems overwhelming that Fred West was the go-between in the scheme with the bookmakers and that he was recommended by Cobb. How is this relationship any different than the friendships that Rose had developed with bookmaker Ron Peters and house guest Tommy Gioiosa, both implicated as placing bets for Rose in Section III of the Dowd Report?

The most damaging of all of the evidence regarding Cobb's guilt or innocence in the investigation of the September 25, 1919, incident is contained in the letter sent by Joe Wood to Dutch Leonard in which Wood states that "we won $420" and that $30 was given to Fred West, leaving three shares of the winnings of $130 for himself (Wood), Leonard, and presumably the third party is Ty Cobb. It appears that there is probable cause to suspect that Cobb did conspire to bet on a game and possibly even fix a game. Nonetheless he is enshrined in Cooperstown and Rose is not. There is something wrong with that kind of unequal justice in the office of the commissioner of baseball.

It does not even seem necessary to go into the well-documented episodes of sociopathic behavior displayed by Cobb during his playing days: his constant and overt displays of racism, violence, tantrums, etc. Pete Rose may have topped Ty Cobb on the all-time hit list, but he will never be capable of topping Cobb in the area of repulsive, vile, disgusting, irresponsible, dysfunctional behavior. Cobb will always be baseball's king of wretched behavior. In fact, Cobb himself remarked to a journalist years after he hung his spikes up that if he had it all to do over again, he would have made a few more friends. When Ty Cobb died on July 17, 1961, there were exactly seven persons in attendance at his funeral.

In closing, on the Cobb-Speaker affair of 1919, one last question remains. If Judge Landis knew of the guilt of Cobb in this sordid affair and decided to sweep it under the rug in the best interest of baseball, that makes Landis himself a co-conspirator, and perhaps someone needs to rethink whether his plaque should continue to hang in the Hall of Fame as well.

Another interesting aspect of the investigation that Landis conducted in 1926 into the September 25, 1919, game-fixing affair is that during the testimony of Joe Wood, he indicated that the Washington Senators were a pack of notorious gamblers. Wood told Landis, "It was not exactly a practice, but it was not uncommon for ballplayers to bet on a game, even in the middle of the season. I recall one instance when the whole Washington team went broke; that is, they lost all the cash they had with them on a ballgame that I pitched and beat Walter Johnson. They won it back the next day, when Bob Groome beat our club."[25] Landis then asked Wood, "Who did they bet on?"[26] Wood replied, "On their own ball club."[27] Of course, this means that the immortal Walter Johnson not only bet on baseball, but also bet on his own team, and yet he still has his plaque hanging in Cooperstown with full honors while Major League Baseball looks the other way and continues to admonish Pete Rose for allegedly doing the same thing. Such hypocrisy.

What's even more shocking than the revelation that "The Big Train" was plunking down cash on baseball games is the nonchalant reaction of Washington Senators club president Clark Griffith to betting on his team. "There was no great crime for the Washington players to bet on their own victory in a 1925 game with the Boston Red Sox,"[28] said Griffith. However, Griffith went on to say in an ambiguous statement that he did not sanction betting on baseball games. The 1925 Washington Senators won the American League pennant, then lost the World Series to the Pittsburgh Pirates four games to three. However, it can be implied that there is a huge taint on that pennant victory when applying the standards that Bud Selig is using to refuse Pete Rose reinstatement to baseball. Included on the roster of the 1925 Washington Senators were five future members of the National Baseball Hall of Fame: Walter Johnson, Stan Coveleski, Goose Goslin, Bucky Harris and Sam Rice, and apparently all five bet on baseball games and bet on their own team.

Of course, betting on baseball is as old as the game itself. Even the immortal Hall of Fame member manager John McGraw admitted to betting on his pennant-winning 1904 New York Giants. So Pete Rose was hardly the first manager in major league baseball history to have bet on his own team.

Between the investigation of the Cobb-Speaker affair in late 1926 and the subsequent ruling on the matter by Judge Landis on January 27, 1927, another scandal had to be investigated by the commissioner as well that became known as the "Risberg Series." Swede Risberg, the former Chicago White Sox shortstop banished from baseball for life by Judge Landis following his alleged evolvement with a conspiracy to throw the 1919 World Series, suddenly reappeared, and on the afternoon of January 1, 1927, in a meeting with Landis, made an accusation that in 1917 the White Sox had bought a four-game series with the Detroit Tigers near the end of the season to guarantee the team the 1917 American League pennant. Immediately Landis launched an investigation, and Risberg, unlike the cowardly Dutch Leonard, was not afraid of being bumped off in the Windy City and came to Chicago to tell his account of the chicanery on the diamond.

On January 5, 1927, Landis summoned nearly the entire 1917 roster of the Chicago White Sox and key players from the Detroit roster to his office in Chicago for a hearing on the matter. At 1:45 PM Swede Risberg arrived and took a seat at the left side of Landis's desk. With Ty Cobb, Ray Schalk, Eddie Collins, Howard Ehmke, Oscar Stanage, George Dauss, Donie Bush, Clarence "Pants" Rowland, Bennie Dyer and others all cramped into the commissioner's office and scowling at Risberg, he looked cool, confident and collected as he became the first witness to testify on the matter. Below is a partial text of Risberg's testimony.

Judge Landis began. "Mr. Risberg, you made a statement here New Year's afternoon. Will you repeat that statement?"[28]

Risberg, smoking a cigarette and blowing the smoke Landis's direction, replied without hesitation. "In 1917 we were playing Detroit, September 2, and I was informed by Mr. Clarence Rowland [manager of the White Sox] that everything was all fixed and we won four games from Detroit. About two weeks later, in the Ansonia hotel, Chick Gandil [White Sox first baseman] and I collected $45 apiece from the boys for the Detroit team. Rowland gave us permission to go to Philadelphia, and there we gave the money we had collected to Bill James [Detroit pitcher]. James said he would give Howard [meaning Ehmke, Detroit pitcher] his share."[30]

LANDIS: What was the first thing you heard about this?

RISBERG: We were down in the dugout the morning of the first game and Rowland said to me: "Everything is all fixed."

LANDIS: Nothing was said at that time about money, was there?

RISBERG: No, there wasn't.

LANDIS: Can you tell me how the talk about money started?

RISBERG: No, I can't.

LANDIS: Who collected the money besides you?

RISBERG: Chick Gandil.

LANDIS: During the first game, did anybody say anything to you about sloughing a game?

RISBERG: No. The only thing I remember was that in the afternoon game, Eddie Collins said, when Bennie Dyer, Detroit shortstop, booted a ball: "That's terrible."

LANDIS: Did it look like Stanage [Detroit catcher] was not trying to cut the base runners off?

RISBERG: It seemed like they were getting an awful lead before Oscar [Stanage] let the ball go.

LANDIS: Do you remember anything peculiar about the two games next day?

RISBERG: No, except the that the pitchers were not putting much on the ball.

LANDIS: Ehmke and James pitched the first game and Boland and James pitched the second game. Don't you recall something about their work?

RISBERG: No, I don't remember. I thought when I was up to bat that the pitchers were pretty easy to hit.[31]

Judge Landis then turned the focus of his questioning of Risberg to whether he could remember anything in particular that would suggest that the Detroit players had not played any of the four games in question in good faith. Risberg replied that he didn't remember any. Landis also asked Risberg if he could remember any talk among the White Sox players after the games about fixing them. Once again Risberg could not recall any such dialogue. Furthermore Risberg could not recall who began the talk about raising the pool for the Detroit players.

RISBERG: All I know was I gave my $45 and collected the money from Fred McMullin and some others.

LANDIS: Did you have anything in your mind about why Detroit gave you those four ballgames?

RISBERG: I don't recall any reason. I was a youngster then, my first year in the major leagues.

LANDIS: Aside from Rowland's remark about "everything's fixed" and Collins's remark "that's terrible," do you remember anything about that series?

RISBERG: No, I don't.

LANDIS: Who first spoke of the collection?

RISBERG: It was Chick Gandil. Gandil's talk with Bill James made the thing clear to me. I was with Gandil when he collected the $45 from Eddie Collins, and Gandil said: "Eddie, we want that $45 for the that pool," and Collins gave Gandil the money with the statement that he would never do it again.

LANDIS: What was that remark Rowland made to you in 1920?

RISBERG: Don't let that 1917 thing out. That was when I was in a scandal myself [the 1919 World Series], and I understood him to mean that I shouldn't tell about that sloughed series.

LANDIS: What was that you told me about those 1919 games?

RISBERG: We paid back Detroit two games. I know I played out of position and Jackson [Shoeless Joe], Gandil and Felsch [Happy] also played out of position.

LANDIS: But you had already paid Detroit in money?

RISBERG: Well, we figured we owed them some games.

LANDIS: What was that Donie Bush talk you had in 1920?

RISBERG: We were in a saloon across from the Sox park and Bush said to me, "I guess the 1917 stuff will be coming out soon."[32]

Landis finished with the questioning of Risberg, turned to the assembled players in his office that were cramped around his desk, and categorically called the roll: Cobb, Stanage, Schalk, Collins, Bush Ehmke, Faber, Rowland and others and asked if any of them wished to question Risberg. All of them declined.

Then, one by one, Judge Landis called the other players up to testify. The first was Clarence "Pants" Rowland, who was in 1917 the manager of the White Sox, but now in 1927 was an American League umpire. Rowland called Risberg's testimony a "damned lie."[33] He denied that he ever told Risberg that any games with Detroit in 1917 were fixed and that it was Gandil who asked him if it would be all right to go to Philadelphia. Furthermore, Rowland

stated that he did not see anything wrong in those games with Detroit and
that the White Sox were two games ahead at that time in the standings with
twenty games to go in the season.

Eddie Collins was called and questioned by Landis. He wanted to know
when Collins had first heard about the pool that was raised for the Detroit
players. Collins stated, "It wasn't at the Ansonia Hotel [New York City],
because I always stayed at my parents' home in Tarrytown [New York]. The
first I heard about any pool was after the season was over and we had come
back to Chicago. Gandil asked me for $45 and I didn't give it to him until I
was satisfied about the pool being actually raised. I asked some of the boys
if they had given their money and they said they had. So after the world's
series was over, October 15, I cashed a check for $100 at the Ansonia Hotel
and gave $45 to Gandil."[34] Collins then rose abruptly from his chair with
veins sticking out on his neck and handed the check stubs to Landis. Trem-
bling as he spoke, he stated, "If anybody says I gave any money to Gandil
at any other time, he is a damned liar."[35] Landis examined the checkbook
and was satisfied that the date was October 16, 1917, and not September as
Risberg had stated. The amount was for $100, with the notation "Gandil $45."

Donie Bush, a Detroit shortstop in 1917 and now in 1927 the new manager of the Pittsburgh Pirates, was next to take the stand. Bush testified that
he did meet Risberg in a saloon in 1920, but never made any such statement
about the 1917 stuff coming out soon. "The first I heard about it was when
the 1919 affair came out in 1920. There was some talk then about the 1917
bonus. All I know was that the games [1917] went along the same as any others. As far as I know, they were on the square. I heard no talk about those
four games being sloughed."[36]

Ty Cobb was the next player to take the witness chair and went off in
pious diatribe about his virtue and honesty as Landis asked him what he
knew about the 1917 incident. The Georgia Peach told Landis, "There never
has been a baseball game in my life that I played in that I knew was fixed. I
remember several years ago, some of our boys were called up to your office
or President Johnson's office [Ban Johnson, president of the American
League] on an investigation about some money they had received, but I
didn't know just what it was about. The first I heard about any sloughed
games was right here. I've played about 3,000 ball games in my life, and I
only remember a very few of them. I can't remember about that series. If
I heard anything about those games being sloughed, I would have looked
for things, but I never heard anything of the kind and so I don't remember
anything about them."[37]

Cobb seemed agitated, and his face became bright red as Landis pressed
him for more detail and asked him to reconsider his amnesia on the incident. When Landis questioned Cobb about a Detroit newspaper interview

where he was quoted as saying that the St. Louis Browns were going to give a series to Detroit in 1923 because those dam Indians [Cleveland] had ridden us all season, Cobb clashed with Landis and denied that he had ever said such a thing and asked Landis if he wanted him to swear on his answer.

One by one the players took the witness chair: Ray Schalk, George Dauss, Oscar Stanage, Howard Ehmke, Bennie Dyer, Harry Heilmann, Eddie Murphy, Ed (Big Ed) Walsh, John Collins, Bernie Boland, Albert E. Reb Russell, George Burns, Ted Jourdan, Harry (Nemo) Liebold, Bob Veach, Joe Benz, Dave Danforth, Kid Gleason (coach on the White Sox in 1917), and even Dickie Kerr, who was not even on the White Sox roster in 1917, testified. All the witnesses followed suit that Swede Risberg's assertion that the games were fixed was an absolute lie; however, none denied that a pool of money collected from the White Sox for the Tigers players had existed. Risberg was vilified, called a pig, a liar, and even worse to the extent that at one point Landis had to remind the assembled witnesses to not use dugout language in his office.

Urban (Red) Faber was still pitching for the White Sox and about to begin his 13th year with the club in 1927. He told Landis that he didn't notice any sloughing in the "Risberg" series and pointed out that he was knocked out of the box in both games. Then Landis questioned Faber about the pool of money collected for the Detroit players. Faber responded, "In New York, during the last of the season [1917], there was some talk of making Detroit pitchers a present for beating Boston. I wrote out a check for $500 to Chick Gandil as my share and the shares of some of the other fellows. I got the money back from the other fellows, all except the money for my own share, which I thought was $50 instead of $45. I thought that the money was for Detroit pitchers for beating Boston. I never heard anything about Detroit sloughing a series to us. That collection was first mentioned to me in Philadelphia. I don't remember who first spoke to me about it."[38]

Even Buck Weaver, the talented White Sox third baseman banned for life from baseball by Judge Landis as one of the eight alleged conspirators to fix the 1919 World Series, appeared and testified. Weaver stated that he was not with the team when the "Risberg" series was played in early September 1917 because he was away from the team with a broken finger. However, he stated, "Gandil and Risberg asked me to give $45 for the Detroit club, and I refused. I said I wouldn't give any money."[39]

Then as Weaver rose from the witness chair, he turned to Landis and said, "Judge, I don't feel that I owe baseball anything, but baseball owes me something. I ask you now for reinstatement."[40] Landis replied, "Drop me a line about that, Buck, and I'll take the matter up."[41] Weaver was still writing letters to the commissioner's office asking for reinstatement almost until the day he died on January 31, 1956. Justice and fairness for Buck Weaver, like Pete Rose, has never come about yet.

The testimony took more than five hours and continued for two more days. Not much came out of it other than that indeed a pool had existed. The testimony produced little more than circumstantial evidence of any fix in the games as alleged by Risberg. The Chicago players' position was that the money raised was a reward to the Detroit pitchers for beating Boston the runners-up in the 1917 pennant race in a previous three-game series, not a bribe to lie down in the early September 1917 series. No one was ever disciplined by Landis in the matter, and it was dropped. Nonetheless, this was a scandal of enormous proportions, with no less than 50 players involved, of which 10 percent were future Hall of Fame members: Ty Cobb, Eddie Collins, Urban (Red) Faber, Harry Heilmann and Ray Schalk. While the check register of Eddie Collins shows that the amount given by him to Chick Gandil was after the fact, the question remains as to whether or not Collins had prior knowledge of the purpose of the money being raised by Gandil.

The relevance of the "Risberg series" to the Pete Rose situation is that the circumstantial evidence in the allegation by the commissioner's office that Rose bet on baseball is similar to the allegation made by Risberg that the September 1917 series with Tigers was fixed. In fact, the allegations of Swede Risberg, when compared to the testimony in the Dowd Report of such characters as Tommy Gioiosa, Ron Peters and Paul Janszen, take on a similar questionable tone as to the reliability of charges made. The Dowd Report states that evidence collected shows that Rose placed bets through a friend, Michael Bertolini, who in turn placed bets on his behalf with an unidentified bookmaker in New York City. The Dowd Report cites as a sort of exhibit A a 1988 tape recording of a conversation between Michael Bertolini and another Rose associate, Paul Janszen. It is alleged that in these conversations Bertolini mentions to Janszen that Rose has incurred a substantial amount of debt with him and the unidentified New York bookmaker (supposedly identified as Val) and that Rose had given Bertolini personal checks that he subsequently cashed and then sent the money to the alleged New York bookmaker. The report further states that Rose's financial records reveal checks made out in the amounts stated by Bertolini to fictitious payees. However, Rose denied placing any bets with Bertolini and denied owing anyone money. Nonetheless, Rose did acknowledge sending eleven $8,000 checks to Bertolini made out to fictitious payees, but stated that these checks were loans to Bertolini to be used as payments to various athletes for baseball card shows.

To critique or raise a point-by-point argument with the Dowd Report is a long and arduous project and would require that one dedicate a book-length work to the task. Nonetheless, there are many points in the report that are arguable on behalf of Rose. For example, in Section III, Results of the Investigation, A: The Rose-Gioiosa-Peters Betting—1985 and 1986, it states that

Tommy Gioiosa usually placed the bets for Rose. However, during the period of 1985–1986 on at least four to six occasions, Rose had contacted Peters directly to place his bets. Furthermore, it states that on one of those occasions, in 1985 or 1986, Rose called Peters to place bets on baseball, including the Cincinnati Reds. Peters recorded the conversation and then played the tape back to Rose. The report states that Rose became upset and asked Peters whey he had taped him. Peters explained to Rose that he wanted an insurance policy to make sure that he would pay his gambling losses. The report then states that the tape in question cannot be located. This is clearly more uncorroborated evidence that is very similar to Swede Risberg stating to Judge Landis that White Sox manager Clarence "Pants" Rowland came to him and stated that the series with Detroit was all fixed.

Tommy Gioiosa doesn't seem to have his story together even 14 years later. In 2001, Gioiosa was interviewed for over 100 hours by Buzz Bissinger for a *Vanity Fair* magazine article published in September 2001. In the article, Gioiosa states that on January 16, 1987, he and Rose spent their last social occasion together at Turfway Racetrack in Florence, Kentucky. That night Rose, Paul Janzsen and others had purchased a Pik-Six ticket. Gioiosa had arrived late and Rose wanted to cut him out of a share of the ticket. According to Janzsen, you could feel a lot of tension between Rose and Gioiosa, and it is believed that Rose was replacing him with Janzsen as his primary gambling gofer. Nonetheless Janzsen agreed to sell Gioiosa a share of his portion of the ticket. As luck would have it, Rose and the other bettors in his group picked the winning horse in six consecutive races, and the Pik-Six ticket paid $47,646. Rose asked Gioiosa to cash the ticket, and Rose divided up the winning shares. Two years later, Gioiosa was indicted by the IRS for filing a false tax return that included winnings on the Pik-Six ticket.

But the point here is not the Pik-Six ticket but rather how credible a witness Tommy Gioiosa is when it comes to answering the question of whether or not Pete Rose bet on baseball. In the same *Vanity Fair* article, it states that Gioiosa fixed Rose up with an Ohio bookie by the name of Ron Peters, who could handle larger bets, as much as $2,000 a game. "At first, as before, the bets Gioiosa placed with Peters were on basketball and football. But at a certain point, Gioiosa says, Rose began to bet on baseball, on several occasions doing it directly from his phone in the clubhouse office as Gioiosa listened."[42]

However, the Dowd Report makes no reference to Tommy Gioiosa being in the Reds' clubhouse listening to any conversations that Rose was alleged to be having with gamblers. The Dowd Report lists conversations that Rose is alleged to have had with gamblers regarding betting on baseball on April 9, 10, 11, 12. Other calls on April 13 and 14 do not directly indicate that Rose was the caller or recipient of the call in question. However, the report does state that on April 10, 1987, according to phone records, Paul Janzsen called Rose in the Reds' clubhouse and that the call lasted for five minutes. Rose allegedly won $2,000 on the Reds that evening and lost $2,800 on Texas, won $2,000 on Minnesota and lost $3,200 on Philadelphia. Regardless of the allegations in the Dowd Report referring to this gambling activity, the burning question is how could Tony Gioiosa be present in the clubhouse and hear Rose's conversation if in his own words the last time he had contact with Pete Rose was at Turfway Park on January 19, 1987, nearly three months previous?

The Dowd Report states that "Pete Rose had denied under oath ever betting on Major League Baseball or associating with anyone who bet on Major League Baseball."[43] Is his statement any less credible than the testimony of fifty or so witnesses, including five players who would eventually be elected to the National Baseball Hall of Fame, Ty Cobb, Eddie Collins, Urban (Red) Faber, Harry Heilmann and Ray Schalk, who all told the commissioner of baseball, Judge Kenesaw Mountain Landis, on January 6, 1927, that a pool of money raised by the players on the Chicago White Sox for the players on the Detroit Tigers was not a bribe, but a gift?

To consider the case for or against the reinstatement of Pete Rose to baseball and his subsequent eligibility for the Hall of Fame, it is prudent to examine the huge skeleton that falls out of the Major League Baseball closet when the name Leo Durocher comes up. Leo Ernest (The Lip) Durocher, the man who coined the phrase "nice guys finish last," was elected posthumously to the National Baseball Hall of Fame in 1994 by the Committee on Baseball Veterans, and a lot baseball fans, writers and historians are still wondering why. As a player, Durocher played 17 years in the big leagues with the New York Yankees (1925–29), Cincinnati Reds (1930–33), St. Louis Cardinals (1933–1937) and Brooklyn Dodgers (1938–1945). He wound up his career with 1,320 hits, 24 home runs and a lifetime batting average of .247, hardly Hall of Fame statistics. However, Durocher was perhaps elected to the Hall of Fame by a sympathetic group of aging writers who felt that his 2,008 career wins as a manager, seventh on the all-time list, outweighed his marginal statistics as a player and lack of character as person.

Leo Durocher's character was in question almost immediately upon his arrival in the big leagues. A story circulating since 1925 is that Durocher, as a rookie with the New York Yankees, was accused of running afoul of the great Babe Ruth. Apparently, on a Yankees road trip, the "Bambino" entered the hotel lobby late one evening loaded to the gills from carousing during one his infamous nights out on the town. The Babe saw Durocher sitting in the lobby and asked him for assistance in getting to his room. Durocher acquiesced. The next morning, Ruth was steaming mad as he accused Durocher of stealing his watch in the process of assisting him to his room.

Durocher was a fast-talking, nattily dressed free spirit who loved walking on the wild side of life. When the Yankees sent him to Cincinnati on waivers in 1930, he found the city's pool halls and the gambling dens of Northern Kentucky just across the Ohio River very accommodating to his lifestyle. Happy Chandler stated he first met Durocher when he was playing for the Reds. "When Leo was a player in Cincinnati, Leo would get all spiffed up, dressed to kill, spending all his money, while his mother was working at the Netherlands Plaza Hotel scrubbing floors."[44] Durocher was traded to St. Louis in 1933 and then Brooklyn in 1937, but his flamboyant and reckless ways followed him.

By 1939, Durocher was the player-manager of the Dodgers, and when Branch Rickey arrived in Brooklyn to become general manager in 1943, baseball commissioner Judge Kenesaw Mountain Landis issued an order to Rickey: "You must break up that nest of horseplayers and card sharks."[45] It had long been a source of irritation to Landis that Durocher freely associated with gamblers, bookmakers, racing handicappers, ticket scalpers and even notorious organized crime figures. Some of these unsavory characters even had access to the Dodgers' clubhouse and dugout. It was also known that three bookmakers had even sued Durocher for uncollected horse racing debts.

By 1947 Judge Landis had been replaced as commissioner of baseball by A. B. (Happy) Chandler, a former Kentucky politician and U.S. Senator. Consequently, Durocher wound up in hot water. Durocher had become friends with movie actor George Raft. Raft usually played gangster roles in the movies, but was also known to hang out with some of the real-life types that he portrayed on film. An incident connecting Raft to Durocher took place in 1945 and came under public scrutiny in the fall of 1946. While the Dodgers were at spring training in 1945, Durocher had allowed Raft to stay in his midtown Manhattan apartment. Raft apparently organized a craps game in the apartment, and a mark by the name of Martin Shurin wound up accusing Raft of bilking him out of $12,500 in the game by using loaded dice. Seven months following the incident, Shurin went to the New York City District Attorney's office and filed a complaint. In October 1946, New York columnist Westbrook Pegler wrote about the crooked dice game that took place in Durocher's apartment and laid out the details, according to Shurin, of how he was cheated by Raft. Raft called Shurin's account of the game false, and later Shurin was arrested for passing bad checks. But in the aftermath of the event, a cloud of suspicion hung over Leo Durocher. Branch Rickey ordered Durocher never again to allow Raft to use his apartment.

In November 1946, Commissioner Chandler held a meeting with Durocher at the Claremont Country Club in Berkley, California, and ordered Durocher to move out of George Raft's Coldwater Canyon home. He also asked Durocher if he knew anyone by the name of Bugsy Siegel or Joe

Addonis. Durocher admitted that he had been a casual acquaintance of both men, who were known mobsters. Consequently, Chandler ordered Leo to immediately disassociate himself from Siegel and Addonis. Bugsy Siegel had grown up in New York City and was the boyhood friend of such notorious organized crime figures as mafia boss Lucky Luciano and mob financial wizard Meyer Lansky. It was Luciano who sent Siegel to California to expand the New York syndicate's crime empire, and eventually Siegel, using his mob muscle and money, moved operations into Las Vegas, Nevada, where he built the Flamingo Hotel and Casino, which opened in December 1946. However, Siegel was suspected of skimming from the Flamingo by his mob bosses and killed, gangland style, in Beverly Hills in June, 1947.

While Durocher attempted to disassociate himself from high-profile gangsters and gamblers, his next act of outrage was to covet his neighbor's wife. In December 1946, Ray Hendricks, who was married to actress Larain Day, accused Durocher of stealing his wife. Against the orders of a California judge, who ordered Durocher and Larain Day to live apart for one year, the couple flew to Juarez, Mexico and were married. This little act of wife-stealing didn't sit well back in Brooklyn with the 50,000-strong Catholic Youth Organization (CYO), which in February 1947 condemned Durocher's act as immoral and threatened to switch their allegiance to the New York Yankees, or worse yet, the Giants.

Then came spring training in 1947, and Leo Durocher imploded. Larry MacPhail was general manager of the Dodgers in 1939 when he named Leo Durocher manager. The relationship between MacPhail and Durocher was volatile until the day MacPhail resigned on September 24, 1942, and Branch Rickey took over the following season. By 1947, MacPhail was back in New York as general manager of the Yankees. Charlie Dressen, also a known gambler, had been Leo Durocher's right-hand man as a coach on the Dodgers, and in 1947, MacPhail induced him to come over to the Yankees. Durocher was beside himself, and when Dodgers were playing an exhibition game against the Yankees in Havana, Cuba in the spring of 1947, Durocher, who had been warned by Happy Chandler the previous fall about the company he kept, became incensed when he saw one of his former gambling cronies by the name of Memphis Engleberg, a well-known bookie, sitting with MacPhail in his box during the game. During the game, Durocher was fuming as he pointed out to sports columnist Dick Young what he saw as a double standard. The next day, when Engelberg was again seated in MacPhail's box, Durocher, through ghost writer Harold Parrot, the Dodgers' road secretary, wrote a derogatory column in the *Brooklyn Eagle* about the event. Consequently, on March 16, 1947 Larry MacPhail filed formal charges defamation against both Durocher and Branch Rickey. In the statement, MacPhail said, "I know Memphis Engleberg, and to my knowledge he never bets on baseball games. He wasn't my guest, but I wouldn't bar him from Yankee Stadium. I go to the races and do not forbid my players from going. Incidentally, Memphis often visits the Dodger clubhouse as a personal friend of Durocher's."[46]

With McPhail's assertion that Leo Durocher had permitted Memphis Engleberg to visit the Dodgers' clubhouse, the roof blew off. If this was true, then Leo was clearly in violation of the order given to him by Commissioner Chandler to disassociate himself from persons detrimental to the integrity of baseball. Consequently, Commissioner Chandler launched an investigation and set a date for a hearing on the matter, to be held March 24 in Sarasota, Florida, and sent out considerable number of summonses.

The hearing began at 2 PM on March 24, and the press was barred from the proceedings as Commissioner Chandler attempted to sort out who said something insulting to whom. Larry MacPhail was on hand to tell his side of the story, and Leo Durocher left his new movie actress bride, Laraine Day, in a nearby motel and testified in front of Chandler for 45 minutes. Durocher was followed by his former Brooklyn associate Chuck Dressen, then Harold Parrott, the Dodgers' road secretary, then Augie Galan, who played for Brooklyn in the 1946 season and over the winter had been traded to Cincinnati. The hearing dragged on for five hours as Chandler attempted to sort out the facts in who said something insulting to Larry MacPhail. However, Chandler decided to continue the hearing after Branch Rickey was unable to attend. Rickey had failed to appear due to the death of his wife's brother John Moulton back in Ohio. On March 28, amid steep growing boredom over the whole matter, Branch Rickey appeared before Chandler and testified. Now everyone was hoping for a quick resolution to the matter by Chandler so that the decks would be cleared for opening day.

Also there was growing anxiety among the baseball owners that a prolonged hearing could have a negative effect on the gate receipts in the wake of an NFL scandal that was now being adjudicated. On December 15, 1946 Alvin J. Paris, David (Pete) Krakauer and Jerome Zarowitz had attempted to bribe two professional football players, Merle Hapes and Frank Filchock of the New York Giants, into throwing the NFL championship game with the Chicago Bears. The Bears won the game 24–14, and Paris turned state's witness against the other two involved in the plot and was convicted in January and sentenced to a year in jail on April 7. Krakuaer and Zarowitz were convicted and sentenced to five to ten years in jail. Hapes and Filchock, who played in the Giants' backfield, were suspended indefinitely from playing professional football by NFL commissioner Bert Bell.

Finally on April 9, 1947 Commissioner A. B. "Happy" Chandler issued his ruling in the MacPhail investigation. In an unprecedented action, Chandler suspended Leo Durocher for the 1947 season. In a statement issued from his office in Cincinnati to the press, Chandler said, "The incident in

Havana, which brought considerable unfavorable comment to baseball generally, was one of a series of publicity-producing affairs in which Manager Durocher has been involved in the last few months. Managers of baseball teams are responsible for the conduct of players on the field. Good managers are able to insure the good conduct of the players on the field and frequently by their example can influence players to be of good conduct off the field. Durocher has not measured up to the standards expected or required of managers of our baseball teams. As a result of the accumulated unpleasant incidents in which he has been involved, which the commissioner construes as detrimental to baseball, Manager Durocher is hereby suspended form participating in professional baseball for the 1947 season."[47]

Also Chandler suspended Chuck Dressen, now a Yankees coach, for 30 days beginning April 15 and fined Harold Parrott, traveling secretary of the Dodgers, $500 for writing a deliberately derogatory newspaper article about persons in baseball and violating his order to remain silent following the hearings. Lastly, both the New York Yankees and Brooklyn Dodgers clubs were fined $2,000 each. Furthermore, the commissioner stated that evidence produced at the hearing on the matter disproved the allegations of Durocher that the two gamblers seated in the box of MacPhail were guests of his. Chandler said that both Durocher and Rickey had admitted that they did indeed make statements accusing Larry MacPhail of sitting with gamblers in Havana. However, Rickey flatly denied that he had made any such comment that "apparently there are rules for Durocher and other rules for the rest of baseball."[48]

No one seemed to be overly traumatized by Durocher's suspension for the season. An article written by the NEA sports editor on April 12, 1947, summarized the feelings of most people. "Commissioner Chandler's office would be flooded with letters of protest if Dodger fans could write, but Brooklyn will not secede from the Union and the incredible Gowanus guys will forget Durocher the first time the Giants show up. Ebbets Field is now cleared of Hollywood characters and baseball is discussed in the clubhouse rather than subjects that provide choice bits for gossip columns. The Lip finally talked himself out of baseball and celebrated double-talkers have been taught to keep their big yaps shut. Now the ballplayers can play ball."[49]

At just about the same time that Durocher was suspended in April 1947, the Dodgers had purchased the contract of Jackie Robinson from the AAA Montreal Royals. In fact, when the news of the commissioner's ruling on Durocher was released, Leo had been in a meeting with Branch Rickey and Dodgers coaches Ray Blades, Clyde Sukeforth and Jake Pitler, along with the manager of the Montreal farm club, discussing the future status of Robinson. When the news of the suspension arrived in Rickey's office, Durocher buried his head in his hands and his eyes filled with tears. As a result of his suspension Durocher was not present with the Dodgers to witness the historic entry of the first African-American player on a major league roster. Clyde Sukeforth managed the Dodgers for one game; then Burt Shotton took over for the balance of the 1947 season. However, Durocher returned to manage Brooklyn for part of 1948 before being fired and moving over to manage the cross-town rival New York Giants through 1955. Durocher would later become a coach with the Los Angeles Dodgers and then manage the Chicago Cubs from 1966 through part of 1972, winding up his managerial career in Houston in late 1972 and 1973.

Leo Durocher's association with gamblers and mobsters is only part of his complex personality. This is the same person who abused his first wife and, along with an Ebbets Field security guard, was arrested in June 1945 for assaulting, with brass knuckles, a fan who had heckled him. Durocher's penchant for violence never seemed to cease; even at age 59 he was still slugging fans. While a coach with the 1964 Los Angeles Dodgers, Durocher was accused of punching a 29-year-old engineer in the jaw outside Dodger Stadium. The man was waiting in line to have a Dodger phonograph record signed. Durocher passed up the fans, got in his car and began to drive off. Then someone yelled, "Durocher, you're a jerk," and he backed the car up and demanded to know who had said that. When Robert Hallsworth said, "Maybe I did," Leo got out of the car and popped him![50]

For all of the alleged transgressions of Pete Rose, one thing is very clear: He was no Leo Durocher. To even attempt to put Rose's blighted associations with Ron Peters, Tommy Gioiosa and Paul Janzsen in the same category with Durocher's buddies, such as Bugsy Siegel, Joey Addonis and George Raft, is ludicrous. While Rose hung out with small-time Ohio gamblers and bookies, Durocher kept company with some of the most notorious organized crime figures and killers in American history. Siegel, for one, was connected with the New York mob infamously referred to as "Murder Inc."

Bob Feller, of course is one of Pete Rose's strongest critics. However, when asked how he felt about the sordid associations of Leo Durocher, Feller was somewhat patronizing and forgiving. "Leo was a good friend of mine; I was fond of him and his wife Larain. He didn't associate with the right people. A one-year suspension was enough."[51]

However, regardless of the many character flaws apparent in Leo Durocher, bigotry was not one of them. When the Dodgers purchased the contract of Jackie Robinson shortly before Durocher's suspension, a few of the Dodgers' players were indicating that they would take up a petition and refuse to play with a black man on the team. When Durocher was informed of the petition, started by Dixie Walker, he told the players circulating it in no uncertain terms where they could they shove it.

If Branch Rickey thought that a double standard of conduct existed in the baseball commissioner's office for Durocher, or Leo thought that himself, it's too bad that they didn't have the chance to see how Pete Rose has been treated. Bob Bonifay, former general manager of the Macon Peaches, said, "They [baseball] had it in for Rose years ago. He had been in the majors only a few years when there was a close play at first base and Pete had an argument with the first base umpire. He was not only thrown out of the game, but the president of the National League suspended him for ten days. Usually an argument like that was cause for a three-day suspension at most."[52] As a matter of fact Bonifay's assertion of a three day suspension is still pretty much the norm in baseball for getting thrown out of a game.

In 1988, Rose was managing the Reds when he got into a heated dispute with home plate umpire Dave Pallone and pushed him. The commissioner's office suspended Rose for 30 days for shoving Pallone. The issue could be raised as to whether the protracted suspension he received was for nothing more than just being Pete Rose. By contrast, consider the fact that in September 2002 there were two incidents of players shoving umpires in major league games in one week, and both received two-day suspensions. On September 15, San Francisco Giants catcher Benito Santiago received a two-day suspension for bumping umpire Mark Hirschbeck, and then later in the week, Kansas City's Brent Mayne was suspended for two games for making contact with umpire Jerry Crawford. Where's the equality of justice for Pete?

The Hall of Fame is not just littered with various gamblers hanging on the walls. When one peruses the Hall of Fame membership list, the number of inductees with abnormal and abhorrent behavior patterns in their pasts simply magnifies the injustice towards Rose. For example: The All-Hall of Fame Alcohol Abuser team reads like a Who's Who in baseball: Grover Cleveland Alexander, Waite Hoyt, Larry MacPhail, Mickey Mantle, Babe Ruth, Paul Waner, Lloyd Waner, Hack Wilson, and a few living members who will remain unnamed.

Mickey Mantle killed himself abusing alcohol. In an interview with *Sports Illustrated* in 1994, Mantle said, "I began some of my mornings the past 10 years with the 'breakfast of champions'—a big glass filled with a shot of brandy, some Kahlua and cream. Billy Martin and I used to drink them all the time, and I named the drink after us. When I was drinking, I thought I was funny—the life of the party. But, as it turned out, nobody could stand to be around me. After one or two drinks, I was real happy. After several, I could be downright nasty."[53]

Mantle's alcohol abuse took a toll on his career. In his retirement years, Mantle admitted to frequently playing games when he was hung over and pointed out in more than one interview that he never again had a decent season after the 1964 campaign, when he was just 33 years old. It is certainly a very sad circumstance when you consider what might have been for Mantle, a player so rich in talent. Notwithstanding the steroids controversy, Barry Bonds hit 73 home runs at the age of 37 and won a batting title at the age of 38. Likewise, Ted Williams won back-to-back batting titles at the age of 39 and 40. Even Pete Rose hit .331 at the age of 38. It simply begs the question: What would the possibilities in the record book have been for a sober Mickey Mantle?

In the name of fairness, it should be mentioned that at least one of the alcohol abusers mentioned above did clean up his act. That was Waite Hoyt, the former New York Yankees pitcher with the infamous 1920s "Murders Row" teams and good friend of notorious guzzler Babe Ruth. After coming to Cincinnati to become the Reds' radio broadcaster in the early 1940s, Hoyt brought his life long hard-drinking ways along with him. Consequently, in June 1945, he found himself face-down, passed out on a Cincinnati street, and was hospitalized for alcoholism. When Hoyt was discharged, he vowed to never touch alcohol again, joined Alcoholics Anonymous, and stayed sober until the day he died on August 25, 1984. Along the way, not only was he elected to the Hall of Fame in 1969 and broadcast Reds games for twenty-three years on the radio, but he also became a good friend of Pete Rose. Hoyt died too soon to witness the wealth of injustice that Major League Baseball has heaped upon Rose. However, it is fairly certain that had he lived, Hoyt would have been in the forefront of seeking fairness for Pete Rose.

Pete Rose was not a drinker. It is true, however, that Rose, like scores of other major leaguers, did take amphetamines commonly known as "greenies" in the 1960s when they were made available by the baseball teams themselves in every major league clubhouse. The amphetamine controversy in major league baseball really came to the fore in 1985 during the cocaine trafficking trial of Curtis Strong a Philadelphia cook who was alleged to have had access to many major league clubhouses for the purpose of distributing cocaine. According to the testimony in the trial by Dale Berra (son of Yogi Berra), who played on 1979 Pittsburgh Pirates world championship team commonly known as "The Family," if he wanted amphetamines he was told to contact either Hall of Fame member Willie Stargell or Bill Madlock, a possible future Hall member who won four National League batting titles and finished his fifteen-year big league career with a .305 lifetime batting average. Berra also stated that he snorted cocaine with teammate Dave Parker, another former player with an outside chance of making the Hall of Fame someday through the Veterans' Committee. Also, future Hall of Fame member Paul Molitor, number eight on the all-time career hits list with 3,319, was a well-known cocaine abuser during his playing days.

It seems that no sort of aberrant behavior has eluded the Hall of Fame membership rolls. There is even a member of the Hall of Fame implicated in drug trafficking. Orlando Cepeda played in the major leagues for 17 years with several clubs, most notably the San Francisco Giants and St. Louis Cardinals, getting 2,351 hits with 379 home runs and a lifetime batting average of .297. A year after his retirement in 1974 federal agents found 160 pounds of marijuana in Cepeda's car parked at the San Juan airport. He was convicted of importing marijuana and sentenced to prison, where he served ten months at the Elgin Air Force base in Florida. Upon his release, he was *not* placed on the ineligible list by the commissioner of Major League Baseball and even returned to the game in 1980 as a coach with the Chicago White Sox. While it seemed that Cepeda was coming up short each year in the Hall of Fame balloting and the baseball writers were holding his conviction against him, he did eventually make into the Hall when he was voted in by the Veterans' Committee in 1999.

In 1980, Texas Rangers pitcher Ferguson Jenkins was arrested at a Canadian airport and charged with drug possession. However, Jenkins alleged that he was set up, and in 1991 he was elected to the Hall of Fame. Furthermore, someday in the near future, those with voting privileges for Hall of Fame entry will have to struggle with the question of whether or not the fence-busting records of Barry Bonds, Sammy Sosa and Mark McGwire were tainted by steroid use.

Steroid use continues to be a considerable problem in the major leagues today. New York Yankees pitcher David Wells wrote in his biography, released in 2003, that 10–25 percent of major leaguers use steroids. Wells, a long-shot future candidate for the Hall of Fame, goes on in his book to state that he pitched his perfect game in 1998 half-drunk with bloodshot eyes, monster breath, and a raging, skull-rattling hangover.

The lists of racists in the Hall of Fame is also long, beginning with Cap Anson, who refused to let a Negro catcher by the name of Fleet Walker play against his Chicago White Stockings in a 1884 exhibition game with Toledo. When Toledo stood its ground, Anson conceded, only to have his way three years later when Chicago was scheduled to play Newark and Walker once again was supposed to be in the lineup. While Anson's plaque hangs in the Hall of Fame, his racial intolerance is widely believed by baseball historians to be the trigger event that barred blacks from major league baseball until 1947.

Another Hall of Fame member, baseball commissioner Judge Kenesaw Mountain Landis, played a large part in keeping blacks out of the major leagues until 1947. He served for 24 years in the commissioner's office and systematically discriminated against black players. His successor, Happy Chandler, said, "For twenty-four years Judge Landis wouldn't let a black man play. I had his records, and I read them, and for twenty-four years Landis consistently blocked any attempts to put blacks and whites together on a big league field. He even refused to let them play exhibition games."[54]

Pete Rose was always more concerned with a fellow player's work ethic than his color. The very first friendships he developed upon arriving in the major leagues were with black players with the Cincinnati Reds, Frank Robinson and Vada Pinson. "Race is no barrier if you are willing to work,"[55] said Rose.

The reality of the Hall of Fame membership is, however, that nearly no one seems to be immune from controversy, not even the immortal "Joltin' Joe" DiMaggio. Author Richard Ben Cramer, who won a Pulitzer Prize for international reporting in 1979, chronicles in his book *Joe DiMaggio: The Hero's Life* how DiMaggio left baseball following the 1951 season to enjoy the good life with a trust fund that had been set up for him by mobster Frank Costello with the Bowery Bank in New York. According to Cramer, every time "Joltin' Joe" made an appearance in one of the many prominent night spots in New York either owned or controlled by Costello, such as the Cotton Club, Copa Cabana, The Stork Club or El Morocco, a deposit of $200 was made by the managers to an account for Joe the following day at the Bowery Bank. The mobsters considered it promotion for "Joltin' Joe" with a classy lady in tow, to appear at one of the clubs they controlled; they felt it gave the joint class, and of course Joe never saw a tab. Ironically, and perhaps with no connection, towards the end of his life DiMaggio made regular commercials for the Bowery Bank. DiMaggio was also supposed to have had close connections with other notorious New York City area gangsters as well, such as Abner (Longy) Zwillman and Richie (The Boot) Boiardo from the first ward in Newark.

New York *Daily News* sports writer Bill Madden, writing an article about the book in 2000, states that, according to Richard Ben Cramer, following the San Francisco earthquake during the 1989 World Series, DiMaggio entered his badly damaged house in the marina district looking for something of special interest. "At the time, Joe talked about how he was searching for his sister. In each of his arms he was holding these huge garbage bags which people assumed were filled with his valuables and baseball mementos. What was really in them was over $600,000 in cash he'd earned from his memorabilia signings."[55] For the record, undeclared income from memorabilia signings is one of the charges that landed Pete Rose in Marion Prison in 1990.

This modest sample of Hall of Fame free spirits clearly represents the double standard that is so apparent when the case Pete Rose and Cooperstown is considered. The Hall of Fame is about baseball players and their achievements on the field. It is not purgatory, nor heaven. Morality is not even a subjective condition for membership. The Hall of Fame membership

Pete Rose. (Photo File, Inc.)

is made up of people with human foibles and frailties, and the fans seem to want Pete Rose in the Hall of Fame. The commissioner and various others, however, want Pete Rose to throw himself prostate before them, confess and beg for their forgiveness. Consequently, it looks as if Pete Rose is going to remain on the outside of the Hall of Fame looking in until the fans, the people with the most influence, make their feelings known on the matter. Until then, the self-righteous commissioner that Bud Selig is, along with dedicated enemies like Bob Feller and Ralph Kiner, will have their way on the matter.

The feelings of the nation in the Pete Rose matter are best summarized by an editorial published in the central New Jersey daily, the *Home New Tribune*, on December 12, 2002, that read in part: "Pete Rose belongs in baseball and his plaque belongs in the Hall of Fame. Anything less is a nod to hypocrisy—the sort the Lords of Baseball have been expert at dispensing for more than a century. Yes Rose is a crude and vulgar man, a liar, an arrogant, self-inflating former star forever in search of the spotlight—hardly ingredients of the ideal American sports hero, the rare athlete blessed with both physical virtuosity and personal value. Rose is banned for life from the sport because he bet on baseball. Baseball has the proof. Yet Rose maintains his innocence—the song of an addict forever in denial. It is a sad and familiar story, but not one punishable for life. It will be a bile-raising moment if ever Rose stands on the steps of Cooperstown to reap his moment of adulation. The man may not have earned it. But the player did. And each has served penance enough."[56]

X

Rumors of Reinstatement

Prior to Pete Rose's being banned for life in 1989, eighteen other players had previously been banned from Major League Baseball. There were, of course, the infamous eight members of the Chicago White Sox who are alleged to have fixed the 1919 World Series: Eddie Cicotte, Happy Felsch, Chick Gandil, "Shoeless Joe" Jackson, Fred McMullin, Swede Risberg, Buck Weaver and Lefty Williams. In addition to those eight players, two others were also banned in the wake of the fallout from the scandal: Bill "Sleepy Bill" Burns, a former major league pitcher, 1908–1912, one of the alleged gamblers in on the plot, and Joe Gedeon, a pitcher who played in just one major league game with the Washington Senators in 1913, but was a friend of Swede Risberg and allegedly had knowledge of the fix. Others banned from baseball included pitcher Jean Dubuc, banned in 1922, and third baseman Heinie Zimmerman, banned in 1919 for allegedly assisting notorious gambler/first basemen Hal Chase to fix games during the 1919 season. Likewise, infielder/outfielder Lee Magee was also banned in 1919 for helping Chase to fix games. Rounding out the banished list are Gene Paulette, 1919, Benny Kauff, 1920, Phil Douglas, 1922, Cozy Dolan, 1924 and Jimmy O'Connell, 1924.

While not one of the previous eighteen players banned has ever been reinstated, Pete Rose applied for reinstatement to Major League Baseball with the commissioner's office in September 1997. However, until 2002, commissioner Bud Selig had not taken the matter up. In fact, it seemed as if Selig was totally ignoring the matter. Everyone seems to have a different

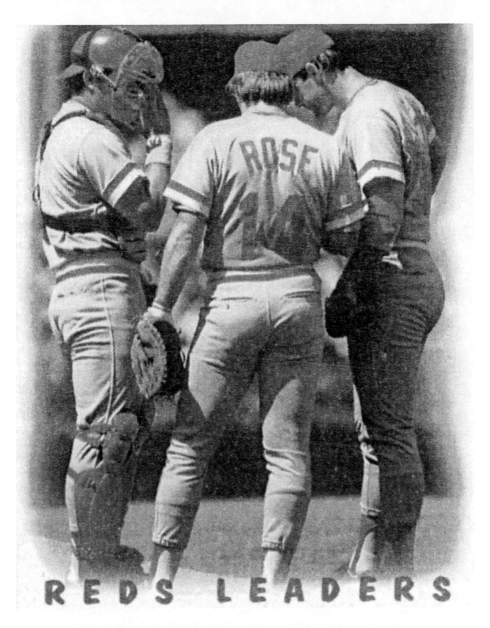

Pete Rose, 1987. (The Topps Company, Inc.)

opinion on what was keeping Bud Selig from reviewing Pete Rose's application for reinstatement. According to former Reds manager Dave Bristol, "If his [Rose's] record doesn't warrant entry into the Hall of Fame, what does? Pete just needs to fess up, and if he did they'd probably let him in."[1] Bob Bonifay, former general manager of the Macon Peaches, takes the case for Rose a step further. "I feel that Bart Giamatti really had it in for Rose. Fact is I think they [Major League Baseball] had it in for him years ago. During his 30-day suspension in 1988, he made a few accusations and gave them a hard time. I don't think they ever forgot that for some reason."[2] One of Rose's severest critics is former Cleveland Indians pitcher and Hall of Fame member Bob Feller. Regarding the Rose matter, Feller states, "I care for baseball and its integrity. Would you buy a ticket to a baseball game that you knew was being gambled on? If you read pages 196 and 197 of the Dowd Report, that will support my opinion."[3]

However, the question of heavy-handed justice in the Rose matter remains. In 1989, major league umpires Rich Garcia and Frank Pulli received two years' probation from commissioner Fay Vincent when it was revealed that they had been betting with bookmakers, yet Rose remains suspended for life for betting with bookmakers. Vincent has maintained that the difference between the circumstances of Garcia and Pulli and those of Rose is that the umpires did not bet on baseball. Tim Sullivan, a writer for the *Cincinnati Enquirer*, believes that the difference between Garcia, Pulli and Rose is that "each time Rose gains a little ground on the road to reinstatement, he is stopped by his own stonewalling. He seeks forgiveness without confession and so far has given commissioner Bud Selig little reason to grant it. In baseball's eyes, Garcia and Pulli came clean while Rose remains muddied."[4]

Muddied perhaps, but notwithstanding his adversaries on the matter such as Bob Feller, Ralph Kiner and Jim Palmer, Rose has turned some former critics into supporters—Joe Morgan, for one. Following the Hall of Fame induction ceremonies at Cooperstown on July 28, 2002, a group of Hall or Fame members, including Joe Morgan and Mike Schmidt requested a meeting with Bud Selig to discuss the issues surrounding the possible reinstatement of Rose. However, Morgan has stated after the fact that he never has asked Selig to reinstate Rose, only to meet with him and evaluate him. Compare him to where he is today as opposed to 13 years ago.

The outpouring of forgiveness and support for Rose displayed by fans at the 2002 World Series got Selig's attention. Baseball, at the moment, is in a crisis. More ball clubs are losing money at the gate, causing unpopular talks about contraction, while the game suffers from an image problem due to its slowness and continued labor relations problems. Perhaps reinstating Rose could be a public relations shot in the arm for the ailing national pastime. Perhaps Rose could even give Bud Selig, an unpopular commissioner with the press and fans alike, a shot in the arm too. Ken Rosenthal of *The Sporting News* wrote, "Most fans don't care that Charlie Hustle turned into Charlie Sleazeball. Rose received the loudest ovation of all the legends introduced at the World Series in San Francisco. His transgressions occurred not when he was a player, but after he became a manager. He belongs in the Hall of Fame."[5]

In Cincinnati the Reds were making plans to open their new ball park on March 31, 2003, and desperately wanted to include Pete Rose in the ceremonies. Following the 2002 World Series, Cincinnati mayor Charlie Luken wrote to Selig twice, on November 13 and 20, urging him to meet with Rose. In his letter to Selig of November 13, Luken wrote: "As you know, Cincinnati is about to open a new ballpark: The Great American Ball Park. It was paid for by Cincinnati taxpayers. These thousands of fans and taxpayers are joined by millions across America in their desire to have Rose reinstated by Major League Baseball. Rose is not perfect. But MLB is no stranger to imperfection. Whatever the crime, time has been served. Whatever agreements were signed years ago are irrelevant today."[6]

After all the years of triumph and tragedy, Pete Rose was still the Cincinnati Kid to his hometown worshipers, and they were now coming forward for him in his time of need. They did indeed believe that their favorite son had paid the price for his transgressions and that it was time for baseball to forgive him. Bud Selig, being ever conscious of his image, was concerned that if he did not reinstate Rose in time for the opening of the Great American Ball Park in Cincinnati, he might be loudly booed by the partisan crowd if he attended the event. However, reports of Rose's continued gambling were troublesome to Selig. It had been reported that during the 2002 World Series, while Rose was receiving the accolades of millions, he was also, according to the New York Daily News, betting $5,000 a game on football. In February 2003, the Daily News, said that the report of Rose's football betting was confirmed by Major League Baseball chief executive officer Bob DuPuy.

Nonetheless, a few days before Thanksgiving, Rose took a Delta flight to Milwaukee and on November 25, 2002, he, Selig and their lawyers held a secret meeting at which they exchanged draft proposals for his reinstatement. Cincinnati television station WXIX-TV reported that former Philadelphia Phillies teammate Mike Schmidt had also accompanied Rose to Milwaukee and participated in the meeting with Selig. Nonetheless, there was no official statement by either party following the meeting, but speculation was that an agreement to reinstate Rose could be reached that would permit him to be back on the eligible list by November 1, 2003, if he signed a document stating that he bet on baseball. On November 27, Cincinnati mayor Charlie Luken placed a follow-up call to Major League Baseball chief executive officer Bob DuPuy and was told that Bud Selig was open and receptive on the subject of Rose's return to baseball.

To some, such as Bob Feller, this is a disgraceful turn of events for the commissioner to arbitrarily consider the reinstatement of Rose based on the economics of the Cincinnati Reds opening a new ball park. "Everything is money today,"[7] said Feller. "Baseball should not be a sounding board for the commissioner, but Bud Selig will do anything for a buck. He needs calcium in his spine. If someone breaks the rules, they should have to pay the consequences. Rose is a felon. Those fans in Cincinnati don't have any respect for the game. If they let him [Rose] back in, they might as well throw away all those signs in the clubhouses."[8] Feller, of course, was referring to the signs posted in major league clubhouses in the aftermath of the Black Sox scandal in the 1919 World Series that warn players that they can be permanently thrown out of baseball for throwing ballgames or consorting with gamblers.

On December 11, 2002, as news of the Rose-Selig reinstatement summit meeting in Milwaukee became public, former baseball commissioner Fay Vincent put his two cents in on the matter, stating that if Bud Selig reinstated Rose, he could expose baseball to future gambling scandals. "The issue is not whether he bet on baseball—he clearly did,"[9] said Vincent. "The issue is whether it's in baseball's best interest to reinstate Pete Rose. Otherwise, if he becomes a manager of the Reds, how do you know he won't bet on baseball again?"[10] Furthermore Vincent believed that Selig was buckling under to enormous pressure from fans and the triumvirate of support from Hall of Fame members Mike Schmidt, Joe Morgan and Johnny Bench. "Seventy-five percent of the public wants him back because we are a nation that forgives everyone, from Richard Nixon to Bill Clinton to Pete Rose,"[11] said Vincent. The most damaging evidence in the Dowd Report, according to Vincent, were the telephone records maintained by the Reds' management. According to Vincent, former Reds owner Marge Schott was angry that her players were using the clubhouse telephones for free and mandated that the operator at Riverfront Stadium keep records of telephone calls. "We found that Pete had made regular calls to a bookie,"[12] said Vincent. Bud Selig's response to the statements of Vincent was that he should mind his own business.

The fact of the matter is that Vincent may have been understating the support that Rose has for reinstatement. Various polls were being taken around the country, and they were all overwhelming in favor of Rose. In a joint poll conducted by the *Cincinnati Enquirer* and local Cincinnati television station WCPO-TV, the results were that 86 percent of 411 residents contacted believed that Rose should be reinstated to Major League Baseball. Furthermore, 50 percent of those residents stated that it did not matter that Rose had gambled on baseball while he was the manager of the Reds. In New York, the *Daily News* conducted a poll on its website, nydailynews.com., and of 1,884 respondents, 75 percent voted "yes" on the question "Should Major League Baseball reinstate Pete Rose?" In an ESPN poll of 21 of the 500 voting members of the Baseball Writers Association of America, all 21 stated that they would vote for Rose if he was on the Hall of Fame ballot. The die was cast for Rose's reinstatement.

Suddenly there was a muzzle put on Rose by his agent Warren Greene, and no interviews of any kind were being accepted. If you tried to reach Rose through Greene's office, you were told that "Right now, Pete is not answering any questions or giving any interviews at this time. I do hope that you understand. It is because of what is going on and the sensitivity of the issue at hand."[13] However, on December 12, Pete Rose, rejuvenated by a groundswell of public support, issued the following statement on his website, www.peterose.com.

> Due to the recent activity in the media surrounding my issues with Major League Baseball, I would like to offer the following statement through my agent, Warren H. Greene, from our corporate offices in Plantation, Florida.
>
> I greatly appreciate the tremendous fan support and interest in my quest for reinstatement back into Major League Baseball. I carry with each of you the passion to enter a new phase of this drama. Since I submitted my application for reinstatement back in 1997, I have looked forward to the opportunity to once again become a part of this great game. I can say today that we have been provided the forum to discuss all of the issues with Major League Baseball. Please respect this delicate process and permit those of us intimate with the details to continue our efforts.[14]
>
> Thank you very much.
>
> Sincerely, Pete.

Suddenly, in late 2002, everyone in the media was projecting that all Pete Rose had to do was bow at the altar of Bud Selig and offer his confession and apologies, then everything would be peaches and cream. In fact, Ronald Blum of the Associated Press reported that secret negotiations between Rose and Selig and been going on for more than a year. However, in the matter of the resurgent popularity of Rose, another point of view was offered by *Daily News* sports columnist Mike Lupica. "He was Pete Rose. He was Charlie Hustle. The people's choice. They loved him in Cincinnati and they loved him in Philadelphia later, and they still loved him when he came back to Cincinnati and was a pretty good manager with the Reds. Between bets. All along, he thought he was so popular with the fans that eventually he would be able to use that popularity like a credit card, buy his way out of trouble. Maybe the same people cheering for him right now will feel differently when he stands up and tells them, straight up, that he has been lying to them for 13 years."[15]

John Dowd was still skeptical, too. "Once he admits he bet on baseball, they have to pick up that deposition I started in April of 1989," Dowd said. "If he's going to be truthful, they have to find who, what, when and how he bet. The debt issue [with the bookmakers] has to be dealt with. There's a lot to this. From a historical sense, I'd be surprised if they reinstated him. But given who's running baseball, I'm not surprised. This isn't just about Pete Rose. This is about the integrity of the game. If they put him back on the field, they have to make sure he's completely clean."[15] "The problem with Pete is one of arrogance,"[17] says Dowd, "He thinks he's a legend, that he's bigger than baseball."[10]

"Rose's possible reinstatement begs a lot questions,"[19] Dowd said. "Because I would like to ask all the questions over where he denied ever betting while he was under oath. I'd like to find out whom he was dealing with and whom he owed money to, and whether he is still indebted to any of those people. I would like to ask him about the cocaine business [in Ohio] and whether he was a cocaine distributor down the line. I would like to know what he has been doing the last 12 years and whether he is still gambling."[20]

Dowd also stated that a person had called him and said that Rose and Selig had come to an agreement that if Rose made the proper admissions, he would manage the Reds again, as the Reds want to get rid of current manager Bob Boone. However, John Allen, chief operating officer of the Reds, denied any such plans were in the works. "There is absolutely nothing to this,"[21] Allen said. "We've had no discussions and I'd know about something like this because I am the COO of this team and I am the liaison to the ownership."[22]

Bob Boone, entering the last year of his contract as the Reds' manager in 2003, stated, "I would think there would be lot of sentiment for him [Rose] to be manager. As soon as I was wrong once, brought in the wrong pitcher, they'll be calling for him to manage."[23] However, Boone, who played with Rose with the 1980 world champion Philadelphia Phillies, also expressed a fondness for him personally. "I really like Pete,"[24] he said. "I'd like to see him back. I think for him not to be in the Hall of Fame hurts the Hall of Fame more than it hurts Pete Rose."[25]

Indeed, while the legalities and ethical issues surrounding the possible reinstatement of Rose were being debated in the press, another issue had come to the fore: Financially speaking, could Pete Rose afford to be reinstated to Major League Baseball? When Shoeless Joe Jackson was banished from baseball in 1921 following the Black Sox scandal, he went back to North Carolina and ran a dry cleaning business and later a liquor store before finally going broke. Teammate Eddie Cicotte changed his name, moved his family to Detroit and worked on an assembly line at the Ford automotive plant, while Lefty Williams operated a pool hall, then moved to California and opened a nursery business. In fact, following the scandal, all eight former White Sox players implicated in the fixing of the 1919 World Series led, as William Shakespeare had once said, "quite lives of desperation." However, this was not to be for the Hit King in his banishment.

On Sunday, December 15, 2002, the *Cincinnati Enquirer* cut right to the chase on the issue, running an article titled "His baseball banishment is his cash cow." For sure Pete Rose had been making more than just a living since his banishment by hawking memorabilia and making public appearances. His website, www.peterose.com, is a slick, well-oiled, state-of-the-art marketing machine that sells autographed balls, bats, photographs, jerseys, whatever, some for hundreds of dollars each. The *Cincinnati Enquirer* reported that the website also lets one know that Rose is available for personal appearances. Quoting the website in the article, the *Enquirer* stated: "Pete Rose is available to appear at many different types of events, including keynote speeches, cocktail parties, golf outings, and many more. If you would like Pete Rose at your event, please fill out the request form. A representative will contact you with further information and quotes on appearance fees and related expenses."[26] The fact of the matter is that the going rate to have Rose appear at a corporate event or at a casino is $20,000.

The article concluded with the proposition: "Somehow, it seems that had Pete Rose never had any trouble with baseball and was a card-carrying member of the Hall of Fame, he'd be just another old ballplayer. Pretty ironic, huh?"[27] While it is a fact that Pete Rose became a multimillionaire from playing major league baseball, conversely it might just be considered that he has been able to maintain his comfortable lifestyle by being banned from baseball. "I think he [Rose] knows he could up his price,"[28] says Brandon Steiner, the owner of sports memorabilia giant Steiner Sports. "He's said he'd rather keep his price down and sign a lot. Every time we've been with him in public situations he's been great. The photos, the babies—he's been great."[29]

Everything was beginning to look promising for Rose, and on December 16, 2002, Bob DuPuy even flew down to Ft. Lauderdale and had a meeting with Rose and his business agent, Warren Greene. While DuPuy, Greene and Rose were mum on the proceedings in that meeting, it is widely believed that some sort of an agreement was reached whereby Rose would admit that he bet on baseball, thereby validating the Dowd Report, and make an apology, thereby clearing his way for some form of reinstatement, be it conditional, probationary, or whatever.

As the momentum continued to swing Rose's way, on December 21, 2002, the *New York Times* reported that Bud Selig was arranging a meeting on January 17, 2003, in Los Angeles with the 58 living members of the Hall of Fame to discuss whether or not Pete Rose should be reinstated by the commissioner's office. One of Selig's worst fears is that if he does not gain sufficient support from the living membership of the Hall of Fame, it could cause a public relations nightmare down the road if Rose were reinstated and a considerable number of Hall of Fame members organized a boycott of a future induction ceremony at Cooperstown. The precedent for this type of event nearly occurred with the Bob Feller and Marty Brennaman incident at the 2000 Hall induction ceremonies.

Selig also knew that the meeting he was planning in Los Angeles had the potential to open up a can of worms between those members of the Hall supporting Rose and those opposed. Jim Palmer, quoted in the *Washington Times* stated, "Nothing has changed in 13 years. He [Rose] hasn't seemed to change his life or done anything different. He's still the same guy he was."[30] Meanwhile Robin Roberts stated that he would take a pass on the meeting. "I don't really want to be part of it,"[31] said Roberts. "That's something to be worked out between the commissioner and Pete. Until he's off the banned list, there's no point talking about it."[32] Of course, while Rose ultra-critic Bob Feller planned to attend the meeting, his position was already well known. According to Feller, "Your character is like your shadow; you're never going to get away from it."[33]

Then on December 23, 2002, just two days after Bud Selig announced that he was going to meet with the living members of the Hall of Fame to poll their opinions on the reinstatement issue, the jaded past of Pete Rose came rolling in like a huge tidal wave. The *Dayton Daily News* and the *Cincinnati Post* were reporting that according to the FBI, one of Pete Rose's former bookies had ties to the Mafia and cocaine trafficking. Worse yet was the fact that the alleged Dayton, Ohio gambling kingpin Richard K. Skinner, aka "The Skin Man," who was believed to control a $1 billion-a-year gambling racket, had Rose on tape.

Skinner was angry at the fact that Rose had not made good on a long overdue gambling debt and decided to visit Rose at his home in Cincinnati in January 1986. Skinner's motivation for taping his conversation with Rose is that he considered it to be insurance in the event that he was arrested. "It seems that he's been dodging me and dodging me for three [expletive] years,"[34] said Skinner as spoke into the tape recorder prior to his meeting with Rose. The tapes were sized by the FBI from Skinner's Dayton, Ohio, home in a second raid on June 29, 1992. Skinner died on February 15, 1996 at the age of 65, but not before he told the *Dayton Daily News* that Rose had never paid him. The debt believed owed to Skinner was alleged to be in the range of $30,000. The conversation on the tape between Skinner and Rose suggests that there may have been gambling leads not known to baseball investigators during their probe of Rose in the late 1980s. Skinner went to Rose's home to collect the alleged debt under the guise of intending to get him to sign a 1975 World Series Yearbook for his nephew. The following are excerpts from the tape:

SKINNER: I couldn't believe, after I met you [expletive], you're one of the nicest guys I've ever met in my life. I can't figure out why you're doing this.

ROSE: I just got caught short, I guess.

SKINNER: Well hell, you could send me two, three thousand at a time or something.

ROSE: I don't like to do it that way.

SKINNER: Well, I understand, but hey … it's been three years.

ROSE: I'll get it straightened out before I go to spring training. I mean, I don't keep cash at the house here.

SKINNER: Oh, I heard that you were firing at the guy in Hamilton there, some Ron [Peters] or somebody.[35]

As Skinner prepares to leave, Rose promises him that he will make good on the debt right after the 1986 Super Bowl is played. The 1986 Super Bowl was to be played in New Orleans between the Chicago Bears and New England Patriots, with the Bears being 10½-point favorites. The Bears won the game 42–10.

SKINNER: Who do you like?

ROSE: Oh, I'll take the points.

SKINNER: Most everybody is, and I know I should.

ROSE: I don't like the way the Bears are acting down there.

SKINNER: I know, man. They're cocky, ain't they?

ROSE: When a team has covered the spot 14 straight times, you've got to go for 'em, don't you? What's your over-and-under? [Over and under refers to a betting proposition of the combined point total scored in the game.]

SKINNER: Thirty-seven and a half.

ROSE: I'm thinking about just betting under instead of trying to pick a te-am.[36]

It is stated in the *Dayton Daily News* article that at this point in the conversation Rose told Skinner that he heard of someone betting $88,000 on the Patriots. Then Skinner changes the subject to baseball, remarking on an odds-line that changed because of a bet.

SKINNER: 'Cause, you know, you remember the time I told you, the first game that [Tom] Seaver pitched in Cincinnati?

ROSE: Yeah.

SKINNER: It was two and a half runs or something, and a buddy of mine, we were in Vegas, and he went down and bet $2,000 on Seaver minus two and a half, and he calls me and I said I'll be right down. [This type of wager pays of if a team wins by three or more runs.] And I was at the pool. Hell, I had my trunks on, I throwed my shirt on and run down there with two grand, and the guy says it's three runs. And hell, they moved it half a run on a $2,000 bet. But the guy knew who I was going to bet, too. You know. So that might have been the difference.

ROSE: Maybe that guy knows something that we don't know.[37]

In addition to bookmaking, Ronald Skinner was alleged to have been involved with the importation and distribution of cocaine and marijuana and the fencing of stolen property. A link between the bookmaking operation of Skinner and Ronald Sacco, who is alleged to have ran a bookmaking operation for La Cosa Nostra that spread across the USA and Dominican Republic, was revealed in a nationwide investigation by the San Francisco division of the FBI in the early 1990s. According to Dayton, Ohio police detective Sgt. Dennis K. Haller, "There's no question that he knew Pete Rose. He was mad at Pete because he claimed Pete had beat him out of about $30,000. He told me that personally."[38]

On January 7, 2003, Gary Carter and Eddie Murray were elected to the Hall of Fame by the Baseball Writers Association of America. Pete Rose, despite being on the ineligible list, received 18 write-in votes, the same number that he had received in the 2002 Hall of Fame election. In fact, Rose has been receiving write-in votes every year since his banishment, and in 1992 he received 42 votes. However, the January 17 date that Bud Selig had set to meet with the living members of the Hall of Fame to hear their positions on the possible reinstatement of Rose was postponed, according to the commissioner's office, due to scheduling conflicts.

Nonetheless, at the same time, the *Daily News* in New York was reporting that sources were telling them that Major League Baseball was still investigating Rose in an attempt to make sure that he was no longer placing bets on sports and that he had severed his personal ties with various unsavory types. There were reports circulating that allegedly Rose had recently been seen gambling at the Bellagio casino in Las Vegas and that he was hanging around the sports book at nearby Caesar's Place. Then on January 24, 2003, it was reported by the *Cincinnati Enquirer* that Rose was in arrears on his federal taxes to the tune of $151,690 and that consequently the Internal Revenue Service had placed a lien on his $1 million condominium in Sherman Oaks, California. In addition, the State of California had also filed a lien because Rose owed them $2,772 in state taxes dating back to 1997. But according to David Stern, an accountant familiar with Rose's circumstances, "We're dealing with the issue.

It is absolutely, 100 percent not related to the stuff that happened in the late '80s and early '90s."[39] Stern emphasized that Rose wasn't attempting to dodge taxes, but simply was unable to pay the full amount when he filed his 1998 tax return.

Meanwhile, S. Arthur Spiegel, the federal judge who had sentenced Rose to prison in 1990, stated, "I think he [Rose] should be in the Hall of Fame for his accomplishments on the field. He fulfilled his sentence as required by law, both in prison and the halfway house, and in community service. The reports I got back on him were all favorable. As far as I'm concerned, he paid his debt to society."[40]

On January 27, 2003, Major League Baseball decided to put the Rose reinstatement issue on hold as they continued to investigate whether or not he was still gambling heavily on sports. The next day Bud Selig also put on hold the meeting he planned with the living Hall of Fame members to discuss the Rose situation. "That meeting was called off,"[41] said Bob Feller. "Selig wants more time, but I think he knows what he's going to do, which is nothing. My guess would be that he's not going to reinstate Pete Rose."[42]

However, Mike Schmidt, a loyal and true friend of Rose, was ever hopeful. "I'm optimistic that things will happen fast enough that you might see Pete at Reds opening day this year,"[43] said Schmidt. "I don't want to become commissioner on this issue, but I'm optimistic."[44]

Nonetheless, as opening day 2003 drew near and the Reds prepared to open their new Great American Ball Park, Pete Rose turned down a request to be the grand marshal of Cincinnati's opening day parade. Mayor Luken had even invited Pete to be his guest at the game on opening day, but the offer was turned down. "I'm not surprised. It was clear Pete wanted to here, but it was clear he wouldn't do anything that would interfere with his attempt to be reinstated into Major League Baseball,"[45] Luken said. "He'll be here in spirit. I'm sure he'll be here sooner or later."[46] So on March 31, 2003 the Cincinnati Reds opened their new Great American Ball Park without Pete Rose and lost to the Pittsburgh Pirates 10–1. Former president George W. Bush threw out the first ceremonial pitch, and Ken Griffey, Jr. got the first hit in the new facility, a double. Bud Selig was there but kept out of the public's view.

Bud Selig is in quandary over the Rose situation; he seems genuinely to want to resolve the issue, but at the same time has a deep fear of making a decision on Rose and then having to face embarrassment from it. He simply tells everyone that we are going to have to let the process play itself out. For Charlie Hustle, that is exactly what has been going on for the past forty-three years since that early summer day in 1960 when he got off the bus in Geneva, New York with a tattered suitcase and two bats ready to challenge the baseball world. The process has just been playing itself out.

Notes

I. Pete's Journey

1. "All I am is my father one generation..." from an article by Mike Lopresti of
the Gannett News Service, published in the
Cincinnati Enquirer, September 12, 1985.

2. "The last series we played was in
Cincinnati..." from *Bums—An Oral History of
the Brooklyn Dodgers*, by Peter Golenbock,
1984, G.P. Putnam's Sons, New York.

3. "If your daddy's a fisherman, then
you'll... from *Hustle—The Myth, Life, and Lies
of Pete Rose*, by Michael Y. Sokolve, 1990,
Fireside, New York.

4. "Yeah, I knew his father." from the
author's interview with Dave Bristol, September 24, 2002.

5. Ibid.

6. "I'm your new second baseman."
from *Pete Rose: My Story*, by Pete Rose and
Roger Kahn, 1989, Macmillan Publishing
Company, New York.

7. "He was not that good a hitter..."
from an article by Bob Hertzel published in
the *Cincinnati Enquirer*, May 1978.

8. "The South Eastern League in
1962..." from the author's interview with
Bob Bonifay, September 18, 2002.

9. "In addition to Rose playing on..."
from the author's interview with Harley
Bowers, September 15, 2002.

10. Ibid.

11. He was a very good player..." from
the author's interview with Dave Bristol,
September 24, 2002.

12. He was a hustler." from the author's
interview with Bob Bonifay, September 18,
2002.

13. Ibid.

14. When I turned in my reports..." from
the author's interview with Dave Bristol,
September 24, 2002.

15. He was just like he was in the
majors..." from the author's interview with
Harley Bowers, September 15, 2002.

16. The old ladies in their 60s and 70s..."
from *Cincinnati Seasons—My 34 Years with the
Reds*, by Earl Lawson, 1987, Diamond Communications, Inc., South Bend, Indiana.

17. Pete Rose, an All-Star infielder if..."
from an article in the *Macon Telegraph*, Friday, August 17, 1962.

18. With only the playoffs remaining..."
from an article by Harley Bowers, published
in the *Macon Telegraph*, August 23, 1962.

II. Cincinnati Kid

1. "That" observed Ford, "is..." from an
article by Ira Berkow, published in the *New
York Times*, Friday, August 25, 1989.

2. "He'll [Rose] have to play good ball..." from an article by Al Heim published in the *Cincinnati Enquirer*, April 9, 1963.

3. "The Reds' Pete Rose..." from an article by Lou Smith published in the *Cincinnati Enquirer*, April 9, 1963.

4. "I couldn't understand why he..." from an article by Allen Lewis published in the *Philadelphia Inquirer*, December 6, 1978.

5. Ibid.

6. "Just Pete's personality sometimes..." from the author's interview with Dave Bristol, September 24, 2002.

7. "Here was this kid..." from *Pete Rose: My Story*, by Pete Rose and Roger Kahn, 1989, Macmillan Publishing Company, New York.

8. "Nobody had to show Pete how to hit..." from an article by Tom Callahan published in *Time*, July 10, 1989.

9. "Robinson and Pinson were both very..." from *Cincinnati and the Big Red Machine*, 1988, Robert Harris Walker, Indiana University Press, Bloomington and Indianapolis.

10. They didn't want a rookie on..." from an interview with Pete Rose by Maury Z. Levy and Samantha Stevenson, published in *Playboy*, vol. 26, no. 9, September 1979.

11. I'd want him to go out to dinner..." from *Cincinnati Seasons—My 34 Years with the Reds*, by Earl Lawson, 1987, Diamond Communications, Inc., South Bend, Indiana.

12. You could feel the loss of Robinson..." from the author's interview with Dave Bristol, September 24, 2002

13. Ibid.

14. Ibid.

15. Ibid.

16. I had a guy posted in the bleachers..." from an article by Earl Lawson published in the *Cincinnati Post*, November 4, 1975.

17. He was a good baseball man." from the author's interview with Dave Bristol, September 24, 2002.

18. Ibid.

III. Rose and Big Red

1. "He came up to me and said..." from an article by Bob Hertzel published in the *Cincinnati Enquirer*, December 4, 1972.

2. "I was playing with guys like Brooks and Frank Robinson..." from an article by John Erardi published in the *Cincinnati Enquirer*, September 22, 2002.

3. "I never saw Pie Traynor play..." from *Greatest Moments in Baseball*, by Joel Zoss, 1987, Bison Books Corp.

4. "He ran with Tommy Helms then..." from an article by Bob Hertzel published in the *Cincinnati Enquirer*, May 1978.

5. "I'm going to manage the Reds..." from *Hustle—The Myth, Life, and Lies of Pete Rose*, by Michael Y. Sokolove, 1990, Fireside, New York, NY.

6. "That night following the game..." from the author's interview with Sparky Anderson, December 12, 2001.

7. "You just ain't as big as you used to be..." from an article by Bob Hertzel published in the *Cincinnati Enquirer*, May 30, 1972.

8. Ibid.

9. Ibid.

10. Ibid.

11. Ibid.

12. "When Bench connected on his home run..." from an article by John Erardi, published in the *Cincinnati Enquirer*, September 22, 2002.

13. "Me sliding hard into Harrelson..." from *Microsoft Complete Baseball*, 1994, Microsoft Corporation.

14. "He looked at me as the team leader..." from *Pete Rose: My Story*, by Roger Kahn, 1989, Macmillan Publishing Company, New York.

15. "This is some kind of game..." from an article by Pat Harmon published in the *Cincinnati Post*, November 4, 1975.

16. "Peter Edward, you're crazy..." from the video *The Official History of the Cincinnati Reds*, 1987, produced by Major League Baseball Productions.

17. Ibid.

18. Ibid.

19. "I'm a young 34 and I intend to play..." from an article by Earl Lawson published in the *Cincinnati Post*, November 4, 1975.

20. *Ibid.*

21. "If everybody just does what their capable of..." from *Reds Greatest Hits—76*, copyright Cincinnati Reds, Inc. 1976, Counterpart Creative Studios, Cincinnati, Ohio, executive producer Richard Wagner.

22. "He comes around when he can..." from an article by Richard Hoffer published in the *Cincinnati Post*, October 25, 1976.

23. Ibid.

24. "I liked Tommy because he reminded

me..." from an article by Buzz Bissinger published in *Vanity Fair*, September 2001.

25. "The Dodgers don't have a finishing kick..." from an article included in *Microsoft Complete Baseball*, 1994, Microsoft Corporation.

26. "That sonofagun is amazing..." from an article by Bob Hertzel published in the *Cincinnati Enquirer*, May 1978.

27. Ibid.

28. "He lives for action..." from an article by Bob Hertzel published in the *Cincinnati Enquirer*, May 6, 1978.

29. "They can go ahead with the..." from an article in the *Cincinnati Enquirer*, May 6, 1978.

30. "Friday night, he says..." from an article by Bob Hertzel published in the *Cincinnati Enquirer*, May 1978.

31. "The greatest competitor I ever saw..." from an article by Tom Callahan published in the *Cincinnati Enquirer*, May 6, 1978.

32. "something we haven't had here since '69..." from an article by Bob Hertzel published in the *Cincinnati Enquirer*, August 1, 1978.

33. "I was a little surprised that in a game..." from an article by Bob Hertzel published in the *Cincinnati Enquirer*, August 2, 1978.

34. Ibid.

IV. Philadelphia Freedom

1. "Let's get together when we get back..." from an article by Pat Harmon published in the *Cincinnati Post*, November 20, 1978.

2. "I told them to go to hell..." from an interview with Maury Z. Levy and Samantha Stevenson, published in *Playboy*, vol. 26, no. 9, September 1979.

3. Ibid.

4. "Over there they call me..." from an article by Pat Harmon published in the *Cincinnati Post*, November 22, 1978.

5. Ibid.

6. "I don't think the shock of not playing..." from an article published in the *Cincinnati Post*, November 27, 1978.

7. Ibid.

8. Ibid.

9. Ibid.

10. Ibid.

11. "I can understand why they can't..." from an article by Earl Lawson published in the *Cincinnati Post*, November 29, 1978.

12. "Mr. Busch wants me to play with..." from an article by Earl Lawson published in the *Cincinnati Post*, November 29, 1978.

13. "Mr. Galbreath told me that walking into..." from an article by Earl Lawson published in the *Cincinnati Post*, November 30, 1978.

14. Ibid.

15. "I feel I have a job to do..." from an article by Earl Lawson published in the *Cincinnati Post*, December 2, 1978.

16. "I can't deny I did that..." from an article published in the *Cincinnati Post*, December 4, 1978.

17. Ibid.

18. "Unless something unbelievable happens..." from an article by the Associated Press published in the *Home News Tribune*, December 5, 1978.

19. "That was one of my prouder moments..." from *50 Phabulous Phillies*, by Skip Clayton and Jeff Moeller, 2000, Sports Publishing, Inc.

20. "I can remember the day when..." from an article by Earl Lawson published in the *Cincinnati Post*, December 5, 1978.

21. Ibid.

22. Ibid.

23. "Mr. Katz told me..." from an article by Don McKee published in the *Philadelphia Inquirer*, December 5, 1978.

24. "Now we can go head to head..." from an article by Frank Dolson published in the *Philadelphia Inquirer*, December 5, 1978.

25. Ibid.

26. "I think this has engulfed baseball..." from an article by Don McKee published in the *Philadelphia Inquirer*, December 5, 1978.

27. "The Truth? This country's screwed up..." from an article by Martin Ralbovsky published in the *Philadelphia Inquirer*, December 5, 1978.

28. "I played with Aaron..." from an article by Frank Dolson published in the *Philadelphia Inquirer*, December 6, 1978.

29. Ibid.

30. "Don't believe that shit," from an article by Buzz Bissinger published in *Vanity Fair*, No 495, September 2001.

31. "Hit the ball where it's pitched." from an article by Richard Fellinger published in the *Philadelphia Weekly*, May 10, 2000.

32. Ibid.

33. "I'd rather go through a divorce hitting..." from an article by Ira Berkow published in the *New York Times*, August 25, 1989.

34. "I know nothing about baseball..." from an article in the *Philadelphia Inquirer*, October 14, 1980.

35. "Everyone always asks me about that play..." from *50 Phabulous Phillies* by Skip Clayton and Jeff Moeller, 2000, Sports Publishing Inc.

36. "I want you to watch..." from an article by Danny Robbins published in the *Philadelphia Inquirer*, August 11, 1981.

37. "He done it..." from an article by Buzz Bissinger published in *Vanity Fair*, No. 495, September 2001.

38. "I talked to our pitchers..." from an article by Danny Robbins published in the *Philadelphia Inquirer*, August 11, 1981.

39. Ibid.

40. Ibid.

41. "I'd as soon get up out of this seat..." from an article by David Zucchino published in the *Philadelphia Inquirer*, August 11, 1981.

42. Ibid.

43. Ibid.

44. Ibid.

45. Ibid.

46. "I've got a feeling there..." from an article by Danny Robbins published in the *Philadelphia Inquirer*, August 11, 1981.

47. "baseball's dishonest season." from a summary of the 1981 season published in *Microsoft Complete Baseball*, Microsoft Corporation, 1994.

48. "As far as I was concerned..." from an article by Jayson Stark published in *Philadelphia Inquirer*, June 22, 1982.

49. Ibid.

50. "He's got things to do..." from an article by Frank Dolson published in *Philadelphia Inquirer*, June 23, 1982.

51. Ibid

52. "There are so many vital differences between..." from an article by Peter Pascarelli published in the *Philadelphia Inquirer*, June 23, 1982.

53. "You quickly notice the certainty..." from an article by Peter Pascarelli published in the *Philadelphia Inquirer*, June 23, 1982.

54. "Pete, I may be an American Leaguer..." from an article by Frank Dolson published in the *Philadelphia Inquirer*, October 13, 1983.

55. Ibid.

56. Ibid.

57. Ibid.

58. Ibid.

59. I want Pete in there for right-handers..." from an article by Peter Pascarelli published in the *Philadelphia Inquirer*, October 15, 1983.

60. Ibid.

61. I know how he feels..." from an article by Frank Dolson published in the *Philadelphia Inquirer*, October 15, 1983.

62. Ibid.

63. "I try not to think or worry about..." from an article by Jayson Stark published in the *Philadelphia Inquirer*, October 17, 1983.

64. Ibid.

65. Ibid.

66. Ibid.

67. Ibid.

V. The Hit King

1. "We hate to lose Pete..." from *Microsoft Complete Baseball*, 1994, Microsoft Corporation.

2. Ibid.

3. "I believe there are a lot good things Pete..." from *Cincinnati Seasons—My 34 Years with the Reds*, by Earl Lawson, 1987, Diamond Communications, Inc. South Bend, Indiana.

4. "I think the situation here is exactly the same..." from an article by Jayson Stark published in the *Philadelphia Inquirer*, January 20, 1984.

5. Ibid.

6. "I can't remember the last time I went..." from an article by the United Press International published in the *Philadelphia Inquirer*, January 21, 1984.

7. "I heard that she had the prettiest bottom..." from *Pete Rose: My Story* by Pete Rose and Roger Kahn, 1989, Macmillan Publishing Company, New York, NY.

8. "The ovation was special to me because..." from an article by the Associated Press published in the *Home News*, April 14, 1984.

9. "Though his playing career was waning..." from *Marge Schott Unleashed* by Mike Bass, 1993, Sagamore Publishing, Champaign, IL.

10. "If that son of a bitch gets that base hit..." from *Marge Schott Unleashed* by Mike Bass, 1993, Sagamore Publishing, Champaign, IL.

11. Ibid.

12. "I went to the Bengal game..." from an article by Terry Flynn published in the *Cincinnati Enquirer*, September 9. 1985.

13. Ibid.

14. "What are you doing, buddy?" from an article by Tim Sullivan published in the *Cincinnati Enquirer*, September 9, 1985.

15. Ibid.

16. Ibid.

17. Ibid.

18. Ibid.

19. Ibid.

20. "I did not want him to break it..." from an article by Michael Paolercio published in the *Cincinnati Enquirer*, September 9, 1985.

21. My philosophy was to mix the pitches up..." from an article by Bob Rathgeber, published in the *Cincinnati Enquirer*, September 11, 1985.

22. Ibid.

23. I did something I usually don't do..." from an article by Greg Hoard, published in the *Cincinnati Enquirer*, September 11, 1985.

24. There's a lot of dissatisfaction..." from an article in the *Cincinnati Enquirer*, September 11, 1985.

25. Ibid.

26. Just think about this a minute..." from an article by Tim Sullivan published in the *Cincinnati Enquirer*, September 11, 1985.

27. Ibid.

28. I don't know what to do..." from an article by Greg Hoard published in *Cincinnati Enquirer*, September 12, 1985.

29. Ibid.

30. I was happy looking at everybody..." from an article by John Eckberg and Bob Harig published in the *Cincinnati Enquirer*, September 12, 1985.

31. I'll sell everyone of these..." from article by Buzz Bissinger published in *Vanity Fair*, No. 495, September 2001.

32. Woofs and licks..." from an article by Rosemary Munsen published in the *Cincinnati Enquirer*, September 12, 1985.

33. Is this Pete Rose..." from an article published in the *Cincinnati Enquirer*, September 12, 1985.

34. My dad would probably have said..." from an article by Tim Sullivan published in the *Cincinnati Enquirer*, September 12, 1985.

35. Tony was in his last year..." from *Pete Rose: My Story*, by Pete Rose and Roger Kahn, 1989, Macmillan Publishing Company, New York, NY.

VI. Lifetime Banishment

1. "I'm guilty of one thing..." from an article in the *Daily News*, August 24, 1989.

2. "was instructed to find Rose another bookie..." from an article by Buzz Bissinger, published in *Vanity Fair*, No. 493, September 2001.

3. "if he knew someone who could take bets..." from the Dowd Report, Report to the Commissioner in the matter of Peter Edward Rose, Manager, Cincinnati Reds Baseball Club, May 9, 1989.

4. "They wanted my input and advice..." from an article in the *Daily News*, August 24, 1989.

5. Ibid.

6. "Do you bet on baseball?..." from *Pete Rose: My Story*, by Pete Rose and Roger Kahn, 1989, Macmillan Publishing Company, New York, NY.

7. Ibid.

8. "You need to show some income..." from an article by Buzz Bissinger published in *Vanity Fair*, No. 493, September 2001.

9. "That's it; it's over..." from an article by John Bannon published in *USA Today*, June 27, 1989.

10. Ibid.

11. Ibid.

12. He was supposed to be betting..." from an article from the News Services of the *Cincinnati Enquirer*, June 28, 1989.

13. claims Rose would not bet when Mario Soto... from an article by Joel Sherman published in the *New York Post*, December 12, 2002.

14. has for several months been conducting..." from an article by Craig Neff published in *Sports Illustrated*, March 27, 1989. Vol. 70, No. 13.

15. Ibid.

16. It is quite significant that Peters and Janszen..." from an article published in USA Today, June 27, 1989.

17. He started talking about, you know..." from an article by Ben L. Kaufman published in the *Cincinnati Enquirer*, June 28, 1989.

18. Ibid.

19. He's a great baseball player." from an article by Buzz Bissinger published in *Vanity Fair*, No. 493, September 2001.

20. Rose said he had a certificate of deposit..." from an article by Howard Wilkerson published in the *Cincinnati Enquirer*, June 28, 1989.

21. Ibid.

22. "He has been candid, forthright..." from an article by the Associated Press published in the *New York Times*, August 25, 1989.

23. Ibid.

24. Ibid.

25. "it didn't mean did-dly squat..." from excerpts from the report on Pete Rose submitted to the commissioner of baseball, in article by the Associated Press published in the *Star-Ledger*, June 27, 1989.

26. Ibid.

27. Ibid.

28. Ibid.

29. Ibid.

30. Ibid.

31. "I was coaching with him that year..." from the author's interview with Dave Bristol, September 24, 2002.

32. Ibid.

33. "You can't stick your head in the sand..." from *Marge Schott Unleashed* by Mike Bass, 1993, Sagamore Publishing, Champaign, IL.

34. Ibid.

35. Ibid.

36. "biased and prejudiced..." from an article published in the *Cincinnati Enquirer*, June 20, 1989.

37. Ibid.

38. Ibid.

39. "Now on behalf of the commissioner..." from an article by Jill Lieber and Craig Neff published in *Sports Illustrated*, Vol. 71, No. 1, July 3, 1989.

40. "For the last several weeks..." from an article by the *Star-Ledger* wire services published in the Star-Ledger, June 27, 1989.

41. "It continues to be our contention..." from an article by Ben L. Kaufman published in the *Cincinnati Enquirer*, June 29, 1989.

42. "It hasn't occupied the dominant part of our time..." from an article by Murray Chass published in the *New York Times*, July 31, 1989.

43. Ibid.

44. Ibid.

45. "that the controversy in this case..." from an article by Murray Chass published in the *New York Times*, August 1, 1989.

46. "is transparent..." from an article by Murray Chass published in the *New York Times*, August 15, 1989.

47. I'm not an expert in shoving umpires..." from an article Jerry Crasnick published in the *Cincinnati Post*, August 17, 1989.

48. The banishment for life of Pete Rose..." from the text of baseball commissioner A. Bartlett Giamatti's statement on August 24, 1989 published by the Associated Press in the *Home News*, August 25, 1989.

49. "There is no deal for reinstatement..." from an article by Ben Walker published in the *Home News*, August 25, 1989.

50. "I made some mistakes..." from an article by Al Salvato published in the *Cincinnati Post*, August 24, 1989.

51. "If you didn't bet on baseball..." from an article by Mike Bass published in the *Cincinnati Post*, August 24, 1989.

52. Ibid.

53. Ibid.

54. "Pete Rose's shadow is going to be..." from an article by Al Salvato and Debra Dennis published in the *Cincinnati Post*, August 24, 1989.

55. "The ticket was really bought by Pete Rose..." from an article in the *Cincinnati Enquirer*, April 20, 1990.

56. "I feel sick about it..." from an article in the *Cincinnati Post*, August 24, 1989.

57. "that son of a bitch..." from an article by Paul Daugherty published in the *Cincinnati Post*, August 24, 1989.

58. "Last night I felt really good..." from an article by Sarah Sturmon published in the *Cincinnati Post*, August 24, 1989.

59. Ibid.

60. "Bart Giamatti was the best commissioner..." from the author's interview with Bob Feller, March 3, 2003.

VII. Charlie Off to Prison

1. "cash money did not have to be claimed..." from the Dowd Report, III. Results of Investigation, published on Baseball1.com., The Baseball Archive.

2. Ibid.

3. "Everybody else involved in this case..." from an article by John Erardi published in the *Cincinnati Enquirer*. April 20, 1990.

4. Ibid.

5. Ibid.

6. Ibid.

7. "Inasmuch as we have a long docket..." from the Transcript of Proceedings Before the Honorable S. Arthur Spiegel, in the case of the United States of America vs. Peter Edward Rose, Criminal No. CR-1–90–44, July 19, 1990.

8. Ibid.

9. Ibid.

10. Ibid.

11. Ibid.

12. Neither one is doing very well..." from an article by John Frardi published in the *Cincinnati Enquirer*, July 20, 1990.

13. Ibid.

14. "I figured he'd get some time..." from an article by Michael Paolercio published in the *Cincinnati Enquirer*, July 20, 1990.

15. Ibid.

16. "We may have acted too quickly..." from an article by Jack Murray published in the *Cincinnati Enquirer*, July 1990.

17. "It's a big deal..." from an article by Timothy W. Smith published in the *Cincinnati Enquirer*, April 20, 1990.

18. Ibid.

19. "I forgot to say a lot of things..." from an article by Joe Morgan published in the *Cincinnati Post*, August 7, 1990.

20. "The toughest part of being in prison..." from an article by Mark Goodman published in *People Magazine*, September 2, 1991.

21. Ibid.

VIII. Life in Exile

1. "Let me tell you; I cried..." from "Another Pete Rose Plays Ball," *48 Hours Investigates*, published on CBSNews.com, June 28, 2001.

2. Ibid.

3. "everything and more..." from an article by Tim Brown published on Enquirer.com, September 2, 1997.

4. "Other than 4,254 major league hits..." from an article by Harvey Araton published in the *New York Times*, August 9, 1998.

5. "It's just mind-boggling to me... from "Another Pete Rose Plays Ball," *48 Hours Investigates*, published on CBSNews.com, June 28, 2001.

6. Ibid.

7. Ibid.

8. "In response to Jim Grey's NBC-TV interview..." from an editorial by B. Lord Martinez published in the *Augusta Chronicle* and on the website opinion@ugusta, November 2, 1999.

9. "You can't keep a guy from making..." from an article by the Associated Press published in the *Macon Telegraph* and on the website Macon.com, November 30, 1999.

10. Ibid.

11. "No. 14 should be here and isn't." from an article by John Delcos published in the *Home News Tribune*, June 11, 2000.

12. Ibid.

13. "The commissioner said Rose can't be here..." from an article by the Associated Press, June 2000.

14. Ibid.

15. "He made me so mad..." from an article by Scott MacGregor published in the *Cincinnati Enquirer* and on the website Cincinnati.com, July 24, 2000.

16. Ibid.

17. Ibid.

18. "Everybody knows I care about Pete Rose..." from an article by John Fay published in the *Cincinnati Enquirer* and on the website Cincinnati.com, July 27, 2000.

19. "If loud mouth Brennaman..." from the author's interview with Bob Feller, March 3, 2003.

20. "Everybody knows I care about Pete...." from an article by John Fay published in the *Cincinnati Enquirer* and on the website Cincinnati.com., July 27, 2000.

21. Ibid.

22. "At first, I was surprised when I heard..." from an article by Andy Furman published in the *Cincinnati Post* and on the website Cincinnati.com, July 28, 2000.

23. Ibid.

24. "For the past 11 years..." from an article by Tim Sullivan of the *Cincinnati Enquirer* published in the *Home News Tribune*, August 9, 2001.

25. Ibid.

26. There'd be fucking cork all over..." from an article by Buzz Bissinger published in *Vanity Fair*, No. 495, September 2001.

27. Ibid.

28. "I've been accused of everything..." from an article by Tim Sullivan of the *Cincinnati Enquirer* published in the *Home News Tribune*, August 9, 2001.

29. Ibid.

30. "are one-sided and refer to events

more..." from an article by John Erardi of the *Cincinnati Enquirer* published on Cincinnati.com, August 7, 2001.

31. "I can't believe I'm seeing this..." from an article by Howard Wilkinson published in the *Cincinnati Enquirer*, September 24, 2002.

32. "The reason my bobblehead doll is a good..." from an article by Paul Daugherty published in the *Cincinnati Enquirer*, September 24, 2002.

33. "I saw Pete play in that softball game..." from the author's interview with Dave Bristol, September 24, 2002.

34. Ibid.

35. "Let's all get together and put Pete Rose..." from an article by Dustin Dow published in the *Cincinnati Enquirer*, September 24, 2002.

36. "Johnny's a big boy..." from an article by John Erardi published in the *Cincinnati Enquirer*, September 24, 2002.

37. Ibid.

38. "All morning long the phones..." from the author's telephone conversation with the office of Warren Greene, September 24, 2002.

39. "The fans voted for the most memorable..." from an article published in the *Cincinnati Enquirer*, December 2002.

IX. Hall of Fame or Shame

1. "I think my dad got screwed." from an article by Richard Fellinger published in the *Philadelphia Weekly*, Vol. XXIX, No. 10, May 10, 2000.

2. Ibid.

3. "Please understand that the Hall of Fame..." from a statement issued to the author by the National Baseball Hall of Fame, September 17, 2002.

4. "Pete Rose will never be reinstated..." from *The 1919 World Series: What Really Happened?* by William A. Cook, 2001, McFarland & Company, Inc., Publishers, Jefferson, NC.

5. "They can't stand the fact that I'm..." from an article by Buzz Bissinger published in *Vanity Fair*, September 2001.

6. "I think he is being mistreated..." from the author's interview with Harley Bowers, September 15, 2002.

7. "Pete and I were the two closest guys..." from an interview by Robert S.

Wieder published in *Playboy* magazine, Vol. 46, no. 10—October 1999.

8. "After the first game between Detroit and Cleveland..." from an article by the Associated Press published in the *Philadelphia Inquirer*, December 22, 1926.

9. Ibid.

10. Ibid.

11. Ibid.

12. Ibid.

13. Ibid.

14. Ibid.

15. Ibid.

16. Ibid.

17. Ibid.

18. Ibid.

19. Ibid.

20. Ibid.

21. Ibid.

22. Ibid.

23. "This is the Cobb-Speaker case..." from an article by the Associated Press published in the *Daily Home News*, January 27, 1927.

24. "No evidence was discovered that Rose..." from the Dowd Report, 1989, Section II. Summary of Report, 3) Footnotes., published by Baseball1.com, The Baseball Archive.

25. "It was not exactly a practice..." from an article by the Associated Press, published in the *Philadelphia Inquirer*, December 22, 1926.

26. Ibid.

27. Ibid.

28. "There was no great crime for the..." from an article by the Associated Press, published in the *Philadelphia Inquirer*, December 22, 1926.

29. "Mr. Risberg, you made a statement..." from an article by the Associated Press, published in the *Cleveland Plain Dealer*, January 6, 1927.

30. Ibid.

31. Ibid.

32. Ibid.

33. Ibid.

34. Ibid.

35. Ibid.

36. Ibid.

37. Ibid.

38. Ibid.

39. "Gandil and Risberg asked me to give..." from an article from the Plain Dealer Wire, published in the *Cleveland Plain Dealer*, January 6, 1927.

40. Ibid.

41. Ibid.

42. "At first, as before, the bets..." from an article by Buzz Bissinger, published in *Vanity Fair*, No. 493, September 2001.

43. "Pete Rose has denied under oath..." from the Dowd Report, II. Summary or Report, published on Baseball 1.com, The Baseball Archive.

44. "When Leo was a player in Cincinnati..." from *Bums—An Oral History of the Brooklyn Dodgers*, by Peter Golenbock, 1984, G.P. Putnam's Sons, New York.

45. Ibid.

46. Ibid.

47. "Durocher has not measured up..." from an article by the Associated Press published in the *Daily Home News*, April 9, 1947.

48. Ibid.

49. "Commissioner Chandler's office would be..." from an article by the NEA Sports Editor published in the *Daily Home News*, April 12, 1947.

50. "Durocher, you're a jerk." from *The Summer of '64—A Pennant Lost*, by William A. Cook, 2002, McFarland & Co., Inc. Publishers, Jefferson, NC.

51. "Leo was a good friend of mine..." from the author's interview with Bob Feller, March 3, 2003.

52. "They had it in for Rose..." from the author's interview with Bob Bonifay, September 18, 2002.

53. "When I was drinking, I thought..." from excerpts of an interview with *Sports Illustrated* magazine, April 18, 1994, published in the *Daily News*, August 14, 1995.

54. "For twenty-four years Judge Landis..." from *Bums—An Oral History of the Brooklyn Dodgers* by Peter Golenbock, 1984, G.P. Putnam's Sons, New York.

55. "Race is no barrier..." from *Cincinnati and the Big Red Machine*, by Robert Harris Walker, 1988, Indiana University Press.

55. "At the time, Joe talked about..." from an article by Bill Madden published in the *Daily News*, October 15, 2000.

56. "Pete Rose belongs in baseball..." from an editorial published in the *Home News Tribune*, December 12, 2002.

X. Rumors of Reinstatement

1. "If his record doesn't warrant entry..." from the author's interview with Dave Bristol, September 24, 2002.

2. "I feel that Bart Giamatti really had it..." from the author's interview with Bob Bonifay, September 18, 2002.

3. "I care for baseball and its integrity..." from the author's interview with Bob Feller, March 3, 2003.

4. "each time Rose gains a little ground on..." from an article by Tim Sullivan published in the *Cincinnati Enquirer*, December 2002.

5. "Most fans don't care that Charlie Hustle..." from an article by Ken Rosenthall of *The Sporting News* published on the website www.msnbc.com/news/, December 18, 2002.

6. "As you know, Cincinnati is about to open..." from an article by John Fay, John Erardi and Gregory Korte published on reds.enquirer.com., December 11, 2002.

7. "Everything is money today..." from the author's interview with Bob Feller, March 3, 2003.

8. Ibid.

9. "The issue is not whether he bet..." from an article by Michael O'Keeffe published in the *Daily News*, December 12, 2002.

10. Ibid.

11. Ibid.

12. Ibid.

13. "Right now, Pete is not answering any..." from the author's inquiry to the office of Warren Greene, December 15, 2002.

14. "Due to the recent activity in the media ... from the statement by Pete Rose published on peterose.com, December 12, 2002.

15. "He was Pete Rose..." from an article by Mike Lupica published in the *Daily News*, December 12, 2002.

16. "Once he admits he bet on baseball..." from an article by John Fay of the *Cincinnati Enquirer* published in the *Home News Tribune*, December 12, 2002.

17. "The problem with Pete is one of arrogance..." from an article by Michael O'Keeffe published in the *Daily News*, December 12, 2002.

18. Ibid.

19. "Rose's possible reinstatement begs a lot of ..." from an article by Joel Sherman published in the *New York Post*, December 12, 2002.

20. Ibid.

21. Ibid.

22. Ibid.

23. "I would think there would be a lot of..." from an article by Jim Salisbury of the *Philadelphia Inquirer* published on the website www.philly.com., December 22, 2002.

24. Ibid.

25. Ibid.

26. "Pete Rose is available to appear at..." from an article published on the *Cincinnati Enquirer* website reds.enquirer.com., December 15, 2002.

27. Ibid.

28. "I think he knows he could up his price..." from article by Michael O'Keeffee and T.J. Quinn of the *Daily News* published on the website www.nydailynews.com., December 22, 2002.

29. Ibid.

30. Ibid.

31. "I don't really want to be part of it..." from an article by the Associated Press published on the website of the *Philadelphia Inquirer*, www.philly.com., December 24, 2002.

32. Ibid.

33. "Your character is like your shadow..." from the author's interview with Bob Feller, March 3, 2003.

34. "It seems that he's been dodging me..." from an article by Wes Hills of the Dayton *Daily News* published in the *Cincinnati Post*, December 23, 2002.

35. Ibid.

36. Ibid.

37. Ibid.

38. Ibid.

39. "We're dealing with the issue..." from an article by the Associated Press published on the website www.sportserver.com., February 3, 2003.

40. "I think he should be in the Hall of Fame..." from an article by the Associated Press published in the *Cincinnati Enquirer*, February 2, 2003.

41. "That meeting was called off..." from an article by Tony Jackson of Scripps Howard News Service published on the website www.sportserver.com., February 3, 2003.

42. Ibid.

43. "I'm optimistic that things..." from an article published in the Home News Tribune, February 24, 2003.

44. Ibid.

45. "I'm not surprised..." from an article published on ESPN.com news service, March 24, 2003.

46. Ibid.

Bibliography

The Baseball Encyclopedia: The Complete and Official Record of Major League Baseball. Eighth Edition. New York: Macmillan, 1990.

The Baseball Encyclopedia: The Complete and Official Record of Major League Baseball. Seventh Edition. Joseph L. Reichler, Editor. New York: Macmillan, 1988.

Bass, Mike. *Marge Schott: Unleashed.* Champaign, IL: Sagamore, 1993.

Bissinger, Buzz. "A Darker Shade of Rose." *Vanity Fair,* no. 492 (September 2001).

Callahan, Tom. "Living Life by the Numbers." *Time,* Vol. 134, no. 2 (July 10, 1989).

The Cincinnati Reds 1973 Yearbook Magazine. Written and edited by Jim Ferguson and Bob Rathgeber.

Clayton, Skip, and Jeff Moeller. *50 Phabulous Phillies.* Champaign, IL: Sports Publishing, 2000.

Cramer, Richard Ben. *Joe DiMaggio: The Hero's Life.* New York: Simon & Schuster, 2000.

"The Dowd Report." *The Baseball Archive,* www.baseball1.com.

Golenbock, Peter. *Bums: An Oral History of the Brooklyn Dodgers.* New York: Putnam, 1984.

Goodman, Mark. "The Swinger from Binger." *Time,* July 10, 1972.

Lawson, Earl. *Cincinnati Seasons—My 34 Years with the Reds.* South Bend, Indiana: Diamond Communications, 1987.

Levy, Maury Z., and Samantha Stevenson. "Pete Rose." *Playboy,* Vol. 26, no. 9 (September 1979).

Lieber, Jill, and Craig Neff. "The Case Against Pete Rose." *Sports Illustrated,* Vol. 71, no. 1 (July 3, 1989).

Microsoft Complete Baseball. Microsoft Corporation, 1994.

Miller, Marvin. *A Whole Different Ball Game.* New York: Fireside, 1991.

Neff, Craig. "The Rose Probe." Edited by Austin Murphy., *Sports Illustrated,* Vol. 70, no. 13 (March 27, 1989).

Neft, David S., Richard M. Cohen, and Michael L. Neft. *The Sports Encyclopedia: Baseball 2000*. New York: St. Martin's Griffin, 2000.

Reston, James. *Collision at Home Plate: The Lives of Pete Rose and Bart Giamatti*. Lincoln: University of Nebraska Press, 1997.

Rose, Pete, and Roger Kahn. *Pete Rose: My Story*. New York: Macmillan, 1989.

Sokolove, Michael Y. *Hustle—The Myth, Life, and Lies of Pete Rose*. New York: Fireside/Simon and Schuster, 1992.

United States of America *vs.* Peter Edward Rose. July 19, 1990, Criminal No. CR-1-90-044, United States District Court, Southern District of Ohio, Western Division.

Walker, Robert Harris. *Cincinnati and the Big Red Machine*. Bloomington and Indianapolis: Indiana University Press, 1988.

Wieder, Robert S. "Twenty Questions: Joe Morgan." *Playboy*, Vol. 46, no. 10 (October 1999).

Will, George F. *Bunts*. New York: Touchstone/Simon and Schuster, 1998.

Zoss, Joel. *Greatest Moments in Baseball*. New York: Exeter, 1987.

Index